ACKNOWLED[GMENTS]

CW01501874

This project started one night in 1994 in Clapton Place in Sydney, Australia. I noticed that an episode of the television series *Lois & Clark* bore a striking resemblance to a Superman story in *Action Comics* #6 (November 1938). I did not realize at the time that I had found a book project, and it took a further eleven years before I did so.

This work benefitted from sabbaticals from my position at the National University of Singapore when I spent time at the University of Melbourne in Australia, the University of North Carolina–Chapel Hill, and New York University. Dan Hunter graciously let me sit in on an "Intellectual Property" master's course he taught at Melbourne, which helped me better grasp concepts of copyright and trademarks. Angela Ndalianis was a great sounding board for a variety of ideas and helped me get to the core of what I was trying to do. In North Carolina, I had a soft landing thanks to my old housemate from Washington, DC, days, Karen Glynn, who let me stay in her house. Robert Allen, Joy and John Kasson, Lloyd Kramer, and Peter Coclanis were all wonderful hosts at Chapel Hill. Andrew Ross and Carolyn Dinshaw facilitated my association with NYU, which proved crucial in finishing this book. Randy Scott at the Michigan State University Library's Special Collections was his usual helpful self, and I was glad to finally return some of his, and Lynn's, hospitality on their visit to Singapore.

My department and the National University of Singapore have supported my work through sabbaticals and in general through a lively intellectual environment. I thank in particular my most recent department heads, Brian Farrell and Yong Mun Cheong, for their support.

ix

This work was supported by the Ministry of Education, Republic of Singapore, AcRF Tier 1 grant R-110-000-18-112.

When I first started working on comics in the early 1990s, it was a rather lonely field. In the years since, there has been a boom in scholarship, and I have been fortunate to attend conferences in the United States, the United Kingdom, Australia, Argentina, Brazil, Singapore, and Europe on comics or with comics-focused sessions. I have benefitted immensely from this contact and thank Bart Beatty, Scott Buktaman, Beatriz Sequeira de Carvalho, Nobu Chinen, Craig Fischer, Jean-Paul Gabillet, Jared Gardner, Karen Green, Lawrence Grove, Charles Hatfield, David Huxley, Gene Kannenberg, Andrew Lesk, Lim Cheng Tju, Dana Mihailescu, Chris Murray, Nick Nguyen, Fusami Ogi, Joan Ormond, Felan Parker, Liber Paz, Barbara Postema, Mihaela Precup, Paulo Ramos, Michael Rhode, Mark C. Rogers, Julia Round, Roger Sabin, Rodrigo Santos, Rebecca Scherr, Matthew Screech, Marc Singer, Waldomiro Vergueiro, Paul Williams, and Rusty Witek for the scholarship, the company, and the humor.

My coeditor on two projects, Matthew P. McAllister, was a delight to work with and such a gracious person that he barely raised an eyebrow when I managed in all my certitude to take the wrong tube in London at a conference. Michael Chaney, Mark Jancovich, James Lyons, Jonathan Gray, Derek Johnston, Lincoln Geraghty, Edward Sewell, Matthew Smith, Randy Duncan, Eric Maigret, and Matteo Stefanelli were all gracious editors, even if not put to the tube test.

Almost thirty years ago in graduate school, I met Charles Shindo. He has been a constant inspiration since for his lack of pretension and his ability to conceptualize a subject and to cut to the heart of a historical issue. I knew this book was taking shape when I felt pleased enough with draft chapters to send them for his comments and suggestions. He and his husband, Michael, have long been welcoming hosts on visits to the United States, and for this and much more, I thank them both.

Beyond academia, the Saturday Afternoon Recreational Softball (SARS) crew have provided much needed diversions in recent years. Thanks Yong, Rickey, Teague Bass, Rug Burn, Hi-Tea, Hor Fun, U-Boat, T. Mick, Joe, Guppie, Sandman, H, Trowels (the elder and younger), Geok, Chano, Collin, The Rube, Johnny Upton, Ziegler, the

SUPERMAN

EDITED BY COREY K. CREEKMUR, CRAIG FISCHER,
CHARLES HATFIELD, JEET HEER, AND ANA MERINO

Volumes in the *Comics Culture* series explore the artistic, historical, social, and cultural significance of newspaper comic strips, comic books, and graphic novels, with individual titles devoted to focused studies of key titles, characters, writers, and artists throughout the history of comics; additional books in the series address major themes or topics in comics studies, including prominent genres, national traditions, and significant historical and theoretical issues. The series recognizes comics of all varieties, from mainstream comic books to graphic nonfiction, produced between the late nineteenth century and the present. The books in the series are intended to contribute significantly to the rapidly expanding field of comics studies but are also designed to appeal to comics fans and casual readers who seek smart critical engagement with the best examples of the form.

SUPERMAN

**THE PERSISTENCE OF
AN AMERICAN ICON**

Ian Gordon

RUTGERS UNIVERSITY PRESS
NEW BRUNSWICK, CAMDEN, AND NEWARK, NEW JERSEY,
AND LONDON

LIBRARY OF CONGRESS CATALOG ING-IN-PUBLICATION DATA

Title: Superman : the persistence of an American icon / Ian Gordon.

Description: New Brunswick, New Jersey : Rutgers University Press, 2017. | Series: Comics culture | Includes bibliographical references and index.

Identifiers: LCCN 2016025796| ISBN 9780813587523 (hardback) | ISBN 9780813587516 (pbk.) | ISBN 9780813587530 (e-book (epub)

Subjects: LCSH: Superman (Fictitious character) | Superman (Comic strip) | Superheroes—Social aspects. | Heroes in mass media. | Myth in mass media. | Popular culture—United States—History. | Comic books, strips, etc.—United States—History and criticism. | BISAC: SOCIAL SCIENCE / Popular Culture. | PERFORMING ARTS / Film & Video / History & Criticism. | LITERARY CRITICISM / Comics & Graphic Novels. | COMICS & GRAPHIC NOVELS / Nonfiction. | SOCIAL SCIENCE / Men's Studies. | LITERARY CRITICISM / American /

General.Classification: LCC PN6728.S9 G67 2017 | DDC 741.5/973—dc23

LC record available at https://lccn.loc.gov/2016025796

A BRITISH CATALOGING-IN-PUBLICATION RECORD FOR THIS BOOK IS AVAILABLE FROM THE BRITISH LIBRARY.

www.rutgerspress.rutgers.edu

Manufactured in the United States of America

For Sandy and Evan

CONTENTS

Sheares Hall team alumni (aka the Zoo), and the floating cast of characters who turn up for the pickup game. Pinsch and McSnooteson
have done their best to provide distractions.

My sister, Sandy, and her husband, Evan, have been the mature
grown-ups in my family for many years. Evan is the brother I never
had, although since I have known him since I was eleven years old,
he seems like just that. Their enjoyment of life and each other's company after over forty years of marriage is a testament to them both.
Their support has been crucial, and I dedicate this book to them
with heartfelt gratitude. Joanne, who told me, "You should dedicate
the Superman book to Sandy and Evan," is the reason for so many
things in my life, including working on my next book to dedicate
to her.

A NOTE ON SOURCES

A good deal of this book draws on legal documents from the various
actions that Siegel and Shuster, and their heirs, launched against DC.
Some of these actions have resulted in reported cases that are available
in printed law reports or online through Lexis. But a good many of
my sources are from legal filings in the cases. My sources for these are
varied, but many can be found on the web at the following two locations: Jeff Trexler's Scribd page at https://www.scribd.com/jefftrexler
and Daniel Best's blog at http://ohdannyboy.blogspot.com.

CREDITS

Chapter 3 draws on previously published material, which I have
reworked and greatly expanded:

> "Nostalgia, Myth, and Ideology: Visions of Superman at the End
> of the American Century." In *Comics and Ideology*, edited by
> Matthew McAllister, Edward Sewell, and Ian Gordon, 177–193.
> New York: Peter Lang, 2001.

> "Superman on the Set: The Market, Nostalgia and Television
> Audiences." In *Quality Popular Television: Cult TV, the Industry,
> and Fans*, edited by Mark Jancovich and James Lyons, 148–162.
> Berkeley: University of California Press, 2003.

> "Smallville: Superhero Mythos and Intellectual Property Regimes."
> In *The Smallville Chronicles: Critical Essays on the Television*

Series, edited by Lincoln Geraghty, 89–108. Lanham, MD: Rowman and Littlefield, 2011.

Chapter 5 draws on previously published material, which I have reworked and greatly expanded:

"Writing to Superman: Towards an Understanding of the Social Networks of Comic-Book Fans." *Participations* 9 (November 2012): 120–132.

SUPERMAN

THE PERSISTENCE OF AN AMERICAN ICON

This book examines the place of Superman in American culture. It is an account of how and why Superman became an icon of American culture and an examination of how a fictional character has sustained that status for some eighty years. Figuring Superman as an icon of American culture is not a process of establishing some essential hallmarks of the character and then tracing these in each and every iteration of the character over the best part of a century. At any given time, or place, in his history, Superman is, and has long been, an amalgam of factors including myth, memory, nostalgia, intellectual property regimes like copyright and trademark, authors, readers, fans, collectors, comic books, comic strips, radio series, movie serials, television shows, animation, toys and collectibles, and feature films. This book shows that an understanding of Superman requires addressing the way these factors figure into any negotiation of Superman's character. Superman's longevity and popularity are not simply reliant on a multiplication of representations across different media. Although this preponderance of representations is important in understanding Superman's popularity, so too are the tropes, such as nostalgia, mythology, and ideology, deployed in Superman's appearance across media. Each Superman media form is an opportunity to marry individual memory to collective memory through a narrative. In part, Superman is an icon because of the sheer amount of material and the competition over which memories are essential to the character. I analyze Superman as a process, rather than as a static, fixed phenomenon. Nonetheless, there is a history to Superman and the character's rise to iconic status.

CREATING SUPERMAN

Jerry Siegel and Joe Shuster's Superman first appeared in comic books in *Action Comics* #1 (June 1938). Not yet fully formed in his first appearance, Superman nonetheless had a dual identity as Clark Kent, worked as a journalist, wore a blue-and-red uniform with a chest insignia, and dated Lois Lane. Superman rapidly became extremely popular with comic book readers and with a more general audience. So popular was the character that by June 1941, the *Saturday Evening Post*, then one of the most widely circulated magazines in America, carried a long feature article on Superman and his creators. Popularity, though, did not equal iconic status, and the piece by John Kobler presented Superman and his creators in a dismissive tone. The "short, plump, heavy spectacled" Jerry Siegel, who stuck "four or five candy bars in his pockets at the cinema," suffered Kobler's ridicule. If the creator of Superman seemed a boob, it was nevertheless hard to deny the success of the character, who by 1941 appeared in the monthly *Action Comics* and the bimonthly *Superman* comic book, a radio serial aired three times a week, and a comic strip carried by 230 newspapers to a combined circulation of twenty-five million readers. In Christmas 1940, 100,000 children paid thirty cents to view Macy's Superman exhibit, there were 250,000 members of the Supermen of America Club, and Paramount Pictures was set to release twelve Fleisher-animated adventures in late 1941. The tone of Kobler's piece suggested that somehow Siegel and Shuster, seeking "psychological compensation" through projecting infantile fantasies, in combination with the sharp business practices of distributor Harry Donenfeld of Independent News and his general manager, Jack Liebowitz, had, at least according to the intellectuals, created "the first authentic cultural hero since Paul Bunyan." It was little matter that Kobler thought Siegel and Shuster unable ever to understand the Nietzschean philosophy through which the *New Republic* magazine analyzed their character; Superman had such an appeal that a cockney boy in London during a heavy air raid scarcely noticed it, so engrossed was he in a Superman comic.[1] But intense media presence and an array of licensed products do not alone turn a character into an icon.

CREATING THE ICON

Superman became an American icon through circumstance and management. The syndication of a Superman comic strip and DC's decision to create a radio version of the character expanded his audience beyond the comic book. But it was probably the advent of World War II that moved Superman from a passing fancy to an iconic status. In doing so, Superman transformed the notion of a superman from something associated with Nazi ideology of racial supremacy to something symbolic of American culture. For instance, the *Los Angeles Times* of December 5, 1941, carried a "Private Lives" panel (an illustrated feature similar to "Ripley's Believe It or Not" but about people) by Edwin Cox that made fun of the Nazi field marshal Wilhelm Keitel, apparently nicknamed "Wittzblatt" or "comic strip general," by noting, "and they don't mean Superman." Although this use clearly referred to Superman, the term still cropped up as a Nazi term, such as in a January 7, 1942, editorial in the *Los Angeles Times*, which wrote of Nazi "supermen," and in Westbrook Pegler's article in the *Washington Post* of January 11, 1942, referring to Hitler sarcastically as "the superman," clearly meaning it in its Nazi sense. When the *Washington Post* of December 10, 1941, reported about the Japanese invasion in the Philippines that an American pilot declared that the Japanese were not the "supermen" that they might seem, the exact reference seems unclear, but increasingly when American newspapers referred to "superman," they meant Superman. These mentions included individuals with sporting prowess being labeled Superman, as in a January 8, 1942, *Washington Post* snippet on the champion bowler Tony Suess, and the sort of qualities required in pilots being described as good but not Superman, in a January 16, 1942, *Post* article on the army's recruitment criteria. Indeed, headline writers very quickly started to associate the fighting ability of American service personnel with Superman. A headline in the February 16, 1942, *Washington Post* read, "One-Man Army Kills 116 Japs in Bataan, Lives to Be Modest about It, Superman Fights for MacArthur." By September 1942, according to a report in the *Nation's Business*, drivers in the US Army called a six-ton truck "the Superman."[2] In early April 1942, the Navy Department decided that Superman comic books were "essential supplies destined for the Marine garrison at Midway Islands," according to a report in *Time*.[3] Indeed, as the war progressed, at one stage the Army Library Services distributed one hundred thousand copies of the Superman comic a month, before giving way to the PX store distribution.[4] Superman comics helped provide Americans with a unified vision of just what the war was about, the defense of a democracy often expressed as the right to consume and abundance of goods and services, something that had already begun to take shape as the American way.

In the many media incarnations of Superman, he avoided direct intervention in the war effort. Rather, he fought saboteurs and fifth columnists on the home front. DC had Superman believe in self-reliance. For instance, in *Action Comics* #41 (October 1941), DC ran a message from Superman in which he promoted self-reliance, telling children, "it is your duty to yourself, your God, your country and your parents to care for yourself in body and mind." This notion of self-reliance fit neatly with Superman's actions of having faith in the spirit of American service men and women. For instance, in a Sunday comic strip from November 21, 1943, Superman, observing two marines attacking three hundred Japanese, says, "How can you beat soldiers with that sort of spirit—the spirit that makes Americans fight against any sort of odds! For me to interfere would be—well, presumptuous."[5] Superman felt this way because DC Comics adhered to the government's view of the war as democracy in action. As Henry Morgenthau, the secretary of the treasury, put it when selling bonds, there were easier ways to finance the war, but selling bonds gave "every one of you a chance to have a financial stake in American democracy—an opportunity to contribute to the defense of that democracy."[6] Superman's intervention would have contravened this faith in American democracy's capacity to triumph.

Arguing causality for something as difficult to define as iconic status is a fraught task. But during World War II, Superman's close alignment with the way the American government presented the mobilization for the war, as that of a democratic people unleashing their wrath at tyranny, would seem to have helped create associations between Superman and a concept of America. After the war, as the generation of men and women who fought that war returned to civilian life and created the baby boom, their view of Superman may have eased the way for their children's engagement with the character.

THE MANY INCARNATIONS OF SUPERMAN

Since first appearing in *Action Comics* #1 (June 1938), Superman has appeared in many media forms. These expanded the reach of the character and quickly turned Superman into something larger than simply a comic book superhero. I discuss many but not all of these incarnations in this book. A Superman daily comic strip commenced publication on January 16, 1939, followed by a Sunday color strip on November 5, 1939. The strip was a result of a contract between DC, Siegel and Shuster, and the McClure syndicate. The comic strip version offered slightly more mature stories for the perceived older newspaper audience. During World War II, the strip ran many episodes aimed at improving the morale both of service personnel and of people on the home front. The rapid success of Superman also led DC to develop a radio serial, *The Adventures of Superman*. DC developed the serial in-house, and it was originally broadcast, commencing February 12, 1940, as a syndicated show on the different radio stations that DC could sell it to across the country. Later, from August 31, 1942, the serial ran on the Mutual Broadcast System before shifting to ABC in 1949 and eventually being canceled in 1951. The radio serial enjoyed solid if not exceptional ratings, drawing audiences as large as three million listeners in the children's afternoon time slot.[7] More importantly, the serial developed what became a standardized description of Superman as its introductory, character-defining, dramatic monologue, a description that later lent itself to many of Superman's familiar catchphrases. In developing this opening, the radio serial drew on yet another version of Superman, a series of animated cartoons from Fleischer Studios that were distributed by Paramount. The studio released the first of these cartoons September 26, 1941, and followed with eight more releases up to August 26, 1942, after which time Paramount took charge of Fleischer Studios, renamed it Famous Studios, and released another eight cartoons between September 18, 1942, and July 30, 1943.[8]

Of all these versions, though, the television series *The Adventures of Superman*, which debuted September 19, 1952, had the most lasting resonance outside of the comic book. The producer of the radio version of Superman, Robert Maxwell, had set his eyes on developing a television version when the early success of the medium undercut radio's audience. By 1951, he was in Los Angeles working at producing the series. Debuting in 1952 and replayed constantly, the six seasons of the series caught successive waves of baby boomers and is deeply ingrained in the cultural fabric. Even though the series has been released in DVD box sets and every streaming format, in 2015 it attracted a loyal following on the nostalgia cable channel MeTV.

The series became a touchstone for readers and audiences of many other versions of Superman. The television series, by using the same opening that the radio serial fixed on in September 1942, cemented the notion that Superman fought for "truth, justice, and the American way."

The 1978 film *Superman*, starring Christopher Reeve, and its first sequel, if not the latter two films of the quartet, saw Superman again standing for the American way. In answer to Lois Lane's question, "Why are you here? There must be a reason for you to be here," Superman replies, "Yes, I am here to fight for truth and justice and the American way." Lois laughs in reply and says, "You are going to end up fighting every elected official in this country," to which Superman responds, "I'm sure you don't really mean that, Lois." And Lois says, "I don't believe this," and Superman replies, "Lois, I never lie." The film essentially retold Superman's basic story but with a slightly more mature version of Superman and Lois Lane's relationship. With a fanfare of publicity ranging from the film's special effects to the salaries of its star hires in supporting roles and a broad marketing campaign, *Superman* became a template for the summer blockbuster film and brought new audiences to the character and reinvigorated an older audience's engagement with Superman.

Numerous other media versions of Superman include two fifteen-part movie serials released in 1948 and 1950, respectively. Superman also appeared in various Saturday-morning television cartoon series. Other television adventures included two television series, *Lois & Clark* and *Smallville*. Two feature films, *Superman Returns* (2006) and *Man of Steel* (2013), attempted to relaunch Superman as a film franchise, but both fell short in revitalizing this dimension of the character's media appearances. Superman also acquired a youthful incarnation as Superboy (a teenage Superman) and a Supergirl cousin, as well as numerous super pets including Krypto the Superdog. All of these incarnations contributed to shaping Superman's place in American culture.

THE BUSINESS OF SUPERMAN

Throughout this book, I predominantly refer to the corporation that controls Superman as DC, or DC Comics. Using "DC" is a convenience that covers the many names and different corporate structures that have controlled Superman. The original contract that Siegel and Shuster signed in 1938 transferring all rights to Superman for $130 was with Detective Comics Inc. Detective Comics Inc. was originally a partnership between Major Malcolm Wheeler-Nicholson's National Allied Publications and his distributor Harry Donenfeld of Independent News, whose accountant Jack S. Liebowitz became coowner. By 1938, though, Wheeler-Nicholson had been removed, and Liebowitz and Donenfeld controlled the company and bought the assets of National Allied Publications. The holding company then went through a series of names including National Comics and by 1961 National Periodical Publications. Along the way, Liebowitz and Donenfeld established Superman Inc. as a separate entity to handle the exploitation of that brand. By 1961, Superman Inc. had become the Licensing Corporation of America, and this entity was part of National Periodical Publications along with the distribution company Independent News. In 1961, National listed on the stock market.[9] In July 1967, the service company Kinney National Service announced it would acquire National Periodicals through an exchange of stock. The *Wall Street Journal* reported that for the previous fiscal year National Periodicals had net income of $3.5 million, or $2.61 per share, on revenue of $65 million. The deal went through by March 1968, and Jack Liebowitz became chairman of Kinney's executive committee.[10] Soon after, Kinney purchased the Warner Bros.–Seven Arts studio for $64 million and restructured its holdings as Warner Communications Inc. Eventually, in 1989, this company became Time Warner, which remains DC's corporate parent.[11] Through all these shifts and changes, DC has mostly been known as just that, or perhaps DC Comics. The name, though, was only formalized in 1977, and since September 2009, DC Comics Inc. has been subsumed under the DC Entertainment division of Time Warner.[12]

THE PERSISTENCE OF AN ICON

Because Superman is so much more than a comic book superhero, tracing and accounting for his iconic status requires something more than a linear history. The same is probably true for most icons. Martin Kemp defines an icon as something "that has achieved wholly exceptional levels of widespread recognizability and has come to carry a rich series of varied associations for very large numbers of people across time and cultures, such that it has to a greater or lesser degree transgressed the parameters of its initial making, function, context, and meaning." Kemp also notes that icons spawn "a huge number of progeny" and that the truly iconic image gathers about it tales that often have a vague relationship with historical evidence, to the point that creators often get caught up in the myths surrounding their creations and believe them to be true.[13] All these features apply to Superman. To examine Superman, I use thematic approaches of myth and history, ideology, nostalgia, production and authorship, readership and audiences, and brands and beyond, because these frameworks allow for an analysis in several registers. For instance, with regard to myth, I can show the way that scholars have used the concept to understand Superman, the way that DC has marketed Superman as mythic, and the way Superman has achieved a certain mythic dimension, while at the same time counterpoising these instances with the history of the character. Likewise, I can discuss the many ways nostalgia impacts the transmission and reception of Superman as an icon. The thorny issue of Superman's authorship is one of the tales around the character that needs unpacking, first, to understand how he became an icon and, second, to understand his persistence as such. The appeal of Superman has some correlation to his availability both as an expression of ideology and as a product. And because the various Superman comic books had letters pages for many years, it is possible to derive some sense of the various associations that audiences brought to the character. All of these phenomena explain the persistence of Superman.

Chapter 1 traces the rise of Superman as an icon and the early history of Superman. Umberto Eco's now-classic piece on Superman has long been a starting point for academic study of the character.[14] The chapter shows the strength and limitations of Eco's piece, which nicely captured a specific moment in Superman's long career but which at the time it appeared in English had already been superseded by changes in the comic book. As a fictional character and a piece of intellectual property, Superman has had multivariant histories. Eco wrote about one of those aspects, the perceived life of a fictional character, who lived in a timeless state. This internal history was in Eco's view a nonhistory in that nothing that happened had any impact on stories that came after. But Superman also had a history as a piece of intellectual property. How the character was developed and marketed over time is one part of a fictional character's external history. And beyond this, there is another aspect of the external history of the character, the understanding that audiences bring to their interactions with Superman, which is based on knowledge of his earlier, albeit timeless, adventures. When the timeless state he lived in would no longer sell comics as readily, Superman's owners moved him to a more linear narrative. And although this may have caused problems for DC in the possibility of exhausting the character by giving him temporality, the company found a solution of sorts in simply rebooting the character whenever he reached the end of a fruitful narrative stream.

A character who fights for the American way would seem to be self-evidently ideological. Chapter 2 examines just what the American way meant for Superman. As a concept, the American way had been very loosely and widely defined before World War II. But during the war, it was codified somewhat around the notion of civility and consensus. This civility was based on the promise of an abundance of goods and services for all, and within that promise lay a space to struggle for the extension of civility to all. Although in the comic books Superman was mostly limited to the small acts of charity that Eco described, in the radio serial he fought against the Ku Klux Klan and for racial justice. But Superman's expressions of ideology extended beyond these aspects of the American way. The post–World War II comic book offered a vision of gendered society with a strong patriarchal tone. And while Superman slipped into consensus and conformity, this state gained a release valve of sorts in an anarchic series of stories featuring a Bizarro Superman that stood many conventions on their head. But, tellingly, these did not include patriarchal conventions of the nuclear family. More importantly, in the 1970s, Superman began to break out of the stasis that Eco had analyzed. Fittingly, in the era of the "Me Generation," Superman's stories started to show a concern with the place and worth of superheroes, and often the answers to these worries lay in forms of individualism.

DC's approach in rebooting, or restarting, Superman afresh might have caused problems for the company in that audiences of earlier versions may have felt abandoned. But Superman engendered much nostalgia, and this not only helped the character remain popular but also became somewhat of a defining feature of Superman. Nostalgia is a form of history in that it is a way of ordering memory. In instance after instance of Superman's appearances across different media forms, his creators wove in memory triggers. Often these were in the form of catchphrases, such as "Look up in the sky," or "Truth, justice, and the American way." In film and television, this has extended to having actors from other versions of Superman appearing in guest or cameo spots. Chapter 3 deals with nostalgia for Superman and DC's use of this nostalgia as both a storytelling and a marketing strategy. Further, both the mythic and ideological dimensions of Superman rely on aspects of the nostalgia for the character.

Superman's origin story, coming from the doomed planet Krypton and being raised by his adoptive parents, the Kents, is one of the most familiar aspects of his story. The story of Superman's creation by Jerry Siegel and Joe Shuster almost rivals that story. So often the story of Superman's creation and success as a character is told as that of Siegel and Shuster losing control of Superman and ending up as destitute before being rescued by the actions of the artists Neal Adams and Jerry Robinson, and the threatened mobilization of public sentiment against DC, in the mid-1970s. This story often achieves the mythic proportions of Superman, with the heroic artists as creative individuals facing off against the monolithic corporation that denied them their rights. Generally these versions ignore that Siegel and Shuster between them made $6 million in 2016 dollars, between 1938 and 1947. Chapter 4 offers a more complex version of this story that traces the rise of Superman through studying the manner in which he was produced. The chapter draws on original correspondence between the various parties involved and on documents from several court cases.

The readers of Superman comics and the audiences for his various other media incarnations have long engaged with the character in ways that go beyond simply consuming him through a purchase. Chapter 5 examines the engagement of different audiences with Superman, the sort of communities they formed, and how these relate to the circulation of Superman. While some scholars, such as Fredric Wertham, Constance Penley, and Henry Jenkins, have explored the way that audiences, readers, and fans step outside simple consumerist roles in the formation of such communities, I argue that there is a double-edged sword and that such communities in turn bind them more closely to the product they consume, even as they as they shape their own level of engagement.[15] For many years, some media companies treated such groups with weary disdain, often demanding that they cease and desist in their activity if it involved the use of images and characters protected by intellectual property laws. But comic book companies like DC encouraged letters to the editor and were happy when fan communities developed. Not only were such communities seen as a source of new talent for the companies, but they helped create value in the characters through practices such as collecting comic books and holding fan conventions. In chapter 5, I examine the letters pages of Superman comic books and argue that these became the site of a broad discussion of the Superman marque, a discussion that extended beyond the comic book Superman and took into account other versions of the character. The letters pages demonstrate that many readers brought other Superman associations to their reading of the comic book stories and that Superman, if not a unified entity across his many incarnations, nonetheless had characteristics that readers and audiences wished to find in different versions, bringing different associations to their engagement with the icon.

Chapter 6 deals with Superman as a consumer product. Superman has been a brand, rather than simply a character, since DC created a radio serial and licensed the character to Daisy toys in 1939. Simply put, not only has Superman sold an array of products from peanut butter to American Express cards, but these products have sold us Superman. Technological changes and the rise of transmedia have thrown this aspect of comic book characters like Superman into sharp relief. This chapter, then, examines the way that DC created Superman's brand. Understanding Superman as a brand helps us better understand his cultural circulation and importance in American and global culture. There is an argument for seeing all forms of Superman, including products like tee shirts and coffee mugs, as forms of media because they circulate the character. Certainly corporations have developed other "characters" deliberately in just this fashion.[16] When so much media content is freely spreadable across file-sharing programs and the like, characters originating in media with more tangible forms of products that are not easily reducible to digital reproduction are all the more valuable. Although 3D printers may soon make this observation obsolete, a purchase is necessary to enjoy products like coffee mugs and tee shirts, whereas comic books, movies, and television series are often available for no cost, albeit illegally. Media is shifting because the ways that money is made from it are shifting. For an iconic character like Superman, whose iconicity in part relies on the widespread availability of products carrying his brand or symbol, shifts and changes in his marketability in this form impact on his status as an icon.

Although over seventy-five years old, Superman remains at the forefront of shifts in the place of superhero characters in American culture, and studying the longevity of his popularity helps explain these developments over the long term. Perhaps no longer the most popular superhero character, Superman retains a sway over the American imagination as an icon that warrants examination.

CHAPTER ONE

SUPERMAN MYTHOS AND HISTORY

Superman's persistence as a figure of popular fiction for close to eighty years rests on a certain relationship to his own history and the ways in which DC has managed that history. Some of the first scholarly efforts at understanding Superman tried to account for this longevity by situating Superman as myth. This chapter, then, reads the mythic dimension of Superman against his history. In an article published in English in 1972 but originally appearing in Italian in 1962, Umberto Eco described Superman as a mythological virtuous archetype locked in a timeless state and thereby never fully consumed by his audience. A key part of Eco's argument, and one captured in the Italian title, was that the Superman comic dissolved time in ways that made it difficult for Superman to be both a mythological archetype with a "fixed nature which renders him easily recognizable" and at the same time a figure of modern fiction in which the story happens as it is told and is marked by "the unpredictable nature of what will happen."[1] To hold this tension in check, Superman's writers could only depict him in ways that broke down the sense of time in the story told. That is, readers had to suspend a sense of time or avoid applying reason to the time consumed in a Superman tale.

For Eco, these strictures explain in part why an omnipotent figure like Superman confined his activities, for the most part, to acts of virtue. Superman's activities implied an ordered society, the wrongs of which could be put right by acts of charity. Superman operated in a setting of clearly identifiable transgressors such as criminal gangs, the odd mad scientist or two, and the occasional intergalactic villain for spice. As Eco concluded, "The plot must be static and evade any development because Superman must make virtue consist of many little activities on a small scale, never achieving a total awareness. Conversely, virtue must be characterized in the accomplishment of only partial acts so that the plot can remain static."[2] In effect, Superman strove to educate Americans about the timelessness of the existing order or the naturalness of an ordered state of being.

Eco does not cite specific examples of Superman stories in his piece; but in an anecdote elsewhere, he says he used two to three hundred issues of Superman comics to prepare the piece, and it seems these were the original American comic books, rather than Italian reprints.[3] The majority of the comics available to Eco, writing in the early 1960s, would have been from the 1950s, along with some 1940s postwar comics. From the perspective of the early twenty-first century, it is easy enough to see postwar America trying to reassure itself of the timelessness and normalness of prosperity after the deprivations of the Great Depression and World War II. The lack of broader notions of virtue, beyond the small and localized, perhaps lay in a deliberate ratcheting down of Superman as an *Übermensch*, if not in terms of his powers, then at least in regard to his actions, as a response to criticism that he represented just the sort of ideology that America had fought a war against.[4] Likewise, the context of the Cold War explains some of the notion of virtue as charity rather than, say, programmatic reform. Indeed, America generally presented its actions in the world as lending a helping hand in the spirit of charity rather than the sort of self-interest that motivated imperial powers.[5]

To a certain extent, in Eco's hands the notions of time and of history are conflated. Moreover, he reduces both history and time to the singular, passing over the existence of several modes of history and historical causality that correspond to different modes of time and temporal explanation. John Cheng discusses some of the way notions of time shifted in fact and fiction, under the impact of Albert Einstein's theories, from pre–World War II concepts of linearity to postwar concepts of time as not necessarily linear.[6] Eco hints that it is the idealized narrative forms and structures of Superman stories that makes the character timeless. By showing us one side of Superman, the timeless structure of a hero/superhero myth, Eco allows us to see a tension in Superman between features that are crystallized— entities such as Superman are God-like and above change—and the experience of writers and readers trying to fit that entity to lived conditions. It is a play between diachronic and synchronic aspects of Superman, with Superman understood here as a phenomenon and as a totality of many aspects: the character, the business of producing comics/television/film (trademarked brand name and copyrighted), and the work of distributing, consuming, and using the marque. Eco might have been right in principle about the totalizing nature of the Superman myth, at least that version extant when he wrote, but there are so many socially and historically relevant variations on the Superman theme that it is useful to pause and think about the application of his methodology.

Eco considered ideal abstractions of Superman as a heroic figure and read them semiotically and symbolically, but his analysis centered on a limited set of Superman comic book stories, even if that amounted to ten years' worth of comic book stories. Eco shows us how these Superman stories structure a myth, in this case the Superman myth, and if we follow Giambattista Vico, we can see this myth as a particular needs projection of 1950s America.[7] But what Eco does not show us is the construction of Superman. That construction is a history that can be tracked and traced, and although like all history it is not possible to offer a complete blow-by-blow account of the development of Superman, it is possible to trace every shift and turn in the comic books and most of the other incarnations of Superman.[8] And thanks to court cases, many documents on the early development of Superman are widely available. To be sure, this is not the story Eco was trying to tell, but it is the story of Superman.

Eco's 1950s Superman was somewhat crystallized within a limited version of virtue. But Eco's interpretation does suggest that, as limited as Superman's virtue might be according to the prevailing social order, numerous possibilities for storytelling focused on virtue existed under different conditions. So Eco's Superman is, then, not totally timeless but can act as an instructive tool for what passes as virtue in society, and Superman's popularity at any given time is probably in direct relationship to his creators' success in capturing a dominant mood. In effect, Superman is a product by which we consume virtue. Nonetheless, such an approach assigns to Superman an a priori status as virtuous, with him being a fixed point of reference. And indeed Superman is virtuous, and that is fixed because he is a work of fiction. The tension in Superman, then, is this: he has fixed qualities like virtue, but he has existed since 1938 and has a history that involves a degree of change and development. Claude Lévi-Strauss's notion that myth recycles earlier versions of the myth as part of its status is a useful observation because it reminds us that such figures must contain the earlier versions of themselves.[9] In this chapter, then, I examine some of the ways Superman manages this feat.

EARLY SUPERMAN

The earliest version of Siegel and Shuster's comic book Superman had a different notion of virtue than that encountered by Eco. Superman of the first two years of *Action Comics* was somewhat of a reformist liberal, albeit one given to direct action. In his early years, Superman saved a woman who had mistakenly been condemned for murder, confronted a wife beater, prevented the United States from becoming embroiled in a European conflict, destroyed slums to force the government to build better housing (well, modern high-rise apartment blocks), tore down a car factory because its shoddy products caused deaths, and fought a corrupt police force. In this version, his creators, Jerry Siegel and Joe Shuster, tied Superman's virtue to Franklin Roosevelt's New Deal politics, America's 1930s isolationism, and the reality of life in Cleveland, where they lived. This somewhat-anarchic Superman captured an audience of young fans who probably reveled in his short-cut solutions to social problems and defiance of conventional authority. But this Superman was short-lived.[10]

Beginning in the latter half of 1940, a combination of factors transformed Superman into a symbol of more general American cultural values in that his individualism was tied to consumerist values. Superman's metamorphosis resulted from the confluence of his success as a comic book character, which brought added attention and opportunities for his creators and publishers, and the way the creators and publishers clashed over realizing the value in those opportunities. This success, and the more general success of comic books, also brought a morality campaign directed at comic books. A heightened patriotism with the growing realization that America would be drawn into the European war also colored this period. This transformation naturalized many aspects of Superman and produced the "timeless" character of which Eco writes. The process of change was traumatic and difficult for Siegel and Shuster. The early Superman with all its raw edges was very much their vision of the character. The rapid success of the character, marked among other things by the introduction of a daily comic strip in January 1939, brought with it fresh demands and a need for change. Correspondence from 1938 to 1941 between Jerry Siegel and Jack Liebowitz, the business manager and later coowner at Detective Comics, shows the tensions in this process.

By all accounts, Siegel, who had shopped Superman around to much rejection, was relieved at first to find a home in *Action Comics*. But six months after assigning all rights to Superman to DC Comics, Siegel sent a letter to DC that Liebowitz said took his breath away. In the letter of September 26, 1938, Siegel asked for, and just stopped short of demanding, fifteen dollars per page for Superman. If Siegel felt hard done by, so too did Liebowitz, who wrote on September 28, "the amount of increase you demand does not hurt me as much as your attitude in the entire matter." Liebowitz went on to suggest that Siegel took such a stance because he was an inexperienced young man. Siegel, for his part, replied on September 30 noting that Liebowitz had explained "many things" to the writers' "complete satisfaction" and returning the new contracts for comic book page rates and for the syndicated comic strip. But whatever goodwill existed at that time seemed to have evaporated rather quickly. Several letters from Liebowitz and later from the DC Comics editor Whitney Ellsworth stress again and again the need for organization and quality control in the production of both the comic strip and the comic book. In April 1939, Liebowitz suggested to Siegel that he and Shuster move to New York so they could be "at a moment's touch" with everything that they did. Liebowitz continued, "I think with a daily routine in an office, you will be able to accomplish a great deal more away from the distractions of working at home."[11]

Much of this correspondence reads like a textbook case of the point Roger Chartier, a French cultural historian, makes that we need to distinguish between "text" and "print." "Text" involves authors writing, and "print" involves publishers publishing. The two may be linked, but they are not one and the same. What writers intend for their work and the ways in which publishers market it may be at odds.[12] And to this point, we can add that publishers of serial narratives need to control production, quality, and delivery of that narrative, and this will

potentially bring them into conflict with creators. The process of creating Superman was a complex piece of business. Liebowitz reminded
Siegel to "invest now in building for the future" and not to become
complacent with his "present monetary results." The McClure syndicate and DC Comics were active partners in shaping Superman,
constantly giving Siegel and Shuster notes on aspects of the character
and rejecting work as substandard. Because Siegel seemed to create
on the fly, Liebowitz urged him to submit synopses of continuities so
they could be edited. In 1940, Liebowitz suggested that Siegel consult
a dictionary, where he would find that "haemophilia is a tendency to
profuse bleeding even from slight wounds" and not, as Siegel thought,
a condition of "a person with lack of blood." And in this same 1940
letter, Liebowitz sent Siegel a synopsis for a Superman story that he
asked Siegel to write "the detailed panel script for," which was probably the first time a Superman story originated with someone other
than Siegel. And again Liebowitz complained about Siegel's inability
to produce the promised five stories a month, calling him "a Superman in reverse."[13] This correspondence between publisher and author
reminds us that this sort of cultural work is cooperative and subject
to the demands of the structure of production and distribution. To
ensure that the latter two parts of this equation flow smoothly, publishers also needed to be sure of their market.

Liebowitz's January 1940 letter to Siegel noted "that at the present
time there seems to be a concentrated drive against movies and comic
books which parent-teachers groups and womens [sic] clubs claim are
harmful for children." The solution to this potential threat to Superman's future lay in an "editorial policy with a view of obtaining the
approval of parents, while still not sacrificing the adventure and the
thrill Superman has always brought to children." Toward the end of
1940, DC Comics instituted an advisory board of psychologists and
child educators in response to this public campaign and the legislation
in some states against comic books that transgressed public morals.
New guidelines for Superman stories prohibited, among other things,
the destruction of private property. What we see here is the process
that made Eco's virtuous Superman and a development that is traceable and situated in specific conditions. And that virtue was defined
in particular terms. In an editorial in the October 1941 issue of *Action
Comics* that introduced the new editorial board, DC explained, "a

deep respect for our obligation to the young people of America and their parents and our responsibility as parents ourselves combine to set our standards of wholesome entertainment."

At the same time, Superman himself had become an important piece of private property. In mid-January 1940, Liebowitz wrote to Siegel that DC planned "to go after various licenses" and that the company had set up a publicity department. He suggested that Siegel do no further interviews, such as the recent misleading interview he had done with the *Cleveland Plain Dealer* boasting of forthcoming Superman products for which no deal existed. Later that month, Liebowitz informed Siegel that DC had signed a deal with "Hecker Products for a radio program." And although the program would lose DC $700 a week, Liebowitz hoped for more stations and a sponsor to turn the loss to profit.[14] Liebowitz needed to get Siegel more organized for the commercialization of Superman to be most successful. One problem that he highlighted to Siegel in February 1940 was that it was difficult to add newspapers to the syndicated strip if Siegel did not provide details on how long a particular story arc (continuity) would run and that no paper would pick up the strip in midstory.[15]

Siegel's enthusiasm for licensing in 1940 seems at odds with his earlier bitter parody of the marketing of Superman products. In a 1938 story, Nick Williams, a shoddy businessman, steals Superman's name to sell a range of goods including bathing suits and automobiles. In a 1983 interview, Jerry Siegel remembered this story in a more positive light, omitting any mention of Superman's name being stolen and his likeness exploited. Instead, he suggested that the story inspired DC to look for licensing opportunities. When I first encountered the story, I read it as a parody of licensing, but the story is perhaps better read as a critique by someone who has no right to the benefits flowing from the licensing value of Superman's name (see figure 1).[16] At the time the story appeared, Siegel and Shuster were negotiating with DC for the right to do the comic strip version of Superman for the McClure syndicate. In each and every contract and codicil to contracts that Siegel and Shuster signed with DC, the company asserted its complete control of the character and ownership of all copyright. Nonetheless, in December 1939, DC granted Siegel and Shuster 5 percent of "all net proceeds which may be derived by [the company] from all commercial exploitation of

FIGURE 1.
Action Comics
#6 (November
1938)

Superman."[17] With this deal in hand, their Superman stories began to contain plugs for various products such as the Superman-themed Daisy Krypto-Raygun (see figure 2).[18] In June 1941, the *Saturday Evening Post* reported that Superman products generated over a million dollars of profit in 1940. For Liebowitz, such a profit vindicated his strategy of selling movie serial rights to Republic Pictures

FIGURE 2.
Action Comics
#32 (January
1941)

for $8,000, "feeling assured" that the low price was justified since, as he wrote to Siegel, "all the publicity we will receive as a result of this venture would aid us materially in building up the radio end promoting the sale of licensed merchandise."[19] Liebowitz understood the benefit of synergy long before Buckminster Fuller gave the word currency.

AMERICAN ICON

The commercialization of Superman was in part responsible for the character becoming an American icon and one imbued with American concepts of virtue. On America's entry into World War II, the defense of the "American way of life," which posited the promise of consumer choice in a market of goods as the basis of a democratic society, became an important cry to rally the troops. Countless advertisements sought to mobilize the nation for war by directing consumption into appropriate expenditures that would assure victory and lay the basis for a postwar democracy of goods. The government and advertisers depicted the war as a test of national resolve to curtail expectations to defend and ensure a way of life. Superman, with his new respect for authority, his anarchic youthful past, and his iconization as a commodity, represented that way of life. The U.S. Army recognized Superman's importance in 1943 and distributed one hundred thousand copies of the comic book to overseas troops every other month until late 1944, when the practice was discontinued because the comic book was readily available through Post Exchange stores. Shortly after the end of the war, the Superman line of comic books averaged monthly sales of 8.5 million.[20]

World War II shaped a particular version of Superman and gave the character a broad familiarity to many Americans. By 1944, a victory for the United States and its allies in the war seemed inevitable. As that victory drew closer and closer, the covers of the Superman comic books grew more and more playful. For instance, of the sixty covers of *Action Comics* from January 1944 to December 1948, forty-five were humorous, nine represented some sort of action with no humorous element, and four showed a war-like scene (two war scenes and two redrawn war scenes because the war was over). Two other covers nicely captured the range of American culture that Superman covered, from popular art to the emerging military industrial complex. The cover of the October 1945 *Action Comics* #89 featured a translucent Superman against a backdrop of concentric multicolored circles, much like a hypnotic swirl. The cover is simply dazzling and looks like a pop art experiment. The cover of the October 1946 issue #101 showed Superman filming an atomic bomb explosion alongside the headline, "In this issue Superman covers Atom Bomb Test," although no such story appeared inside the book. What I refer to as

FIGURE 3.
Action Comics
#85 (June 1945)

humorous covers displayed a range of playful depictions, from Superman cracking wise that "massage is so stimulating for the scalp" as he
is fed head first to a buzz saw (#85, June 1945; see figure 3) to Superman
providing the breeze to propel an ice sail sled (#118, March 1948). In
the bimonthly *Superman* comic book, twenty-five of the thirty covers
in this same period were humorous, and the war disappeared from

the cover after the January–February 1944 issue #26 showed Superman taunting Heinrich Himmler with the Liberty Bell. During this time, some of Superman's major foes, in addition to Lex Luthor and other evil scientist types, were the Prankster, the Toyman, and the fifth-dimension trickster Mr. Mxyzptlk. In general, DC created a more humorous Superman, who reverted to the joker of Siegel and Shuster's original version, but without the destruction of property and with more respect for the rule of law. Gerard Jones in *Men of Tomorrow* argues that DC was positioning itself as part of the children's entertainment industry and the lighthearted tone of the covers and many of the stories certainly support his thesis. Indeed, DC's introduction of a younger version of Superman, the teenaged Superboy, in 1944 may have been part of this effort to appeal to a younger audience.[21]

Eco's postwar Superman already had been through two prior incarnations and, far from being an unchanging figure, was one with a history. Moreover, the *Superman* that Eco read was increasingly one produced for younger readers than the war audience. If DC Comics was prescient in realizing that comic books after World War II would need to appeal to children as a prime audience, other publishers were not so astute. In the years directly after the war, comic book publishers tried to find audiences for numerous genres of comics, including crime and horror comics. The psychiatrist and liberal activist Fredric Wertham believed that comics in general were harmful to children, and he launched an anti-comic-book campaign in the 1950s that culminated in his book *Seduction of the Innocent* and the related 1954 Senate Subcommittee to Investigate Juvenile Delinquency comic book hearings. Whatever the intentions of Wertham and the subcommittee, and there were some comics clearly not suitable for children, they essentially characterized the medium of comic books as the province of only children. Comic book publishers responded to the campaign by establishing the industry-based Comic Code Authority (CCA), which created standards to which publishers had to conform or else risk losing the CCA mark of approval and hence be more open to attack from parents, social do-gooders, and the usual array of would-be regulators. Such industry self-regulation followed the Hollywood model of the Hay Office and represented a uniquely American solution. In other countries such as Britain and Australia, comic books ran afoul of government intervention and censorship.[22] These actions transformed the medium of comic books from one with diverse appeal and audiences to a children's medium with childish tales.

These developments in American comic books, and the Superman comic books in particular, add a further contextual wrinkle to Eco's theory but do not diminish the strength of his argument about the didactic nature of the comics he read. Indeed, that the comics were for children makes Eco's argument about their pedagogical nature all the more pertinent. For Eco, readers related to Superman by abandoning "control of temporal relationships and renounc[ing] the need to reason on their basis." Eco hammered home the possible consequences of such modes of thought:

> In growing accustomed to the idea of events happening in an ever-continuing present, the reader loses track of the fact that they should develop according to the dictates of time. Losing consciousness of it, he forgets the problems which are at its base; that is, the existence of freedom, the possibility of planning, the necessity of carrying plans out, the sorrow that such planning entails, the responsibility that it implies, and finally, the existence of an entire human community whose progressiveness is based on making plans.[23]

COLD WAR SUPERMAN

Superman comics in the 1950s further compounded the loss of temporal time because stories from this period often envisioned American life as a universal norm across time and space. For instance, in a 1958 story, Krypton families brought their children up in what seem to be suburban homes with rooms with curtains and cribs, and Superman met a scientist who was a "roommate in college" with Jor-El, Superman's father (see figure 4). At one level, this representation is risible, but these sort of normative projections of the American way as a universal way shaped Superman as an icon of American culture. A telling example of such normative representations occurred in "The Bride of Bizarro," published in August 1959. The Bizarro concept, an imperfect copy of Superman with a face like a reflection in a broken mirror and who does everything the opposite of Superman, brought back some of the earlier anarchic humor to Superman but, even so, conformed to social norms of the 1950s. In this story, Bizarro Superman declares his

FIGURE 4.
Action Comics
#242 (July 1958)

love for Lois Lane and his desire to marry her. To be sure, that was the opposite of Superman's behavior. To rid herself of Bizarro's unwanted attentions, Lois creates a Bizarro Lois. Given that Lois was intent on wedding Superman, one would expect that Bizarro Lois would do the opposite and have no desire to wed Bizarro, but she is only too happy to do so and eventually has Bizarro children. The projected social norm of a woman wanting to marry and settle into a nuclear family was so much a norm that even in a world turned topsy-turvy, it still seemed natural. In another story, "The Shame of the Bizarro Family," Bizarro Superman Junior has problems in his school because he keeps passing his tests. The story is a lesson in American civics and culture, such as the colors of the flag, the presidents' faces carved on Mount Rushmore, and the rules of baseball. Bizarro Junior eventually manages to successfully fail his test by carving a replica of Mount Rushmore with the faces of classic horror villains. Indeed, most Bizarro episodes offered lessons in appropriate behavior and social norms by reversing them, but nonetheless, Bizarro Superman lived in the most quintessential norm of 1950s America, the nuclear suburban family.[24]

The Comic Code constrained a lot of storytelling possibilities and helps explain some of the dimensions of timelessness that Eco analyzed. When Superman did confront one of his more sinister opponents in these years, the stories often seemed bland to their readers. In a letter to the Metropolis Mailbag page in the August 1970 issue of *Superman*, Doris Koehler of Pacifica, California, inquired why it was that villains like Lex Luthor and Brainiac hardly harmed anyone except Superman and certainly never killed, although they were supposedly evil. The editors replied that, evil though these characters were, they had to obey the Comic Code Authority. But by the late 1960s, the Code started to break down, and the story lines shifted a little. In a 1963 story, "The Showdown between Luthor and Superman," the supposedly evil Luthor shows a compassionate side, letting a disempowered Superman beat him in a duel so that a planet's population will survive. To be sure, Luthor motivation is part vanity but also part basic human decency. In a 1972 story, "The Man Who Murdered the Earth," Luthor again shows his essential humanity and the need for human society—but not before the entire population of the world has been apparently slaughtered, and his humanity lacks the expressed compassion from the 1960s and mostly revolves around his own need for company (see figure 5). Given that the Comic Code was still in effect, such mass violence was not allowed, and it turns out that Superman has protected everyone by shifting them to another dimension. But a decided shift in tone is evident in that mass violence is presented, if only momentarily, and it is nonetheless necessary for the reader to emotionally connect to that mass violence, and the nature of evil that would commit such an act, for the story to make sense. The story shows some of the impact of the American war in Vietnam, in that mass violence is more readily contemplated and not so shocking, given the nightly news body count. The story also captures the dilemma for Superman writers in this period: horrific violence was basically not allowed, but what else could threaten an invulnerable man? There were only so many times that the writers could use Kryptonite or magic to make Superman vulnerable. Also, a Superman without powers essentially runs counter to the whole concept, unless he is in Clark Kent mode, but in those years, Clark Kent was more of a plot device than a fleshed-out character.[25]

The CCA eventually unraveled because of the changing nature of the economies of comic book production and readership, which by the early years of the twenty-first century made it mostly irrelevant. But that process took some forty years. Along with violence, sexuality was the other great concern of the CCA. In keeping with the code, Superman eschewed such matters. The absence of a mature relationship held Superman in a timeless stasis in the 1950s and beyond. In *Men of Tomorrow: Geeks, Gangsters, and the Birth of the Comic Book*, Gerard Jones depicts Jerry Siegel and Joe Shuster as boy-men who graduated from high school late and retained an innocent, immature worldview well into their twenties. In Jones's account, both the geeks and gangsters who shaped the early comic book industry had some trouble in sustained emotional relations with women. The early Superman comic books incorporated a tough-guy and film noir *Weltanschauung* that dames are trouble. These attitudes continued throughout the 1950s and 1960s. In these years, DC published imaginary tales in which Lois and Clark/Superman marry. DC also published stories about Lois's constant pursuit of Superman both romantically and in search of his secret identity. The problem with dames, then, for Superman is their curiosity. Indeed, the way DC presented the matter, a woman's curiosity about a man could be resolved for her only in marriage, where she could control the man and so limit his ability to present her with things to be curious about. A 1963 story, "The Romance of Superbaby and Baby Lois," shows Lois's curiosity about Superman's identity, and because of a personality change brought on by a car crash, she blackmails Superman into marrying her, which Superman forestalls by using a rejuvenating spray to make them both regress back to babies. At the end of the story, when normalcy is returned and Lois and Superman remain unmarried, Lois dreamily says, "If I ever get

FIGURE 5.
Superman
#248
(February
1972)

him to that altar because he *really* loves me, he won't get away again!"
On overhearing this statement, Superman thinks, "Something tells me
I'd better get out of here while the going is good!"[26]

As Superman entered the 1970s, his comic book adventures were a
mixed bag. *Superman* #222 in December 1969 consisted of reprints from
the early 1960s, which by that stage looked to be a different century.
Mort Weisinger, an apparently less than pleasant editor with a sense that
he knew best, remained at the helm of most of the DC comic books

with Superman stories, as he had been since the 1940s. The February 1970 issue of *Superman* carried an imaginary tale of a married Superman and Lois having a super intelligent, but evil, Superbaby who has an enlarged cranium. Although the images show a shift in fashion styles, in most ways the story is more of the same old stuff and indistinguishable from the much-earlier material reprinted in the December 1969 issue. By this time, *Superman* sales were falling. Between 1968 and 1969, sales dropped by 20 percent. By March 1973, sales had fallen by 50 percent from 1968.[27] The limits of Superman's timeless state were beginning to show, and just at the time that Eco's piece appeared in English, Superman's frozen state became unstuck, albeit at an almost glacial pace. The structured world of Superman stories in the 1950s and into the 1960s was part of a business model that worked for DC Comic. When that no longer attracted as many readers, Superman had to change.

DC tried to hold its readers through a series of changes. Toward the end of 1970, Weisinger retired or was shown the door, and Julius Schwartz replaced him as editor of *Superman* and was listed as such in the January 1971 issue. With sales hemorrhaging, Schwartz also took charge of *Action Comics* by 1972. The change after Weisinger departed was noticeable. Under Schwartz and others, such as the editorial director Carmine Infantino, DC tried to adjust to changing readership tastes.[28] Three stories from this period vividly demonstrate this shift. A November 1970 story by Robert Kanigher, who was also the author of the evil Superbaby story, had Lois Lane spend a day as an African American. The story replicated *Black Like Me*, a work by the journalist John Howard Griffin, who in the late 1950s traveled through some southern states with medically induced darkened skin and wrote of his experience of race and racism.[29] Lois's comic book version compresses the action into a day and offers a pat conclusion. The story's naïve liberalism was almost a prerequisite for the media of the day, and the story is more important in showing that DC was trying to reposition itself and catch up with its competitor Marvel Comics, which was starting to take a greater share of comic book sales and which had taken a liberal "tackle the issues" approach in its books. That DC hired one of Marvel's star auteurs, Jack Kirby, makes it clear that the corporation was trying to hold off Marvel's assault on its sales. Kirby set to work re-creating the Newsboy Legion feature that he had originally produced for DC with Joe Simon in the 1940s, but updating it with the type of fabulous technologies and characters he had done for Marvel, as can be seen in the October 1970 story "Jimmy Olsen Brings Back the Newsboy Legion."[30]

DC also began to give Clark Kent more attention as a character and in the January 1972 issue of *Superman* commenced a series of stories titled "The Private Life of Clark Kent." Again such a representation of Clark was an attempt to follow in Marvel's footsteps, with more focus on the secret identity of characters. In Spider-Man, Iron Man, Thor, and the Fantastic Four, Marvel had an array of superheroes whose secret and not-so-secret identities were as much a part of their stories as their powers. A 1973 story, "I Can't Go Home Again," has a nostalgic Clark preventing the demolition of his childhood family home by gently leading his old friend and now geological surveyor Pete Ross to the discovery that "remains of an Indian civilization" were buried beneath the house, a theme later picked up by the television series *Smallville*. Clark's nostalgia and desire to "still go home again" reveal to Pete, who unbeknown to Clark knows he is Superman, that Superman is really human. The writer, Elliot Maggin, has Pete say, "a wise man once said, 'we must be very careful about what we pretend to be because some day we may wake up to find that's what we are!'" The sentiments are Kurt Vonnegut's, but not surprisingly, he put it better and more succinctly in the introduction to *Mother Night*: "We are what we pretend to be, so we must be careful what we pretend to be." In DC's view, Clark/Superman was not only one entity but at this stage deeply human.[31]

INDUSTRY ISSUES

These shifts were part of broader developments in the comic book industry that included a move away from self-contained stories to continuity. In a wide-ranging essay on comic books, their received history, and issues of genre, among other things, Henry Jenkins notes that in the early 1970s a shift began from self-contained stories to serialization. This development was part of a broader shift, with comic book readers on average being older and reading comics "over a longer span of their lives." Readers placed "a high value on consistency and continuity, appraising both themselves and the authors on their mastery of past events and the web of character relationships within any given franchise." Such was the extent of "this principle of continuity" that it applied "not just within any individual book but also across all of the books by a particular publisher so that people talk about the DC and Marvel universes."[32]

Sheer economics also played a role in this shift to continuity, or so the story goes. Prior to the development of a direct sales market to comic book specialty stores in the 1980s, comic books were mostly distributed on a sell-or-return basis to newsstands. For sales of just over 500,000 copies per month of *Superman* in 1969, DC produced almost a million copies per issue. DC then printed twice the number of copies that the magazine sold. By 1975, sales had fallen to under 300,000 per month. In 1965, DC had sold 823,829 copies of the comic book per issue, so sales had fallen by close to 65 percent over ten years. DC must have been concerned about this decline and the associated decline in profits from comic books. If print runs could be calibrated more closely to sales, DC's profit margin would increase. That falling sales coincided with the industry shift to continuity stories suggests an economic dimension to this change, and the most likely explanation is that such stories were designed to retain a sales base among fans since they had the sort of specialist knowledge necessary to enjoy such stories most completely. Continuity stories would also potentially lock in more sales since curiosity about how a story ended might cause a casual reader to buy succeeding issues. And of course, once DC introduced continuity to Superman, the character gained another layer of history as one that moved forward through linear time, whereas earlier most of his history existed outside of the comic book narratives.

The issues of *Superman* in the mid-1970s give an indication of just how desperate DC was becoming to stem the slide in sales. Many feature topical subjects woven into stories as subplots. For instance, the May 1974 issue of *Superman* has a subtheme of Japanese technology not performing in the United States, which demonstrates the anxieties caused by the rampaging Japanese economy and particularly the threat posed to the US automobile industry from a superior Japanese product. Likewise, the 1970s oil crisis triggered the September 1974 issue, which has a subtheme of oil shortages causing economic difficulties. Eerily, given the terrorist attacks on New York in 2001, the story has a plot device of a skyscraper near the Twin Towers about to collapse and Superman having to rescue the situation because no fire-truck ladder could reach people in a building that high (see figure 6). In this story by Elliot Maggin, the criminal mastermind is an oil-company tycoon who uses the

FIGURE 6. *Superman* #279 (September 1974)

Twin Towers as his headquarters. The July 1975 issue of *Superman* has one of the strangest Superman comic book covers. A photomontage shows a drawn Superman tackling a phantom horseman, against a photographed street-scene backdrop in which the DC staffers Bob Rozakis, Cary Bates, Jack C. Harris, Carl Gafford, and E. Nelson Bridwell appear. Some of the staffers are shown prepared for action in kung fu poses. I am not sure if these stances were meant to induce laughter or awe. Readers of Marvel comics would probably have recognized this self-aggrandizement, possibly masked as self-depreciation, as on par with the antics of Stan "The Man" Lee, who from time to time appeared in the books he wrote. This issue also features the Metropolitan Revolutionary

Army (the previous year, Patty Hearst had been kidnapped by the Symbionese Liberation Army), John Wayne, and the Roller Derby. In many ways, these stories were 1970s versions of Jerry Siegel's 1938 Superman, who tackled many national concerns, as well as local Cleveland issues, head-on. DC's writers and editors in the 1970s touched every base they could to make the comic book relevant. In 1975, they turned to continuity stories.

The first substantial Superman story with continuity occurred in the four issues of *Superman* leading up to the three hundredth issue in June 1976. These stories would have been planned and plotted in 1975. In these issues, the question of Superman's identity as one or the other of Clark or Superman plays a central theme. As part of this theme, Clark for a short time displays a more dynamic personality and even enjoys a serious romantic interlude with Lois Lane, which culminates in a passionate exchange in issue #297 in March 1976. Some fans took this romance and the way it played out to suggest that Lois and Clark had sex, but such an inference is just that, an inference, because the panels depicting the relationship are highly ambiguous.[33] To be sure, Clark and Lois enjoy a passionate kiss, but from the representation of the kiss, one can not even determine whether it is open-mouthed or not. But in these stories, still very much under the strictures of the CCA, Superman develops a broader, more adult personality and appeal. Significantly, at the end of the series in the May 1976 issue of *Superman*, he says to himself, "I tried to decide whether Clark Kent or Superman is more important and realized that to do away with one would be to kill half of myself."

Despite the introduction of continuity, sales continued to fall. By October 1983, the sales of *Superman* had fallen to 126,279 an issue, on average, on a print run of over 300,000 copies; by October 1985, that figure had fallen to a little over 100,000. The constant decline in sales must have been a worrying trend; even with sales guaranteed beforehand and printing costs lowered, DC needed to reinvigorate *Superman* and other comic book titles.

REBOOT

In 1985, DC Comics initiated a *Crisis on Infinite Earths* series of twelve issues spread over a year to celebrate its fiftieth anniversary and in part to give order to its vast array of characters. Shortly after the *Crisis* run ended, DC decided to finish off a version of Superman in *Superman* #423 and *Action Comics* #583, both with a cover date of September 1986, with a story by Alan Moore titled "Whatever Happened to the Man of Tomorrow?" As Paul Kuppenberg, an editor at DC, put it in an introduction to a 1997 reprint of these two issues, *Crisis on Infinite Earths* offered DC an opportunity to relaunch its major characters with a "blank slate" as far as the backstory went, and Moore's story was the consequence. This was to be the first of many reboots or rebirths for Superman in which DC consciously chose to update the character in some fashion. *Crisis* demonstrated that some DC executives, editors, and writers thought the way to stave off the real crisis in slumping circulation was to emulate Marvel Comics' notion of a single Marvel universe where all characters had at least a tidy backstory and lived within some notion of temporality. Moore's story, on the other hand, suggested another route and one that DC did not immediately recognize. Moore prefaced his story with the line, "This is an imaginary story . . . Aren't they all?"[34] Moore offered a simple-enough proposition that what DC needed to do was create stories that appealed to readers and not look to structural solutions like tidying up the complex nature of its many-universed existence. So while readers may well have enjoyed finding logic and meaning in well-structured universes, part of this pleasure lay in the incongruities and inconsistencies that engaged readers, something that editors and writers had known of their 1961 audience for *Superman* #145, which contained a story full of deliberate mistakes and a challenge to readers to spot them.[35] The explanation for discrepancies in any given universe could simply be that they are stories.

Mythology allows the hero to appear in different guises and forms and yet remain the hero—well, at least if readers are active agents in shaping mythologies. Angela Ndalianis has argued just this point in her 2009 essay "Enter the Aleph." Ndalianis argues that a significant shift has taken place in the presentation of Superman and that "the temporal paradox, which, according to Eco, 'should not be obvious to the reader' now *is* obvious and, in fact, becomes an integral part of a narrative game that the audience is invited to engage with." Basically she argues that for the commercial product that is the superhero comic book genre to survive, it must contain its own past, "make way for the present and look towards its future. However, for a genre to achieve

FIGURE 7. *The Man of Steel* #6 (December 1986)

this it requires an audience that's familiar with its conventions and rules, and that . . . engages in a dialogic relationship with its process of construction."[36] Whereas Eco, writing in 1962, believed that Superman as myth would collapse if the reader did not lose "control of the temporal relationships and renounce the need to reason on their basis," Ndalianis suggests that the mythical dimension is sustained because readers can recognize it as a construct and enjoy the play of stories that undermine that construct.[37] Janet Murray points to "a sophistication on the part of the audience, an eagerness to transpose and reassemble the separate elements of a story and an ability to keep in mind multiple alternate versions of the same fictional world."[38]

A six-part miniseries in 1986 by the writer/artist John Byrne followed Moore's story and relaunched Superman by retelling the familiar tale of his origin. Byrne's version owed something to the Superman movies that preceded it and laid the basis for the *Lois & Clark* television series that followed. Byrne touched on many of the major themes of Superman, including the commercialism associated with celebrity. While trimming away some of "the barnacles" that DC had attached to Superman, Byrne retained and expanded the role of his adoptive parents, Martha and Jonathan Kent. In the final episode of the series, Byrne highlights the immigrant status of Superman, who concludes, "[America/Earth] gave me all that I am" and "all that matters."[39] Such a conclusion addressed Superman's history. Although the narrative begins anew, it also recycles the past, and the "all that I am" includes the many prior incarnations of the character (see figure 7).

In the introduction to the collected Ballantine Books edition of the series, Byrne wrote of his childhood memories of Superman. Born in England in 1950, Byrne first encountered the character in the 1950s television show and later in black-and-white comic book reprints. For Byrne, it was a window into another world. Byrne saw as the task at hand in the series to "re-create Superman as a character more in tune with the needs of the modern comic book audience." He also hoped that his version of the character would inspire some readers to follow in his own footsteps and discover a lifetime's work through the window.[40] Byrne's nostalgia about his childhood encounter with Superman, the dreams it inspired, and his eventual arrival in the United States, by way of Canada, suggest that his Superman's "humanity" rests in Byrne's own journey. If that is the case, then Byrne's vision of Superman rests on a version of America, or the America of the imagination, as a land of opportunity for immigrants. At the same time, though, Byrne presents Superman's sense of self as deriving from values instilled in him by his parents and a place: America/Kansas/ Smallville. The Superman story, then, also embodies an ideology of assimilation. That this tale was originally sketched by two Jewish teens, Siegel and Shuster, perhaps adds a dimension to this feature, but the important point is how stories told and retold retain their symbolic features. Superman demonstrates that being American is a state of mind achievable by adopting a set of values. The ideological dimensions of this are multivariant. Such an ideology might shut off competing notions of America, or it might open up a debate on what values are American. On another register, though, this aspect of Superman suggests to his non-US readers that they too can be Americans if they so choose.

CONCLUSION

Superman burst out of the timeless constraints that Eco so wonderfully analyzed. But DC faced tensions in managing the character. Storytelling opportunities are essential to a character with a regular monthly appearance. Character development over time is one such narrative strategy. But developing a character over time may well lead to inconsistencies and indeed exhaust story lines. The comic book reboot is, then, not just a method of tidying up a fictional universe but also a means of telling and retelling stories in a new, timeless fashion. When the consequences of a story line or years of narrative make Superman seem tired, DC simply reboots him in a new incarnation. Nonetheless, Superman remains constrained by his Americanness and the notion of his every action as virtuous that goes along with that identity.

CHAPTER TWO

IDEOLOGY AND MORALITY

The anthropologist Clifford Geertz argued, "ideologies transform sentiment into significance."[1] Such an understanding offers a fluid and broad view of ideologies and reminds us that ideologies are not fixed sets of precepts but social practices that result from human action. Superman as a character and commodity is conditioned by mythology and nostalgia, and both of these are ideological practices. They also inform and are informed by other ideological practices. Superman rarely directly engages in conscious ideological displays, particularly since World War II, but ideology is entwined in the threads that make up the weft and weave of Superman's fabric. Superman's persistence is in part reliant on his identification with a broad notion of what is best about America.

THE AMERICAN WAY

Superman famously fights for "truth, justice, and the American way." Although the American way seems like it is something that should be codified in a book by a consensus historian from the 1950s and early 1960, say, Daniel Boorstin, it lacks a clear enunciation. Perhaps Arthur M. Schlesinger Jr.'s *The Vital Center* comes close to capturing some aspects of the American way, at least as a liberal democracy confronting a global context: "its mortal international enemies— fascism to the right, communism to the left." But as Schlesinger later made very explicit, he was not talking about a putative "middle of the road."[2] The American way, then, is a very general concept that in part entered the public consciousness through a Depression-era campaign by the National Association of Manufacturers aimed at heading off some of the thrust of Franklin Roosevelt's New Deal. The campaign suggested that the American way was freedom of religion and speech, opportunity, representative democracy, and private enterprise. Ironically, the campaign is perhaps best remembered through a 1937 Margaret Bourke-White photograph of another billboard boasting that the American way meant the highest standard of living in the world, in front of which a line of African Americans queued for relief after the Ohio River flood. But in the mid- to late 1930s, as Wendy Wall has shown, the phrase was everywhere, with all hues of the political spectrum contributing their take. For instance, Henry Wallace, Roosevelt's secretary of agriculture and later vice president, published an article titled "The Search for the American Way" in the July 1936 issue of *Scribner's*. A month earlier, Roosevelt himself had used the term "an American way of life" in his renomination speech for the presidency. Such was the widespread and divergent use of "the American way" that in 1937 *Harper's* ran an essay contest seeking clarification on the term. The 1,570 submitted pieces did little to solve the dilemma and covered a wide array of divergent views.[3]

Not surprisingly, this diverse articulation of a concept lacking accepted meaning was, as Wall argues, the result of a crisis of confidence triggered by the Great Depression. And, as she shows, the 1930s saw a debate over the political economy of America and the cultural definition of "American." This national argument was further complicated by America's entry into World War II and the resulting efforts at categorizing America's foe. In this atmosphere, the American way came to mean a national consensus, but nonetheless the matter of what consensus meant was not settled. On the one hand, some sectors of society promoted consensus as a concept of civility across all divisions in society, while others regarded consensus as a force that could be mobilized to address power imbalances and to produce equality. Consensus was a fragile compromise holding together American diversity as a hallmark of democracy, but not descending into the anarchy of "unchecked difference" that seemed to many American intellectuals a trait of European countries in the interwar period.[4] Much of the U.S. war effort was driven by appeals to the American way, and worries about power imbalances were perhaps abated by the promise of postwar prosperity for all.

Not withstanding this history, it is probable that when most people hear the phrase "the American way," the first association they make is with Superman. The producers of the Superman radio serial added the phrase to the show's opening in 1942 for the first episode of the third season, broadcast on August 31. It was the capstone phrase to an introductory narration that had developed both in the earlier two seasons of the serial and a series of animated shorts produced by Fleischer Studios for Paramount. The credit for this final wording belongs to Olga Druce, a graduate of Smith College and later the producer of the children's television show *Captain Video*. Robert Maxwell, the producer of the Superman radio serial, later carried this opening over to the 1950s television series that he also produced. That series enjoyed global exposure and wide syndication for many years and was still being rerun on cable in the early years of the twenty-first century.[5] As a consequence, "truth, justice, and the American way" is so closely associated with Superman that its absence from the 2006 movie *Superman Returns* was cause of some consternation to many aging baby boomers, including most notably the American Fox News personality Bill O'Reilly.[6]

If the phrase had been vague enough to encompass divergent believes before World War II, Superman gave it some firmer meaning in the pages of the various Superman comics and on the air in the radio serial. Although Superman never spoke the phrase "the American way," in this period, he did represent what it entailed. First, on the covers of comic books and in the comic strip, he actively promoted buying war bonds. Second, he fought the enemies of tolerance, generally fifth columnists and fascist types, on the home front. Moreover, the general tone of the comic book suggested that America was a land of plenty and that Americans needed only to delay gratification by abstaining from consumer purchases as much as possible during the war to ensure victory. Many American businesses promoted these sentiments during the war, and Superman did his part. For instance, in one memorable 1943 story, "Million Dollar Marathon," Superman, faced with the challenge of spending a million dollars in twenty-four hours, manages to do so in a virtuous way that supports charities and reminds readers of the war effort. Likewise, department stores encouraged conscious decision making, rather than outright consumerism, in the name of the American way. A unity of purpose underlay this concern, and a 1945 Bullock's department store advertisement captured this nicely: veering "neither to the 'Right' or 'Left' . . . lies the American Way. It is winning the war. It can win the peace."[7]

Across Superman's multimedia incarnations, which at this stage included the two comic book titles, a comic strip, the radio serial, and a series of animated cartoons, he participated in this wartime construction of the American way as unity directed against America's enemies. Whether in the 1942 Paramount animation *Japoteurs*, with its racist caricature, or on the cover of *Action Comics* #58 (March 1943) urging Americans to "Slap a Jap," albeit metaphorically through buying war bonds, with its similarly racist depiction, this unity evoked racial hatred. Robert Maxwell, the producer of the Superman radio serial, saw himself as "formulating ideologies for these youngsters" against America's enemies. He told the Office of War Information that he was "teaching this vast audience to hate" an enemy for whom there was no difference "between the individual and the state whose ideology he defends. A German is a Nazi and a Jap is the little yellow man who 'knifed us in the back at Pearl Harbor.'" The American way, while promoting internal unity and tolerance, did not tolerate external enemies and was not above characterizing them in racial terms. Moreover, as Wall argues, the wartime promotion of tolerance and American unity were shallow when it came to racial minorities, especially Japanese Americans and African Americans.[8]

Superman's identification with this ideology during World War II shaped his postwar existence in his various incarnations. As the war wound down, the covers of *Action Comics* and *Superman* often showed him in a domestic setting or a humorous suburban setting. These covers in many ways replicated the sort of American norms and values that Norman Rockwell so often drew for the *Saturday Evening Post*. The stories inside were the ones that Umberto Eco found locked in stasis, with Superman's moral world defined by charity so as not to challenge the status quo of private property.[9] In *Superman* #54 (July–August 1948), over the signature of "Lois Lane," DC editorialized that Superman has hung up "an enviable record as a crusader for the American way of life." Among Superman's contributions was his cooperation "with all branches of the armed forces during the war, on public relations, information, and educational projects." Moreover, Superman had helped out the Greater Cleveland Hospital Fund and the Episcopal Church and had addressed the dental needs of children and assisted in a campaign against slot-machine operators cheating children. For DC, then, such activities defined the American way in the immediate postwar years.

Over the years, writers of letters to the editor made mention of Superman fighting for the American way. In a letter published in *Superman* #142 (January 1961), Anne Zeek wrote that a story, "The Jolly Jailhouse," in #139 (August 1960) presented "a 'true' picture of the condition in many Communist-infiltrated countries today, . . . countries where freedom of the press is non-existent. The story is an eloquent spokesman for the American way of life." That one reader at least understood a generic story about a country where a political prison existed under the command of a colonel, who could arbitrarily arrest people and order executions and yet himself be removed for corruption by other forces, as being about the dangers of communism and the importance of a free press to the American way probably says something about the strength and orientation of civics education in America at that time. Indeed, the August 1960 issue carried an advertisement form the National Social Welfare Assembly, in which Superman helped promote the United Nations World Refugee Year. Another advertisement from that agency, which appeared in *Superman* #80 (January–February 1953) and #138 (July 1960) and *Action Comics* #266 (July 1960), explicitly mentioned the American way in a didactic message about the conduct of politics in America, which involves letting the other fellow have his say and not engaging in dirty tricks such as pulling down an opponent's posters. Given that the comics appeared on the newsstands three months before the cover publication date, these advertisements coincided with the 1952 and 1960 federal elections, although the subject of the ad was local politics and a mayoral race. The first time this ad ran in 1953 in *Superman* #80, the issue contained another, similar one-page plug for the National Rifle Association's Hagerstown, Maryland, Air-Rifle Clubs competition that had Superboy endorse the idea. The advertisement featured Tom Campbell from the local Civitan Club, who had conceived the idea, and was based on an article from the *Hagerstown Morning Herald*.[10] Superboy discovered from Campbell that his was "a project to make better citizens of Hagerstown youngsters," and he urged parents to get their civic-service clubs involved in such ventures.

In these actions, it seems that Superman's owners, DC Comics, used him to promote the American way as a consensus around civility, but Superman was not entirely hidebound in his support of the American way as simply status quo. The story of Superman taking on the Ku Klux Klan–like Guardians of America in *The Adventures of Superman* radio serial in April 1946 and then much more directly in June 1946 against the Clan of the Fiery Cross is so well known that it rated a section in the 2005 best-selling *Freakonomics*.[11] Many versions of this tale rely on secondary accounts, rather than listening to the broadcasts, and suggest that the radio series passed on secret Klan passwords, which it did not.[12] The real significance of the Klan story arc was not the sort of imagined childish heroics of Stetson Kennedy, who liked to relate his role and significance, but rather, as Wall notes, that Superman engaged with an American way that promoted tolerance. Superman, then, embodied this tension within the American way between consensus as simply civility and consensus and as a struggle for tolerance. Because Superman existed in several forms of media, understanding this tension and how it was received is helped by analyzing audience reception of Superman across media. This is no easy task. But letters to the editor of Superman comic books mentioning the American way gives some sense of his audience seeing him in a broader sense than just his comic book representation.

As Anne Zeek's letter in January 1961 showed, one norm that readers expected of Superman was that his support for the American way went hand-in-hand with opposition to communism and Russia. But almost inevitably, one reader at least wondered how things might have been different. In *Action Comics* #339 (July 1966), Victoria Phillips, of Long Beach, California, wrote, "I dare you to do a story in which you show what would have happened if Superbaby had landed in Russia instead of America, and had been brought up as a Communist. I doubt that you'll have the courage to print this letter, much less publish such a tale." The editors replied, "It isn't lack of courage that nixes our using your idea—just that it's against our policy to indulge in politics. Our stories are strictly for entertainment—even though we'd bet the Man of Steel would crash through the Iron Curtain to show his contempt of Russia's dictators."

In January 1967, Richard Laurent wrote to *Action Comics* (#345) replying to Victoria Phillips's letter and suggesting that a Soviet version would have had the rocket land outside a town named "Malenkiysyelo

(Smallville), in the eastern Ukraine," and the baby inside be found by the "Ivanovs (Johnsons), who named the baby Yuri." Later, he saw Yuri becoming "a reporter on the staff of Pravda (Truth), the Soviet Union's largest newspaper," alongside "Vera Shimitrov (Lois Lane), Ivan Shubayev (Jimmy Olsen) and editor Perisko Beliy (Perry White). He changes to Perechelovek (Superman) in the zapaskomnata (storeroom) and flies out to catch prestoopnikiy (criminals)." Laurent suggested that it was unlikely that this Superman "would be a Communist, since only about 4% of the population belong to the party. It's true that he would be taught from infancy that the Communist way of life was the best in the world. But aren't American children taught the same thing about their government?" The DC editors felt the need to insist that "Superman, with his super-senses, would be able to get the truth about America and other countries, proving that an Iron Curtain can't confine a Man of Steel!" In April 1967, Jim Doody from Altadena, California, wrote to *Action Comics* (#349) noting that "Stalin" translated to English as "Man of Steel" and warned DC, "Watch it, before the F.B.I. accuses you and *your* Man of Steel of Communism!" DC replied, "Have no fear! Despite that *red* cape he wears, anyone can see that Superman is true-*blue*. And everyone knows that accusing him of being un-American would be an F.I.B.!"

DC may have had a policy not to engage in politics, but these statements, and indeed the 1960 story to which Zeek was responding, were highly political. DC replied in a charged political manner to a April 1962 letter from a reader in *Superman* #152 inquiring about the accuracy of depicting Lex Luthor in solitary confinement in prison but having a window, a radio, and a book. The editor wrote, "The purpose of prison is to rehabilitate, not punish. Cells such as you describe are used by tyrants and dictators to brainwash their prisoner!! In America, solitary confinement does not mean depriving a man of simple comforts. He is only deprived of companionship, because he is considered to be too dangerous to mix with other inmates." Perhaps the DC editor genuinely believed this to be the case, which would have been rather naïve, but this seems more like Cold War propaganda, based on liberal ideals. That DC supported the American efforts in the Cold War is not that astounding. Nor perhaps is it surprising that the company presented itself as nonpolitical.

In a letter in *Superman* #205 (April 1968), Tom L. Smith worried about a story in the January 1968 issue. In the story, Superman, disguised as the devil, tricks two criminals into confessing their crimes. Smith complained that the American way "must of necessity result in a balanced approach. And yet, in this story, Superman is so over-zealous in his pursuit of criminals that he is willing to cut the very foundations from under our American institutions. The suspected guilt of any individual is irrelevant to the protection of his basic civil guarantees." DC laughed this off with the comment, "Maybe Superman was a bit overzealous . . . but when this happens, someone like you will always 'horn in' and give us the Devil!" Both Smith's and Zeek's letters imported the concept of Superman standing for the American way from radio and/or television incarnations, since the line had almost certainly never seen print in the comic book.

In *Superman* #356 (February 1981), Alicia A. Suarez praised a story in the September 1980 issue that had promoted racial tolerance toward a child Cuban immigrant. For Suarez, the story had special meaning since she too had come from Cuba and had improved her English by reading Superman comics. For her, such stories taught "the real meaning of truth, justice, and the American way." These examples and several other instances, in which letter writers refer to Superman standing for the American way, show that that phrase resonated with Superman's broad audiences and that they used the term to indicate that Superman stood for civility, tolerance, and the struggle to extend just who was tolerated. These sort of identifications of the American way with Superman also suggest that he did not simply represent it but helped shape and articulate its meaning. For many readers, Superman personified the sentiment.

AMERICAN NORMS: DOMESTICITY

Superman comics from the mid-1940s to the mid-1960s offer some low-hanging fruit for a scholar on the hunt for ideological expression. In issue after issue, Lois Lane plots to expose Clark Kent as Superman and is constantly foiled. Likewise, she is foiled in her quest to have Superman admit his love for her and propose marriage. These stories, many of which end with Superman expressing relief at having avoided Lois's wiles, offer a vision in which a working journalist like Lois Lane could be understood only as a nosy woman and one out to get married. These sorts of stories began with a series of covers just

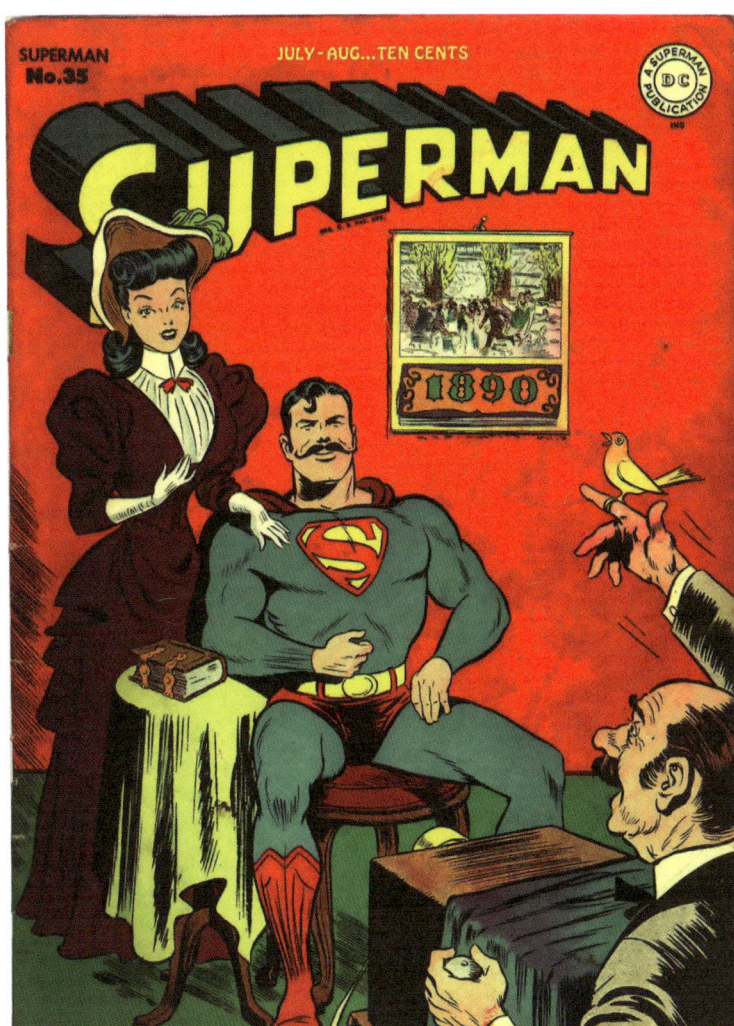

FIGURE 8.
Superman #35
(July–August
1945)

after World War II that promoted domesticity. The war had only just ended in 1945 when Superman and Lois Lane appeared on the cover of *Superman* #35 (July–August 1945) posing for a photographic portrait in a domestic setting evoking 1890 (see figure 8). In the very next issue, in September–October, the two appear before a refrigerator, of which Superman seems to have nonchalantly rammed a finger into the freezer, breaking the cooling element. Lois, with hands on hips

FIGURE 9.
Superman #45
(March–April
1947)

and carrying a hammer and a small pick, stares at him with contempt.
At the conclusion of a story in *Superman* #45 (March–April 1947), the
writer Alvin Schwartz has Lois say that she hates men who try to keep
women "weak and defenseless," to which Superman thinks, "Whew!
Whoever understands a woman is a better man than Superman" (see
figure 9). On the cover of *Superman* #51 (March–April 1948), Lois
takes freshly baked cookies from the oven. One has dropped on Super-

man's foot, and he hops is pain with the sore foot throbbing. And on the cover of *Action Comics* #127 (December 1948), Superman appears with the host of the radio program *Truth or Consequences*. Superman wears and apron and carries a feather duster and is being squirted with seltzer. Not all of these covers relate to stories within the comic, and clearly some of them are just attempts at playful jokes; but in a very real sense, they foreshadow the domestication of Superman and move Lois and her schemes to the fore of the comic book, and indeed of the Superman franchise as a whole, as a sort of meta plot device. Jokes about domesticity such as these tell us what the editors of *Superman* thought would appeal to a comic-buying public.

The importance of Lois Lane to the Superman mythos in the 1950s was so great that she received her own comic book, but as the title made clear, she was "Superman's girlfriend Lois Lane" and not just simply "Lois Lane." In #12 of that comic in October 1959, Lois suffers a terrible accident, and to save her life, a surgeon turns her into a mermaid. Although Aquaman becomes her new boyfriend, she pines for Superman. Superman, with his fabulous superbrain, is able to reverse the mermaid operation and fully restore Lois, who tells Superman that she is back where she belongs, in his arms. Nonetheless, all was not smooth sailing, and in *Superman* #139 (August 1960), Lois receives a marriage proposal from an old college friend, whose love for Lois has inspired him to great success. Overhearing the proposal, Superman determines to make Lois believe she has no chance of ever marrying him. He then fakes a romance with Lori, a mermaid, whom he knew during his college years. Lois, though, has her heart set on Superman and refuses to be involved with any man if she cannot be with Superman. At the end of the story, she thinks, "If Superman went to all that trouble it proves I mean a lot to him! Maybe he'll marry me yet, some day?"

These Superman stories might read simply like male editors and writers asserting patriarchal norms, and as much as that is true and obvious from these tales, there was more at play in the postwar comic books. World War II was a total war, and America's mobilization for its conduct opened previously closed workplaces to woman. At war's end, women did not necessarily wish to return to other roles, and significant campaigns were waged to move them out of some of the jobs, such as riveters, that they occupied. Some women at least resisted this process.[13] At the same time, the baby boom is adequate testament that many men and women started families. These two developments are not mutually exclusive, and my point here is that, rather than simply checking off a list of postwar changes and developments, it is important to understand the process and the role of comic books and superheroes like Superman in that development. Abstract notions like the American way as a war aim, and even Roosevelt's more formally stated concept of an America grounded in four freedoms (speech, worship, from fear, and from want), were fine, but giving expression to these in concrete form postwar was another matter entirely. The ways in which the abstractions were filled with meaning were multiple and manifested in things as diverse as the GI Bill, the interstate freeway plan, suburbanization, the civil rights movement that took shape in part around *Brown v. Board of Education*, marketing strategies that produced "teenagers" as a market and an identity, and the many industries that developed to supply that identity with defining products. The developing consensus could tolerate neither horror and crime comic books nor particularly virulent Jim Crow laws. These changes and developments did not unfold according to some vast master plan conceived during the war but rather as individuals, corporations, and organizations struggled to realize their version of America. Indeed, in the immediate aftermath of the war in 1946, America witnessed the most widespread strike action ever in its history, with slightly over 7 percent of the workforce striking in that year.[14] Listing a few of these things does not help us understand change, but it does help us understand the array of developments and something of the manner of the historical process. When Superman's comic book version offered a view of an American norm, it did not simply reflect that norm but was a constituent element in the creation of that vision of society. Superman comics displayed not only a version of domesticity but also a broader vision of American society.

In the 1950s, Superman gained a backstory in which he had been raised in small-town America and taught values by caring parents, Ma and Pa Kent. In this past, he performed deeds as Superboy. He also acquired a pet dog, Krypto. In Superman stories, writers revealed that Clark Kent had attended college, something his creators had not done. In the 1950s, in comic books and in the *Adventures of Superman* television show, Kent's employment as a reporter on the *Daily*

Planet became more important as a plot device. Superman held a job, answered to a boss (Perry White), earned an income, and lived in an apartment. All this helped to define Superman and put him at the center of the American way. At the same time, DC managed to offer a version of Superman that had some of the raw humor of his original 1930s version. This Superman, seemingly an anarchic, bizarre opposite, demonstrates some of the ways that Superman underpinned the social norms of the 1950s and early 1960s.

THE NORM AND ITS BIZARRE VERSION

One way to see the ideological assumptions of Superman is to look at how writers approach writing topsy-turvy, world-turned-upside-down, stories about Superman. Much of the ideology expressed in Superman happens in matter-of-fact ways and against the backdrop of superhero adventures and so may not be immediately noticeable. From the late 1950s and throughout most of the 1960s, DC ran "Imaginary Stories" that stood outside the normal stories of the comic book. Many of these featured some version of Superman and Lois marrying, sometimes to each other and at other times to someone else. These stories, although outside the continuity of Superman, did not radically differ in their assumptions about the character but rather offered a glimpse of something that, as the editors were wont to say, "may or may not happen one day." But other stories, which involved some sort of fundamental, deliberate reversal of Superman's world, are a useful way of seeing how Superman supported social norms. Seeing social norms as a form of ideology is a common enough occurrence that is perhaps best explained by pointing to the rule of law as a form of ideology. If the rule of law supports individual property rights, then those who oppose such rights, say communists, are in ideological opposition to the norm of the rule of law. Such ideological framing of norms does not require such extreme examples, and generally any conflict over change will reveal ideological stakes in supporting and maintaining a norm.[15] The Bizarro Superman stories from the 1950s and 1960s are one such world-turned-upside-down version of Superman in which some norms were stood on their head.

Bizarro Superman is an imperfect copy of Superman. Bizarros had white, as opposed to pinkish, skin and were drawn in what looks like a caricature of cubist style. Originally created for the Superman newspaper comic strip, in which a Bizarro adventure ran from August 25, 1958, to December 13, 1958, the character had another incarnation in the *Superboy* comic book before taking shape as a figure of some bathos in *Action Comics* #254–255 in July and August 1959 (see figure 10). Then, in the hands of Superman's creator, Jerry Siegel, the character featured as a regular backup to Superboy in *Adventure Comics* in 1961 and 1962. In this series, Bizarro Superman had created a whole planet of Bizarro Supermen and Lois Lanes, with the originals being designated "No. 1." In *Adventure Comics* #285 (June 1961), Siegel outlined the Bizarro code: "Us do opposite of all earthly things; us hate beauty; us love ugliness; is big crime to make anything perfect on Bizarro World." In the same issue, a Bizarro boss fires a hardworking Bizarro and gives a sleeping Bizarro a raise. This is a rather simplistic reversal of common expectations that hard work should be rewarded. Likewise, in another simple inversion, Bizarro Superman celebrates when the price of his share holdings declines. These obvious inversions of common expectations are whimsical and more than anything impart a lesson to the comic book's readers about social norms. Although these stories were most likely conceived as satire by Siegel, rather than as a form of pedagogy, young readers of the stories nonetheless probably received them didactically. Also and not so immediately obvious, most Bizarro stories showed an adherence to social norms even in a world where everything was supposedly reversed. For instance, the original Bizarro, now labeled Bizarro Superman No. 1 and Bizarro Lois No. 1, are married in these stories.

At the time of writing these stories, Siegel had lost his copyright case against DC for ownership of Superman. He wrote the stories unaccredited and under the sufferance of editors whom he had known when they were all teenagers. Although he did not originate the Bizarro version of Superman, it is tempting to see Siegel's vein of creativity as deriving, in part, from his situation. Just as Superman was out of Siegel's control, so too seemingly were the Bizarros beyond the bounds of normal logic, or at least that was the conceit of the plot device. Whether intentional or not, the character's reversal of the norm satirized much of Superman and the squeaky-clean do-gooder he had become. In so doing, the comic owed something to the satire of *Mad*. Indeed *Mad*'s satire of Superman, "Superduperman," in issue #4 (April–May 1953) set the stage for such an anarchic version of the

FIGURE 10.
Action Comics
#254 (July 1959)

character. But the most radical difference in these Bizarro world stories was the absence of Clark Kent. This absence did indeed mark the
Bizarro world stories as a world turned upside down, because in all
other versions of Superman, Clark Kent is a key part of the character's
being. The Bizarro Superman represents an ontological shift and a sin-
gularity, which just as much as Bizarro's physical appearance, tells the
reader that this is not the "real" Superman. And usually in the Bizarro
stories, Superman had to intervene and put right Bizarro's actions.

These Bizarro stories offered a small-scale and, save for the absence of Clark Kent, a rather limited reimagining of Superman and one more playful than challenging. Mostly Superman remained locked in a timeless state, but the social upheaval of the 1960s and the coming of age of the baby-boom generation eventually led to some change in Superman. Gradually authors created subtle modifications in Superman's ideological underpinnings and shifted from the somewhat amorphous notion of the American way to an equally inchoate form of individualism. Superman's individualism left him open to seemingly incompatible views and stances.

FROM STASIS TO INDIVIDUALISM

As the writers and artists of Superman began to break him out of the stasis that Eco described, Superman's search for his identity became something of a trope. In *Superman* #247 (January 1972), DC introduced a series of stories titled "The Private Life of Clark Kent," which ran on and off until July 1982. As the series title suggests, these stories explored the Clark Kent persona and fleshed out some of his character more than had been typical. In that same January 1972 issue, in another story, "Must There Be a Superman?," the writer Elliot Maggin raised the issue of Superman's presence on Earth impeding human development, since too many people looked to Superman to solve their problems (see figure 11). While Superman did not exactly experience a crisis of confidence, he did begin to be more reflective. The introduction of this sort of introspection to the character of Superman predated Tom Wolfe's essay "The 'Me' Decade and the Third Great Awakening," in the August 23, 1976, issue of *New York* magazine, from which the notion of a "Me Generation" arose. Wolfe exclaimed of those who were searching for themselves, "they've created the greatest age of individualism in American history!"[16] Although Wolfe did not make the connection explicit, the Me Generation's search for self in ever-increasing individualism relied in part on a concept of social mobility and self-improvement that stretched back to Benjamin Franklin, through Horatio Alger's stories, on to F. Scott Fitzgerald's Jay Gatsby, and eventually to the self-help section in bookstores. One of the great promises of America has been the ability to make oneself over, although to be sure, such transformations do not always work out for the best. The *New York Times* described the concept of social mobility in America as a "civil religion."[17]

FIGURE 11.
Superman #247
(January 1972)

Superman's path to the Me Generation version of individualism lay in his dual nature as Clark Kent and Superman. To understand the basis of Superman's growing individualism over the years, it is first necessary to understand that his creators, and many writers and artists that followed, highlighted his human traits. Although Siegel and Shuster did not fill out the details of Superman's origins on his debut in *Action Comics* #1 in June 1938, they provided a little more detail in the summer of 1939 in the first issue of the new *Superman* comic book. In this story, the narrator tells us, "the love and guidance of his kindly foster-parents was to become an important factor in the shaping of the boy's future." Pa Kent tells the child Clark that he must hide his great strength or people will be scared of him. Ma Kent adds, "but when the proper time comes, you must use it to assist humanity." Although not human, Clark has been raised that way, with human values. But until the 1970s, this theme of his humanity was mostly unexplored. When Superman writers began using this theme, the stories generally involved Superman's search for a sense of self. The mid-1970s stories from *Superman* #296–299, had Superman explore the theme of his identity, eventually deciding that he was both Clark and Superman. In *Superman* #309 (March 1977), Superman's identity again comes into question, with his passion for Earth being seen as a substitute mechanism for coping with the destruction of Krypton. Rather than being determined by a displaced grieving, Superman affirms that his love for Earth flows from its being his home, albeit an adopted home, but indeed all the stronger a bond for that reason (see figure 12). That is, Superman chooses humanity. One way that writers had Superman ponder his identity was by remembering his adoptive parents. In *Superman* #161 (May 1963), the writer Leo Dorfman, in "The Last Days of Ma and Pa Kent," has Superman recall the death of his parents from a mysterious fever plague contracted on a vacation to the Caribbean. For various reasons, he had been unable to save them, but he honors their memory every year. In *Superman* #363 (September 1981), Cary Bates used this earlier story as a basis and has Lana Lang and Lois Lane both infected with the same plague, but Superman is able to derive a cure. Mourning the loss of parents and concern for loved ones are part of Superman's human characteristics. Using this aspect of Superman as a plot device, Bates wrote another story, for *Superman* #369 (March 1982), in which a depressed Superman tries to cope with Christmas alone by remembering his adoptive parents.

Readers absorbed these stories as lessons in Superman's essential humanity. As the reader Dan Coakley noted in a letter to the editor printed in *Superman* #367 (January 1982), "Superman is especially a victim of his own humanity . . . [because] as Superman has put it himself, 'What good is all this power if I can't use it to save the people I love?'" Another reader, Lyle Watson, wrote to the editor in *Superman* #374 (August 1982) stressing, "Clark Kent has always been a basic and necessary part of the Superman persona. Take away Clark and

FIGURE 12. *Superman* #309 (March 1977)

you eliminate Superman's humanity. Superman is Clark and Clark is Superman. Neither can function without the other. . . . Clark is not just a disguise and facade Superman hides behind, but a way Superman can live the way we live and share the experiences all humans share." Such a view of Superman ran counter to another perspective. In 1965, the cartoonist and playwright Jules Feiffer argued in his history of comic book heroes that Superman chose Clark Kent as a disguise and, in so doing, revealed his view of humans as downtrodden, meek weaklings.[18] Quentin Tarantino echoed this sentiment through Bill in the film *Kill Bill*.[19] Dan Coakley, though, seems to have a better grasp of Superman when he notes Superman's capacity to love and his frustration that his power is sometimes useless to help the people he loves.

In Richard Donner's 1978 film *Superman*, the search for self is a key element. The first quarter of the film shows the destruction of Krypton, Superman's voyage to Earth and discovery by the Kents, his early years, and then, following the death of Pa Kent from a heart attack, his decision to go in search of himself. This quest leads Clark Kent north. In his pack, he carries the crystal-like material that accompanied him from Krypton in his craft. On reaching the Arctic circle, he throws this crystal into the water, and it generates a new structure, a Fortress of Solitude, within which he is able to communicate with a disembodied form of his dead father, Jor-El. Having left Kansas in search of himself, Clark first asks of Jor-El, "Who am I?"[20] In the movie, it is as Clark Kent that Superman grapples with the problems of his super powers. When Clark asks this question of Jor-El, it is about another part of him and one that is developing as he grows older and that he must learn to control. It is not hard to see such a struggle as a metaphor for puberty, but since Clark is eighteen in the film when this meeting takes place, it is puberty delayed. Nonetheless, it is metaphorically similar since he has to master what it means to be an adult, a super man. Clark then undergoes several years' tutelage from his ghostly father in order for him to be Superman. Christopher Reeve in the Superman suit does not appear until fifty minutes into a two-and-a-half-hour movie. Superman, too, had to struggle to realize himself.

When Superman eventually arrives in Metropolis in the film, what spurs him to action, to reveal himself to the world, is the threatened death of Lois Lane, a woman who we of course know is his love interest but whom in the movie he has just met. To be sure, he goes on to perform a number of heroic acts in that same evening, including saving Air Force One from a likely crash landing and stopping various minor criminal acts. But it is saving Lois from a potential fall to her death, following a mishap with a helicopter on the roof of the *Daily Planet* building that is central to the arrival of Superman. In other words, Superman's sole motivation to act is self-interest centered on Lois. Once having acted, he enjoys the adulation, a point, to be sure, Donner wished to make, since the 2001 DVD release of the movie includes a deleted scene in which Superman, having performed a night of super deeds, returns to the Fortress of Solitude to talk again with the ghostly image of his father. Jor-El asks in a rhetorical fashion, "You enjoyed it?" and then advises, "Don't punish yourself for your feelings of vanity. . . . Simply control it."[21] Here, then, was Superman's destiny in the 1970s, simply controlling his feelings of vanity. The language of the script coveys an uncertainty about whether vanity is something to overly concern oneself with since it is "feelings of vanity," not vanity itself, that Superman needs to contain. And lest that seem like a simple-enough thing surely for Superman to do, in the denouement of the film, he fails to do so and yet still emerges as a triumphant hero. Twice in the course of the film, Jor-El tells his son that he must not interfere with human history: first, in his rocket ship on the way to Earth and, second, during the instructional period at the Fortress of Solitude. But when Lois Lane is suffocated in her car because of an earthquake, Superman, despite already having saved millions of people and prevented major and minor disasters, decides to reverse the course of history by spinning the Earth backward and so reversing history. He does this despite again hearing in his mind Jor-El's command not to interfere, as he sets off on his task. Again, it is not the sheer improbability of such actions and events that is worth discussing but rather the morality of the moment. Superman's love for Lois Lane, or perhaps it is his need for Lois Lane's attention and affection, causes him to break a strict command from his father. That Superman's motive is about his desire and his desire alone is demonstrated in that, having discovered that he can reverse history, he does not reverse it so that his adoptive father, Jonathan Kent, does not suffer the heart failure that is brought on earlier in the film by playfully racing with young Clark. It is not the unfettered love of a son for his parents that motivates Superman's actions but the romantic and sexual love of a man for a woman.

The movie was the first time Superman used his time-traveling ability to consciously change history. In the 1963 story "The Last Days of Ma and Pa Kent," he discovers the cause of his parents' death, but rather than travel back in time and prevent it from happening, he mourns the event. And during one of his earlier travels, Superboy tells his father, Jonathan, that they must not "do anything to change history." In another Superboy story, from 1960, he decides to travel back in time and save Lincoln, but the writers have him realize that trying to change the past is futile.[22] In 1963, Superman's writers felt that for him to interfere with history would be morally repugnant; and they believed that history was contiguous, and an event changed in the past would have unknown consequences in the future. Whatever the course of humanity, it was understood that what had happened had happened. Implied in these stories was that humans indeed made their own history, and any being that had the luxury of transgressing time needed a moral code of leaving humanity to its free will. By 1978, sexual love was a good-enough reason to ignore these dictates, even as they were enunciated over and over. In the course of this change, the nature of human free will shifted by implication from the unfettered outcome of human action, be it good or bad (let us call that history), to an abstract, rights-based individual human's unfettered actions. These tensions also unfolded in the comic book version.

The three hundredth issue of *Superman* imagined what would have happened if he arrived on Earth in 1976 and what the world would be like in 2001 when he reached maturity as Superman. This story used a well-worn device of having Superman forgo his identity for some time and contemplate living simply as Clark Kent. But humans being humans, Superman must fulfill his destiny and defeat a false claimant to the title of savior of humanity. He then duly informs the mob of humans that they had been saved from destruction not by this creature but by someone else: "someone who wanted you to look not to heroes and false gods for salvation . . . someone who has enough faith to know your salvation is within you . . all of you!" This despite the fact that five panels earlier Superman had told the same mob, "wise up gullible fools." Superman stands triumphantly on the wrecked shell of his android opponent, with arms outstretched messiah-like. The crowd looks on and exclaims, "That man, power runs through his very being! Unlimited power! Who was he? Where did he come from? He's shown us what we all can be if we try! Yes he was a *Superman*!" And the citizens erect a statue of him, as the narrative voice in the book puts it, "the man who surely is the greatest hero of all" (see figure 13). In this story, DC was of course celebrating a milestone for the character. The story also served as a means of denoting that Superman and what he stood for were timeless. In this instance, the use of the stock catch phrase "Look up in the sky! It's a bird . . ." reminds the reader that, after all, this is Superman. That he lives in America, having been contested over by the United States and the USSR, and yet nonetheless ensures peace between the nations shows that he, like America, has only the best intentions. And his humility in demanding that humans look to themselves instead of heroes shows his rugged individualism. It is just these qualities—a super power in denial of its own impact on the world and refusal to acknowledge inconsistencies

FIGURE 13.
Superman #300
(June 1976)

and incongruities in demanding at the point of violence that people not worship false heroes and gods and choose instead to think and act for themselves—that makes Superman so American and America so troubling, particularly for those who are not interested in adopting the American way writ large. That Superman addresses the crowd gathered as "gullible fools" perhaps says a lot about the writers' and America's state of mind about those who put their faith in anyone other than themselves, except of course superheroes. This sort of dilemma for comic book writers arguing for individual self-reliance and yet writing superhero stories was the sort of tension that Eco pointed to in part, and if, as he said, there were limits to the scope of Superman's actions, there were at least rich narrative possibilities in this tension, something Alan Moore demonstrated spectacularly in his 1986 *Watchmen*. To be sure, the writers of this story, Cary Bates and Elliot Maggin, were liberals and interested in social change, but that is just the point about American liberalism: it is bereft of any ideology as far as what America stands for that is separate and distinct from American conservatism. For Maggin, Superman stood for all that is best about America, so much so that he thought of running for office on the slogan "truth, justice, and the American way."[23]

INDIVIDUALISM

In the 1960s and indeed for many years, DC did not dare follow Victoria Phillip's suggestion in 1966 and attempt a story depicting the outcome of the baby Superman's rocket from Krypton landing in the Soviet Union. But in 2003, twelve years after the final dissolution of the Soviet Union, DC offered such a story. The story was not so much about Cold War issues of containment and the like but rather about underlying ideologies. *Superman: Red Son*, published in a three-part miniseries in 2003 and collected in a trade paperback in 2004, is not as lighthearted in its reversals as the Bizarro-world stories. Author Mark Millar's narrative is far more complex and deeply ideological than Siegel could attempt or would have considered attempting in his Bizarro stories. One key reason for this shift to more complex stories was a shift in the age of readers, with increasingly more adult audiences being the vast majority of readers. Indeed, a 2012 survey of readers of DC Comics' reboot titles *The New 52*, with some six thousand respondents, found 85 percent of comic book readers were twenty-five or older and only 1 percent of the respondents were under eighteen.[24]

In *Red Son*, the Soviet Union announces to the world the existence of Superman in the 1950s. Superman, although not interested in politics, is on friendly terms with Stalin, who treats him like a son. On Stalin's death, Superman eventually sees it as his duty to take charge of the Soviet Union and use his power for the betterment of the people. His success causes the United States to suffer economic setbacks. In the United States, Lex Luthor, in conjunction with the government and agencies like the CIA, tries to develop weapons capable of defeating Superman. Eventually Lex Luthor becomes president of the United States and dramatically improves the economy. He then defeats Superman by making him see that his efforts at betterment are really exercises in subjugating human will. Freed of Superman's shackles and under the leadership of Luthor and his heirs, who have been sired with Lois Lane, to whom Luthor has long been married, humanity develops at an amazing pace. Eventually, after millennia have passed, the society is exhausted and complacent in the face of a dying planet, and one of Luthor's heirs, Jor-L, sends his infant son back in time. In the course of the story, Wonder Woman appears as a love interest for Superman. A Russian Batman features as an underground resistance fighter. Millar also includes a brief reference to the presence of American nuclear weapons in the United Kingdom, an issue that had taxed his mentor, fellow Scottish writer Grant Morrison.[25]

In the introduction to the paperback edition, Tom DeSanto, the producer of *The X-Men* and *Transformers* movie franchises and a comic book fan, praises the moral shades of gray that Millar brings to the story. The story, as DeSanto sees it, reminds readers of the sentiment that Benjamin Franklin expressed when he wrote (or at least as DeSanto would have us believe he "once wrote"), "Those who would sacrifice their freedom for safety will find they inherit neither." DeSanto sees the story as forcing people to change the way they think and to understand that giving up the right to think for yourself and challenge the system, in exchange for security, is no real freedom. DeSanto says, "I don't think Ben Franklin would have liked that idea."[26] DeSanto distills the story to its essence of individual freedom, which although not wholly an American ideology, is one that finds particular voice in America. In many ways, it is immaterial that Franklin actually wrote, "those who can give up essential liberty, to purchase a little temporary safety, deserve neither liberty nor safety," since DeSanto's rewrite captures the sentiment of individual rights that Franklin's words have been used to support in a more concise and direct manner.[27] But, as Benjamin Wittes of the Brookings Institution notes, Franklin wrote the words at a specific moment and meant by the expression "essential liberty" the right of a self-governing people to define a polis and levy tax on the citizenry, that is, an argument for state power, albeit shaped by self-determination, rather than against it.[28] The meaning of Franklin's utterance has been lost in the mobilization of his words as an expression of the ideology of individual freedom.

If there are moral grays in Millar's story, they center on a particular conflict: Superman's underlying belief that he acts for the good of the people and Lex Luthor's narcissistic self-regard. Millar here seems to be echoing the notion of his fellow Scot Adam Smith that public good results from private greed, or as Smith put it, an individual "by pursuing his own interest . . . frequently promotes that of the society more effectually than when he really intends to promote it."[29] Luthor's version triumphs after a long struggle, and Superman, thought to be dead but in reality reduced to observing the wonder of humanity empowered by Luthor's wisdom, realizes the "resourcefulness" of humans. Nonetheless, the most resourceful of all humans over billions of years are the descendants of Luthor. By revealing Superman as Luthor's descendant, Millar rounds out the yin-yang-like nature of his Superman-Luthor morality tale. The ending suggests the two sides as a representation of humanity. Whether or not the ideology of individualism on display here is Millar's is largely irrelevant. *Red Son* is a world-turned-upside-down story, and the way to frame that story is to counterpoise a communal, ends-justifies-the-means Superman with an individually focused Luthor. But on the other hand, the story has at its core the flawed, imperfectible nature of humans—both Superman and Luthor are not likeable characters in this story—and it is the perception of just this imperfectability that drives ideologies of individualism. Furthermore, Luthor's particular narcissistic trajectory happens in this story because Superman is not in America to negate him or limit him. In essence, the story leaves the reader thinking, Superman has an inherent need to do good, but in doing so, does he limit humanity, or does he challenge us to do better?

CONCLUSION

DC has rebooted Superman several more times in comics since John Byrne's 1986 relaunch in the *Man of Steel* miniseries. The infamous death of Superman in 1993, although not a reboot, did change the character, as did Clark Kent and Lois Lane's wedding in 1996. From a range of familiar-enough plot devices, DC has had Superman's powers transform, be lost entirely, and overwhelm him to the point of his abandoning his Clark Kent identity.[30] In 2003–2004, Superman received a reboot of sorts with *Birthright* by Mark Waid, which gave him a new backstory on his development from teenager to man. In 2005–2006, this version was shunted aside in light of another reshaping of DC's world with *Infinite Crisis*. In 2007, in *Action Comics* #850, DC rebooted Superman yet again. And in 2011, DC relaunched all its characters in a series called *The New 52*. In addition, there are many alternate versions of Superman in miniseries like *Red Son*, such as *Secret Identity*, *All Star Superman*, and even a piece of metafiction, *It's a Bird*, which makes a tendentious connection between a writer's struggles and the hope that Superman offers humanity. In *Action Comics* #900 (June 2011), a few months before the *New 52* reboot, Superman renounced his American citizenship, telling a startled official, "'truth, justice and the *American* way'—It's not *enough* anymore." But what that means and how that might play out for Superman is something that DC has not attempted and, one expects, will never attempt at length, because it would take Superman beyond just trying to be good. Indeed, when authors have used the phrase "truth, justice, and the American way" in comic books in the past twenty years, it has been more of a throwaway line or as an evocation of some unenumerated quality.[31] The British-born and American-based literary scholar Benjamin Saunders has said of Superman that he constantly strives for but never quite reaches "absolute virtue." Superman is, as Saunders says, "a representation of the good whose entire career suggests that good can only be gestured toward, but never represented." Saunders equates Superman with our own morality and "the frequent disparity between our moral intent and the results of our actions."[32] Within the internal confines of Superman's stories, it seems that "good" needs to be confined to the limited acts of charity in the sort of stasis that Eco identified. When Superman exists in a world with consequences, even his fictional world, this constant inability to move beyond attempts to do good plays out, and the character has to be rebooted. In stories that have writers take Superman to his logical conclusion, the character finds resolution only by subsuming his identity in Clark Kent or by disappearing. Appealing to nostalgia for the character is a means of sidestepping this problem of narrative exhaustion and of ensuring that Superman persists.

CHAPTER THREE

SUPERMAN: THE OBJECT OF NOSTALGIA

In a special issue of *Time* magazine devoted to Superman's fiftieth anniversary in 1988, the Harvard-educated staff writer and former editor of the *Saturday Evening Post* Otto Friedrich wrote that "one of the odd paradoxes about Superman . . . is that while he is a hero of nostalgia, the constant changes in his character keep destroying the qualities that make him an object of nostalgia." Oddly enough for someone trained in history, Friedrich thought this nostalgia "came out of nowhere" simply because it involved things that the "nostalgia lovers were too young" to know.[1] Nostalgia, to be sure, is a form of memory, and it seems reasonable to expect folks to at least have memories related to what they are nostalgic about. In the years subsequent to Friedrich's piece, the nostalgia for Superman has, if anything, grown, and the lovers of this nostalgia are even more removed from that which Friedrich thought them too young to know. But in addition to being a form of memory, nostalgia in the right hands is a commodity that can be sold, and it was this aspect that Friedrich ironically missed or misunderstood. He was after all engaged in selling that nostalgia in his article.

Nostalgia takes many forms, but academic engagement with it commonly involves a critique of its ahistoricism. Fredric Jameson saw such a situation as "an alarming and pathological symptom of a society that has become incapable of dealing with time and history."[2] Other social commentators have pointed to the ahistoricism of nostalgia. Indeed, Christopher Lasch has noted that both nostalgia and antinostalgia deny history, the former by romanticizing it and the latter by demanding that life be lived in the here and now.[3] Susan Stewart has suggested that nostalgia is a construction that denies the past except as a narrative meditation.[4] Svetlana Boym's concept of nostalgia acknowledges its ahistoricism and capacity, in an unreflective state, for producing monsters. But by reminding us of the utopian impulses within nostalgia and through an etymological dissection, she recovers possibilities of human agency within nostalgia. Boym writes, "restorative nostalgia puts emphasis on *nostos* and proposes to rebuild the lost home and patch up the memory gaps," whereas "reflective nostalgia dwells in *algia*, in longing and loss, the imperfect process of remembrance." Boym stresses that these two types of nostalgia are tendencies and not absolutes, but she does suggest that reflective nostalgia opens a playfulness in which the longing, or the consciousness of distance, is more important than any perceived homecoming. She sums this up nicely: "a modern nostalgic can be homesick and sick of home at the same time." All of this is to say that longing and critical thinking can go hand-in-hand.[5]

Reflective nostalgia can lead in other directions than those proposed by Boym. When Lasch criticizes critics of nostalgia for demanding we live in the present, he speaks as a historian and one already starting to develop a telling case against assumptions that the passage of time equals progress.[6] Nostalgia is to a certain extent a reaction against presentism that emphasizes the positives of now, in that nostalgia remembers what was lost and longs for it. The critique of nostalgia carries an assumption that such longing neglects context and complexity. So one might long for the past but conveniently forget, for instance, that antibiotics are a relatively recent development. But sometimes such longings are warranted, and context and complexity shade off in their importance. Take, for instance, one way the word "nostalgia" entered the English language. During James Cook's extended voyage in the South Pacific from 1768 to 1771, the men on board his ship developed an acute longing for home, which according to Sir Joseph Banks, the ship's surgeon named as a new disease: nostalgia.[7] Cook's sailors were on a long and difficult voyage, in waters dangerous to Europeans, and their longing for home, far from being wistful or pathological, may well have been eminently sensible. Nonetheless, when nostalgia becomes a commodity, all such context and complexity is, if not deliberately stripped away, then at least only held in place as some vague reference through which to understand that being marketed. A clear example is the persistence of the image of Che as a symbol of some kind of radicalism, now so thoroughly commodified that the link to Che Guevara the communist guerrilla warrior of the Cuban revolution and failed Bolivian adventure is something that only spoilsport historians are wont to point out. Ironically enough, both the left and the right of politics can probably agree that Che has been stripped of politics and become a vague symbol of rebelliousness. Superman has suffered a similar fate, albeit he is a vague symbol of the heroic. But because there is no essential real figure, referents to a historical Superman are more helpful than harmful to his value.

Che as a free-floating symbol of rebelliousness stripped of historical referents is but one manner in which a commodified nostalgia works. In the remarkable 1984 work *On Longing*, Susan Stewart discusses the way in which souvenirs move "history into private time." Using the example of a ribbon from a corsage and a miniature Eiffel Tower, Stewart argues that such souvenirs connect to not just the corsage or the Eiffel Tower but the things and events surrounding them, such as, in the case of the corsage, the dress and the dance and so on. But as she notes, the souvenir only evokes and never recovers fully the experience. She reminds us that the souvenir "will not function without the supplementary narrative discourse that both attaches it to its origins and creates a myth with regard to those origins." And that is what she means by nostalgia as a narrative meditation.[8] The public edifice of the Eiffel Tower becomes a private memory of a trip to Paris in such a process. There is a jangle of memories that take narratives to sort and order. Much the same can be said for Superman, with one difference, in that many of the narratives, which sort and order the memories and history of Superman, are themselves "souvenirs" of Superman.

Nostalgia for earlier versions of the character has been part of the sales pitch of various incarnations of Superman stemming from at least 1978. The *Superman* movie released in December of that year played to baby-boomer memories of Superman. In a key scene in the movie in which the audience and Lois learn much about Superman's powers and character through her interview with him, she asks, "Why are you here? There must be a reason for you to be here." And Superman replies, "Yes, I am here to fight for truth and justice and the American way." This phrase, first introduced as the opening of the Superman radio serial in 1942 and then used in the opening of the 1950s television series *The Adventures of Superman*, linked Christopher Reeve's portrayal of Superman to earlier versions. Indeed, Reeve told the reporter Susan Heller Anderson that "what makes [Superman] a hero is how he uses his powers. It's about believing, rather than being cynical. . . . [Superman is] here fighting for truth, justice, and the American way."[9] In 2002, in the first season of the *Smallville* television series, in the eighteenth episode, Lex Luthor suggests to Clark Kent that he run for student president under the slogan "Man of Tomorrow," and Clark replies that he stands for "truth, justice and other stuff."

COMIC BOOKS AND NOSTALGIA

The use of these types of catchphrases in film and television might seem like passing references, but they do build associations across generations. Likewise, in comic books, referencing "the American way" creates nostalgic associations. In 1996, DC published *Kingdom Come*, a special series of four comic books in its "Elseworlds" series. As DC puts it, "In Elseworlds, heroes are taken from their usual settings and put into strange times and places—some that have existed or might have existed, and others that can't, couldn't or shouldn't exist."[10] The story strengthened and enhanced the mythological dimensions of Superman by demonstrating the symbolic values at the character's core. The production values of the book, in which the art was painted rather than drawn and colored, indicated the audience and expectations DC had for it. DC gathered together and published the series as a hardback, complete with introduction and an "Apocrypha" section, which suggests that DC takes its claims that Superman is a new god rather seriously.[11] In the superlative-laden introduction, Elliot Maggin writes, "This Is The Iliad. . . . This is a story about truth obscured, justice deferred and the American way distorted in the hands of petty semanticists." Here Maggin deliberately evokes the 1950s television show to stir memories of Superman. Maggin goes on to declare *Kingdom Come* a message of values and iconography to future generations. *Kingdom Come*, as Maggin states explicitly, is about filling out the values associated with Superman.[12]

Kingdom Come is s story of the hero in exile and pretenders occupying his place. For the mythological dimensions of the story, it matters little that Superman has imposed this exile on himself and that the pretenders are also superheroes. In an era when a glut of massively muscled gung-ho superheroes and villains have challenged the market strength of earlier generations of comic book heroes, this aspect of the story can

FIGURE 14. *Kingdom Come* (New York: DC Comics, 1997)

be viewed as yet another level of nostalgia for simple times. In *Kingdom Come*, an earlier generation of superheroes has retired, dismayed by Superman's abandoning his "never-ending battle." The use of this phrase, also drawn from the 1950s television show, highlighted in bold, drives home the message that the Superman of *Kingdom Come* is an aged version of the 1950s character, whose parents and wife have died and who wears the mantle of his "humanity" heavily (see figure 14).

The hero returns from his exile, as inevitably he must in such mythology. Superman's return is triggered when an errant latter-day superhero named Magog carelessly savages a super-powered opponent who, in reaction, manages to attack and "split open" another hero, Captain Atom, resulting in a nuclear explosion. This battle occurs in Kansas, and the entire state becomes a nuclear wasteland as a result of the explosion. In most workings of Superman's origins, Kansas is his boyhood home. After the destruction of Kansas, the remaining superheroes lose all sense of responsibility. A preacher, the story's choral figure, observing this state of affairs, suggests, "now more than ever we need hope!" And then a gust of wind and the words "Look!"

"Up in the sky!"—words introduced to the Superman mythos by the radio serial—lead to a full-page panel of Superman. But although he has returned, all is not well because of the rage he contains, which is cued visually by the background of the red *S* on his costume being black instead of the usual yellow. Humanity, represented by the United Nations Council, is not altogether happy with this return and the realities of power it reveals.

The story builds to a conflict between humanity and superheroes. Superman is deeply conflicted but retains a moral code: he does not kill. In yet another piece of nostalgia, Superman reminds Batman of when they were the World's Finest team, a reference to a DC Comic that featured team adventures of the two and also a reference to their common humanity. When the United Nations seeks to restore order by destroying super humans, who despite Superman's presence threaten humanity through their conflicts, Superman seeks revenge on the UN but is quickly brought back to Earth by a reminder of his humanity. In the denouement, Superman dons his Clark Kent glasses, which are not so much a disguise but a reminder of his humanity. In the epilogue, Superman and Wonder Woman announce to Batman that they want him to raise their soon-to-be-born child to ensure his humanity. And in the penultimate panel, the three decide that he or she will be a "battler for truth, justice, and a new American way" (see figure 15).

FIGURE 15. *Kingdom Come* (New York: DC Comics, 1997)

TELEVISION AND NOSTALGIA

Alex Ross's art for *Kingdom Come* employs a style that might best be described as *la mode rétro*. Jameson discussed this mode in his analysis of pastiche films, such as *Body Heat*, which he saw as blurring the contemporary into some dehistoricized vision of the past. As Jameson noted, this blurring of time in movies and the creation of a visual pastness developed alongside a range of nostalgic movies such as *American Graffiti* (nostalgia for the 1950s), *Star Wars* and *Raiders of the Lost Ark* (nostalgia for 1950s movie serials), and *Chinatown* (nostalgia for the moody ambiance of film noir).[13] Ross's art looks like a 1950s version of imagined futures. There is a difference, of course, between the painted art of Alex Ross and the imagery of live-action film and television. But the producers of two live-action television series based on Superman used *la mode rétro* in varying degrees. The series *Lois & Clark* (1993–1997) blurs time both through a use of visual appropriation and by playing with the history of Superman as an icon of American culture, making use of earlier comic book, television, and movie incarnations of the characters to create a new pastiche. The series *Smallville* (2001–2011) deploys a small-town setting and a color palette aimed at producing a similar effect.

Lois & Clark: The New Adventures of Superman

Lois & Clark's original producer and creator, Deborah Joy LeVine, acknowledged the importance of Superman's history to the television series. She read over three hundred comic books in her preparation for the show. She took as her model the series of Superman movies starring Christopher Reeve and Margot Kidder, in which the sexual tension between the characters was a central theme. The earlier television series *The Adventures of Superman*, of which 104 episodes were made between 1951 and 1957, was another key source for *Lois & Clark*'s pastiche, and referents to that series crop up in several early episodes of *Lois & Clark*. In using these three earlier versions of Superman, the producers of *Lois & Clark* created a version of the character with diverse audience appeal because the deployment of earlier versions lent the series an authenticity as part of a broader narrative of Superman. As LeVine noted, she owed it to the comic book fans to know the history, and she knew them to be an important component of her audience even as she focused the show on the human relationship of the two title characters rather than the action-centered plots of the comic book.[14]

Lois & Clark premiered on September 12, 1993, and introduced the main characters and the standard features of the Superman story. As in any retelling, some aspects of the story varied. In *Lois & Clark*, Superman's nemesis, Lex Luthor, is a suave businessman somewhat in the mold of Richard Branson, rather than the mad-scientist type of the comic book or the buffoon figure of the 1970s movies. Jonathan and Martha Kent are still alive in Smallville, and Clark visits them for advice. Rather than exploding "Great Caesar's ghost" when astounded, as Perry White had done in *The Adventures of Superman*, the new Perry says "Great shades of Elvis," which incidentally gave the series another dimension of nostalgia on which to play. Other incidental features retained from the 1950s television series include the verbal sparring between Perry White and Jimmy Olsen and the police inspector Henderson, a character not generally sighted in other versions of Superman.

Originally, the series had a slightly more adult orientation in the manner of the 1970s movie version of Superman, in which Lois was a woman of experience as opposed to Clark's more naïve Smallville boy. For instance, in the first episode, Lois confesses to Clark that a former colleague, with whom she has had an affair, has betrayed her. As the first season developed, the producers played down the sexuality of Lois and later dropped another character, Cat, played by Tracey Scoggins, whose main function was to up the sexual tension, almost certainly because of the Sunday-evening family time slot assigned by ABC.[15]

The visual design of the series also helped create an aura of timelessness. The main set for the show, the *Daily Planet* newsroom, with its heavy emphasis on wood, gilt-lettered names on doors, and marginalization of computers, looks more like a 1930s newsroom, at least as depicted in movies such as *His Girl Friday* (1940). To be sure, computers and the ubiquitous coffee pot and other such modern appliances are present, but the overall visualization of the show serves to blur their presence. For instance, in the third episode, when Lex Luthor checks the morning papers, the front page of the

Daily Planet is composed in a retro style with narrow columns and no photographs, at least above the fold. Luther is served by Asabi, a South Asian manservant reminiscent of Daddy Warbucks's "mysterious Oriental" servant, Punjab, in Harold Gray's 1920s comic strip *Little Orphan Annie*. These visual devices are then set against Luthor's curiosity about Superman when he poses a set of questions using phrases from the 1950s television show: Can Superman "leap tall buildings in a single bound?" Is Superman, say, "more powerful than a locomotive?" Later Luthor discovers some answers: Superman is "faster than a speeding bullet" and a "man of steel." The use of key phrases from previous incarnations of Superman helped give *Lois & Clark* a timeless feel. In the first episode, spectators seeing Superman fly exclaim, "Is it a bird? Is it a plane?" In the second episode, Lois prompts Superman in an answer about what he means by helping people with "like fighting for truth and justice."

Other episodes added to the series's timelessness. In the sixth episode, both Lois and Clark work undercover in a nightclub owned by gangsters. Although the plot has the quasi-feminist sister of a gang boss forcing her brother out of the gang because his old-fashioned way of doing things does not match her MBA business skills, the nightclub has torch singers, dancing showgirls, and cigarette-girl-like waitresses. Perhaps such clubs existed in the United States somewhere in the 1990s—certainly casinos offer this type of entertainment, but they are considerably larger than clubs. But the heyday of that sort of nightclub came and went sometime between the end of Prohibition and the 1960s. *Lois & Clark* sometimes appealed more directly to nostalgia. In the ninth episode, about a heat wave, Sonny Bono, then between jobs as mayor of Palm Springs and his later seat in the House of Representatives, appears briefly as the mayor, making references to his hit songs of the 1960s, with "and the heat goes on" about the heat wave and "I got you babe" in answer to a question from Lois Lane. Phyllis Coates, who played Lois Lane in the first twenty-six episodes of *The Adventures of Superman*, appears as Lois Lane's mother in the final episode of the first season. In the fourth season, Jack Larson, who had played Jimmie Olsen in the 1950s series, makes a guest appearance.[16]

The point of all this nostalgia was an appeal not so much to a past but to some narrative of the past. For instance, in the sixth episode,

the evocation of an earlier nightclub era could not be accurately represented complete with cigarette girls because the attitude to cigarette
smoking was no longer the same and it could have been construed as
an advertisement for smoking. Moreover, smoking in places that sell
food is banned in many American states. Lois & Clark's producers did
not always maintain the timelessness of the show. In the third episode,
reference is made to a "drive-by shooting," and Lois Lane watches a
television set that shows what appears to be the infamous Rodney
King video and footage of the Waco debacle of 1993. Although only
shown for a total of five seconds and within the context of the need for
heroes such as Superman, this "reality" is a disconcerting intrusion
into the visualization and timelessness of the series and is not repeated
in any other episodes.

The nostalgic references served a purpose of making the show popular and profitable rather than an exercise in self-reflexive postmodernism. The show's producers did, however, occasionally have to address
the issue of Superman's longevity as a character and his commercial
presence in American culture in a manner relevant to the series's story
lines. For instance, in the fourth episode of Lois & Clark, the producers
used a story line about merchandising Superman products from a 1938
comic book as a subplot. In the episode, Clark/Superman struggles to
find his true self as his fame has resulted in numerous Superman products such as dolls and soft drinks. An agent, straight out of vaudeville,
approaches Superman with commercial endorsement offers including
one to go to Cleveland—an in-joke recognizable to viewers aware that
Jerry Siegel and Joe Shuster created Superman while teenagers living
in Cleveland. Eventually, Clark/Superman decides that he controls his
own destiny and that no manner of commercial product would affect
his true self. Nonetheless, he agrees to the licensing of his name provided that the profits go to charity. The episode neatly fit the developing narrative of Lois & Clark with the commodity status of Superman
as a trademark and much-licensed product.[17]

Lois & Clark's narrative structure, that is, the stories it tells and the
manner in which it tells (visualized) those stories, is nostalgic. If we
regard this as a failure to represent current experience at the popular
level of a television show, then we might want to join Jameson and
see such a situation as a "pathological symptom." Or perhaps if we
agree with Boym and see nostalgia as having the possibility for critical

reflection, did *Lois & Clark* allow its audience, or at least a segment of its diverse audience, to long for something lost and address that longing in a critical manner?

The Internet offers ample evidence that *Lois & Clark* resonated deeply enough with a section of its audience that it engaged them in an active relationship with the series. There are thousands of pages of *Lois & Clark* material on the web. This interaction with the series extends from scanned photographs of the stars, through episode guides and detailed summaries, to fan fiction. In early 2016, there were 3,973 fan-written stories centered on the *Lois & Clark* television series available through the web-based Lois & Clark Fanfic Archives. Stories had been added at regular intervals up to April 3, 2016.[18] This site has received over half a million visits since May 1996. Fans have also written episodes for the fifth season that never was and posted them on several websites.[19] There are also several thousand postings to various *Lois & Clark* bulletin boards.[20] To be sure, not all of this activity could be classed as critical thinking, but diverse scholars, such as the anti-comic-book campaigner psychiatrist Fredric Wertham and the feminist film theorist Constance Penley, have suggested that fan magazines (fanzines) and fiction (fanfic, slash) empower their creators since they let fans slip outside mass-mediated experience. Wertham empathetically noted that these fans refuse to accept "the processing and manipulation of people. . . . In all of this there is definitely an implied social criticism."[21]

At the same time, though, the fans' dedication to the series and their use of it for their own purposes gave *Lois & Clark* an afterlife on cable television. In 2001 and 2002, the US cable network TNT showed the series at eight in the morning Monday to Friday. The TNT website for the series included extensive links to fan sites.[22] Given the legal actions of Viacom and Twentieth Century Fox to shut down fan websites for series such as *The X-Files*, *Millennium*, *The Simpsons*, and *Star Trek* and the prior aggressive stance of DC Comics and its parent company, Time Warner, in defense of their trademarked property, Superman, as well as the extensive legal notice elsewhere on the site, it is stunning to see the Time Warner–owned cable network TNT promoting such sites with only the minimal disclaimer "external sites are not endorsed by TNT."[23] At the very least, this occurrence suggests that the fan activity and the fan longing feed the commercial worth of *Lois & Clark* and other Superman-linked products in sufficient degree that the corporation must run the risk of undermining its legal claims to sole control of the character in order to market it better. Indeed, *Smallville*, yet another incarnation of Superman from yet another arm of Time Warner, the teenager/young-adult-oriented cable network The WB (now The CW), had a webpage that listed fan sites and invited participation in a discussion forum when it had not yet commenced airing the series, save for one episode in a few test markets.[24]

Originally aimed at a specific audience segment that enjoyed light romance, *Lois & Clark*'s US time slot caused a rethink of format and a search for more diverse appeal. Nostalgia formed a useful way of drawing varied audiences. The series then sold the older segment of the audience its own memories. The series introduced a fictional narrative that had existed in many versions over sixty years to a younger audience. A large part of the series's appeal, then, lay in its ability to unite past and present, to elide history, and to offer a disembodied past in the form of a commodity for consumption. In Australia, this helped the show to dramatic ratings success in its first two seasons. At the same time, the use of nostalgia and *la mode rétro* opened possibilities for reflective nostalgia and creative engagement with the series. Nonetheless, even these aspects have been incorporated into the marketing of the series beyond its original broadcasts. In an era of increased audience segmentation, in the 1990s because of cable television and now because of so many delivery platforms, *Lois & Clark* demonstrates that timelessness has a diverse appeal and can draw audiences from outside a particular target segment.

Smallville

Smallville debuted on The WB, a network owned by the Time Warner Corporation, on October 16, 2001. The WB was a fledging network that focused on the teen/young-adult market and was at various times the home to such teen-focused series as *Dawson's Creek, Roswell, Buffy the Vampire Slayer*, and *Gilmore Girls*. *Smallville*, as one critic put it, was "located just a mile or so upstream from *Dawson's Creek*" and centered on the struggles of a teenage Clark Kent.[25] The series, set in the mythical Kansas hometown of Clark Kent / Superman, contains the basic features of the Superman story: his parents send him as an infant in a rocket to escape the doomed planet Krypton, Martha and Jonathan Kent find him in the rocket and adopt him, and he develops super strength and speed. Some other aspects of the series come from the Superboy comics, the adventures of Superman as a teenager. For instance, just as in the Superboy comic book and the Superman movies, Lana Lang is Clark Kent / Superman's initial love interest. And as in the Superboy comic books, Clark and Lex Luthor are friends, and Lex is not predestined for evil. But in *Smallville*, Clark Kent does not don the familiar Superman suit, nor in general does he fly. The series, then, is both a teen "angst-filled" drama and part of the Superman mythology. Importantly, the series appealed to a youthful audience that could learn about Superman through this ten-season-long bildungsroman.

In the absence of the familiar markers of Superman, such as his superhero costume, *Smallville* uses colors, symbols, and associations to tie the series to Superman. The producers and writers clearly derived much of their settings and characters from long-standing features of Superman and appealed to a generalized nostalgia for the character. Without the emblematic Superman costume, *Smallville*'s producers replicated its color scheme of dominant red and blue simply and nonintrusively by having Clark Kent wear blue jeans with a red tee shirt. When Warner released seasons of *Smallville* in DVD boxed sets, red and blue dominated the design. "*Smallville*" always appears in the same bold red as Superman's costume on the DVD covers, and Tom Welling, who plays Clark Kent in the series, more often than not appears in either a blue or red tee shirt.

Smallville contains numerous other connections to earlier versions of Superman. These include Annette O'Toole, who played Lana Lang in the movie *Superman II* and appears as Clark Kent's mother in *Smallville*. Guest appearances by Christopher Reeve, Margot Kidder, and Terrence Stamp—respectively, Superman, Lois Lane, and General Zod in the movies—also establish a connection to earlier versions. Although these actors play different characters—in Stamp's case moving from Superman's enemy General Zod to his father, Jor-El—their presence evokes broader dimensions of Superman. Many other playful references in the series link it to Superman. In the pilot episode,

Clark Kent reads a copy of Friedrich Nietzsche's *The Will to Power*, which contains the phrase "Behold the Superman," and Lana Lang asks him whether he is man or superman. In the seventeenth episode of the first season, Lex Luthor says he received a copy of the book for his tenth birthday. In the second season's fifth episode, Lana refers jokingly to Clark Kent as a "man of steel." In that season, many of the episodes feature music that "quotes" the Superman movie theme by John Williams. In the third season, a police chief says to the journalist Perry White, "Don't call me chief," which references the 1950s television series's Perry White telling Jimmy Olsen not to call him chief.

And the list goes on, with key phrases, powers, and events from Superman's back catalogue trotted out at regular intervals. Catchphrases from Superman's many incarnations, such as "What is it? A bird? A plane?" "faster than a speeding bullet," "powers and abilities far beyond those of mortal men," "up, up, and away," "truth, justice and the American way," "strange visitor from another planet," and "able to leap tall buildings at a single bound," appear in numerous episodes.[26] The series also has references to other versions of characters: Lois Lane cannot spell (as in the movies), a character is told to "kneel before Zod" (a favorite fan line from *Superman II*), Princeton scouts come to view Clark play football (Dean Cain, who played Superman in the series *Lois & Clark*, went to Princeton, where he played football), Clark squeezes coal into a diamond (an oft-repeated trick in the comic book), and Clark's friend Chloe, who knows his secret, wonders, what next, "spin the earth backwards on its axis"?—a reference to the 1978 *Superman* movie.[27] Likewise, appearances by numerous characters from DC Comics locate the series within a broader framework of Superman's history. Characters such as the Flash, Green Arrow, Aquaman, and Bruce Wayne appear in the show. And in one episode, a dog, seemingly with super powers, arrives at the Kent house, and for a moment, Clark toys with naming him Krypto, the name of Superboy's super pet dog in the 1950s and 1960s comic books. All of this suggests that *Smallville* is not just highly derivative of the original Superman but part of a broader circulation of nostalgia for Superman as a constituent element of the character in recent incarnations. As the Australian academic Angela Ndalianis has argued, "the *telling* of the myth has become *as* important as the myth that is told."[28]

The 1978 movie *Superman* reinvigorated Superman. In addition to three sequels, it also gave rise to the two television series just discussed. The film rehearsed some of the key parameters of the Superman story and added some new twists. It provided a template for comic book movies that followed, particularly in its use of star actors like Marlon Brando and Gene Hackman to generate publicity, and consequently raise capital, for the film.[29] As already mentioned, *Superman* evoked earlier forms of the character by using catchphrases like "truth, justice and the American way," and indeed the hiring of the actor Christopher Reeve, whose name was similar enough to that of George Reeves, also played to such nostalgia. The 2006 film *Superman Returns* does not announce itself directly as a sequel to the earlier Superman movies, but it makes enough subtle and not-so-subtle references to those movies that the connection is obvious. Like DC stable-mate Batman, Superman was in need of an overhaul following disastrous third and fourth outings in movies. In Batman's case, producers and executives decided to begin anew with the aptly named 2005 movie *Batman Begins*, whereas Superman returned. *Superman Returns* opens with the voice of the late Marlon Brando as Jor-El saying farewell to his son, Kal-El. The audio is from the original *Superman* movie directed by Richard Donner and can also be heard in his director's cut of *Superman II*. As Krypton explodes, the camera pulls back, with the scattering fragments and the opening credits rolling over the top of the John Williams *Superman* score. The opening, then, is a pastiche of the first movie, a quick recap and then opening credits rendered in almost exactly the same style as *Superman*, mostly using the same neon-blue outline font and the design form that zooms in and then dissolves. To be sure, in the first movie, the credits zoomed in and then dissolved, but only up to the appearance of the Superman logo and the movie title after the text "A Richard Donner Film," after which they zoomed out and dissolved. In *Superman Returns*, they zoom in all the way through, but after the text "A Bryan Singer Film" and the Superman logo and movie title, they momentarily turn red for the names of Brandon Routh and Kate Bosworth. Also in *Superman*, Brando's and Hackman's names appear above the title. The movie title order, a key to Hollywood status, demonstrates that Superman is the real star of the movie; that is, by 2006, Superman's star outshone those of actors.

The homage continues throughout *Superman Returns*; for instance, Lex Luthor is shown in his library just as in *Superman* and later, when Luthor visits the Fortress of Solitude, his familiarity with it leads his girlfriend, Kitty Kowalski, to remark, "It's like you have been here before," which of course he has in *Superman II*. And just as Luthor had been in *Superman*, he is obsessed with real estate and creating new value. The level of homage is such that a whole sequence features a miniature train-set world that is disrupted by a Krypton crystal, causing earthquake-like events and the destruction of one face on the miniature Mount Rushmore, which directly references the first two Superman movies, in which Superman saves a train from destruction and General Zod destroys a face on Mount Rushmore. The scene indirectly comments on the extensive use of miniatures for the special effects in the original movies. Indeed, the first appearance of Superman in costume and performing heroic deeds replicates the first movie in that he saves Lois Lane from an air disaster. Whereas in the first movie he saved Lois from a helicopter accident and then later saved Air Force One, in *Superman Returns* the events are collapsed into one, with Superman saving a jet that has Lois Lane on board. And because the jet is attached to a space shuttle whose launch from atop the jet has gone wrong, the movie evokes real-life space-shuttle tragedies. Just to reinforce the connection, after saving the passengers, Superman gives the same speech about flying still being the safest way to travel as he gave to Lois in *Superman*. The list goes on: as in the first two movies and *Smallville*, Lois can not spell; exiting the *Daily Planet* building, Clark has trouble negotiating talking while walking with Lois and using a revolving door; and Metropolis is still basically New York City. Lois lives at 312 Riverside Drive, and there are matte aerial shots showing the Brooklyn and Manhattan Bridges and glistening shots of the Manhattan financial district from across the waters of the harbor, unaware of an impending threat, which eerily evokes 9/11, although the film was shot in Sydney, Australia. *Superman Returns* even reproduces classic scenes from the comic books, reaching back to the cover of *Action Comics* #1 (June 1938) to show Superman holding a car aloft at just the right angle, a photograph of which Perry White later labels as iconic. The very astute fan will notice at 40 minutes and 16 seconds

FIGURE 16. *Superman Returns* (2006)

into the film, in the wreckage of the model train set, a replica of the exact model of car that Superman held over his head in his first comic book appearance and a collapsed Smallville railroad-station sign (see figure 16).

These playful tributes, pastiches, and in-jokes have, since the television series *The Simpsons*, become de rigueur for an American entertainment product. They engage audiences in the play of spotting the references and make the viewing experience potentially more interactive. The film's creators use these techniques to engage audiences, whose reception of the film is potentially made more pleasurable by being the recipients of the insider jokes and references. For instance, in the character Kitty Kowalski, the creators of *Superman Returns* may have authored a complex in-joke. The alliteration of the name follows that of Lois Lane; Kitty is somewhat older in fact and dress than Lois in the movie, so her initial letters naturally enough precede Lois's in the alphabet. The alliteration also provides a clue to another connection. In the 1960s, the Canadian-born wrestler Killer Kowalski, who had obtained some fame in the United States, toured Australia on a regular basis. The joke here is the Canada-America-Australia link shared by Superman through the artist Joe Shuster, who was born in Canada; the obvious American icon status of Superman; and the film's having been shot in Australia. The other level of the joke is that the 1950s television Superman George Reeves wrestled a little and died the same night as going to a wresting match. Such textual strategies are yet another addition to the polysemic character that a work created for mass circulation needs to contain to achieve its intended broad demographic appeal. Whether or not the Kowalski connection was deliberate is not as important as someone making it and thus deepening his or her relationship with the film, and all the other in-jokes raise the possibility and encourage these sorts of connections. Beyond such industry tricks of the trade, DC has increasingly built Superman as a character around its concept of him as mythological. At times, it seems as if some bright, young executive at DC read the 1972 translation of Umberto Eco's article on Superman as myth, possibly at college, and decided yes, this is what Superman is and how we shall promote and sell him. For instance, in 1983, Jenette Kahn, then-president of DC Comics, described Superman as "the first god of a new mythology."[30] And indeed, in *Superman Returns*, Lex Luthor describes Superman as a god and compares himself to Prometheus. If a mythological tale is simply the telling of something already known, it makes it easier to dismiss a story that does not work as simply that: a failed retelling of the already-known story. So the viewer can consign *Superman III* and *Superman IV* to the dustbin of mythology. *Superman Returns* builds on story elements from the last successful film telling of Superman, in *Superman II*, and as Matt Yockey has noted, the film could "be read as both a vague remake of and a sequel" to the two earlier Superman movies.[31]

Superman Returns is the classical mythological tale. Mostly it simply retells us the story we already know, and much of it is told in a form we already know from the first two Superman movies. As such, the movie assembles the key elements that make Superman Superman and that make a successful Superman movie a Superman movie. There is only one new element in the film, and although this takes up a rather small amount of time in the movie, it is the key element of the film and the part that potentially set up a sequel and a new series of Superman films, even if this film's failure destroyed that chance. Early in the film, when Clark Kent returns to his job at the *Daily Planet*, he and we discover that Lois Lane is now a mother of a boy she has named Jason White. Although not wed, she lives with the apparent father of her child, Richard White, Perry White's nephew. As the film progresses, Jason's powers are revealed, and it is apparent that although unaffected by Kryptonite, he is indeed Superman's son. The only way it makes sense for Lois to have borne Superman's son is that the events of Richard Lester's *Superman II* were the antecedents of this film. There are slight problems here because Superman wiped Lois Lane's memory of their encounter with each other because, as well as sexual intercourse, it involved the revelation of his Clark Kent identity. So with Lois having found herself pregnant, she must surely have wondered how she arrived in that state. Lois Lane has been many things over numerous incarnations of Superman, but she has never been one to sleep around. But the major problem for the movie is that for this story line to make sense, the audience has to be familiar with the plot specifics of *Superman II* up to a point, to accept Lois and Superman having sex, and to be willing to forget the conclusion of the film, but again this asks those who do remember the ending to actively forget and so help construct the ongoing mythological tale themselves. Nonetheless, Superman's son is the emotional core of *Superman Returns*. The movie begins with a prologue: Jor-El's voice intones over a shot of Krypton, "You will travel far, my little Kal-El. But we will never leave you, even in the face of our death. You will make my strength your own. You will see my life through your eyes, as your life will be seen through mine. The son becomes the father, the father becomes the son." Two and one-quarter hours later, at the end of the film, Superman intones these words to his sleeping son. Having acknowledged his son, Superman then sets out to depart, but on encountering Lois, she asks of him, "Will we see you around?" and he replies, "I'm always around." And then he flies off, circles around in a manner reminiscent of Christopher Reeve at the end of *Superman*, and comes back toward the camera.

Superman Returns's version of Superman did not pan out as Time Warner and DC hoped. But the revenue generated from the box office and various licensed products, not to mention renewed interest in earlier versions of the character, all made the movie a worthwhile outing for the corporation. *Superman Returns* offered a return to a smaller scale of virtuous males conveying values to their sons, albeit in a world with a different set of moral values. The movie, then, seemed deeply nostalgic for some ideal time when such things supposedly happened.

MAN OF STEEL AND BATMAN V. SUPERMAN

Released in 2013 to coincide with the seventy-fifth anniversary of Superman's initial appearance in *Action Comics* #1 in June 1938, *Man of Steel* is on the surface the least nostalgic of Superman's recent screen appearances. The film does indeed tell the standard origin story of his Krypton birth and journey away from the doomed planet to an idyllic small-town American childhood with adoptive parents. But it tells it in a different color palette and a somewhat different tone. The film critic Joe Williams summed up the response of many viewers and critics when he complained that, "instead of the primary colors from the classic comic books, the dominant hue is pewter," and linked this darker shade to the film's overall character, in which "every opportunity for humor, compassion or plausible responses to otherworldly phenomena is buried beneath product placements and CGI special effects." He called the film a "desecration . . . disguised as a Superman film."[32] Such a comment suggests that some notion of a Superman movie exists above and beyond the *Man of Steel*, and from the context, that is clearly *Superman* and *Superman II*, directed by Richard Donner and Richard Lester, respectively.

Man of Steel avoids the nostalgic winks and asides of catchphrases and cameo appearances that many of the screen iterations of Superman have contained. In a sense, the film does not need a set of built-in nostalgia triggers because the anniversary celebrations created many such referents. Moreover, the damming criticism of *Superman Returns* for its abundant nostalgia made it commercially logical to avoid such references. But the media reception of the film was perhaps inevitably ensnared in recollections of earlier versions of Superman that went beyond acknowledging the long history of the character. To note that these engagements involved large dollops of nostalgia is not to suggest that the discursive framework around the film simply amounted to such dealings. Superman is in and of itself a rich paratext involving audiences, industry, and an array of texts and artifacts, and the meaning of the character lies in a constant process of negotiating this assemblage. Joe Williams at the *St. Louis Post-Dispatch* adopted a strategy to guide him through this process. He made Donner's 1978 film a standard for Superman movies against which all other versions would be judged. Reviewing *Man of Steel* in Singapore, Dylan Tan wrote, "Call it nostalgia but there's a certain old school charm about Richard Donner's Superman movies. The costumes were tacky and the special effects may be cheesy by today's standards but it's undeniable the moment Christopher Reeve took to the skies, the make-believe was magical enough to light up the audience's faces." In London, Ben Childs noted that the film "introduces a navel-gazing Superman, eschews the spiky humour of the Christopher Reeve films in favour of jaw-dropping spectacle and imagines a Lois Lane who doesn't seem to share much chemistry with Clark Kent." And in Dublin, Gavin Burke said, "So we got a little bit of Richard Donner's Superman, some of Richard Lester's Superman II, and no Lex Luthor. . . . While this new kind of superhero movie is welcome, there is an argument for a return to the more simplistic—and fun—variation. After all, this will be the first Superman experience for some kids and they're going to wonder why everything has to be so serious." And Reagan Gavin Rasquinha for the *Times of India* suggested, "many of the usual Superman tropes are deliberately avoided. In fact, he barely even smiles and the quips of past films are studiously avoided."[33]

The critics here were occupied in unreflective nostalgia, in which their memories of earlier Superman films as superior to that under review involve no examination of the context or indeed of the manner in which the different films engaged with the broader history of Superman. To be fair to these writers, most of these reviews were short pieces and used the earlier film as a hook for the article. But then again, that is my point: the most familiar hook they all reached for was nostalgia even when discussing a movie that deliberately sought not to play to that sentiment. The only critic who saw something beyond this framework was Manohla Dargis at the *New York Times*, who wrote,

> This superhero flambé aside, the oil platform is most notable for the workingmen Superman rescues, laboring brothers to the trapped coal miners who figure into one of his first comic-book outings in 1938. One of the pleasures of the Christopher Reeve "Superman" series, which took off in 1978 and bottomed out in 1987, was how the movies managed to be both charmingly old-fashioned and of their contemporary moment. There are a number of overt references to the past in "Man of Steel," a title that itself summons up America's lost industrial history. There's even a scene in which Jor-El narrates Krypton's rise and calamitous fall using immersive, metallic-gray images that morph and scroll across the frame like an animated version of a W.P.A. bas-relief mural.[34]

But in noting how *Man of Steel*, contrary to general opinion, does play with the history of Superman, or at least with his origins in the

1930s, Dargis still wraps it in a cover of the Reeve films, which seems a sly nod to nostalgia and its charms.

The 2016 film *Batman v. Superman* is not solely a Superman film, but it does function as a sequel of sorts to *Man of Steel* in that a good part of the film and its setup relies on the events of *Man of Steel* seen from the perspective of Bruce Wayne / Batman. Like *Man of Steel*, *Batman v. Superman* is not overt in its use of nostalgic reference points. Rather, the film has several "Easter eggs." Easter eggs are a slightly different order of nostalgia, trading on fan knowledge rather than generally circulated catchphrases such as "truth, justice, and the American way." Easter eggs are vague references: signs that appear in the background, blink-and-you-will-miss-it moments, and story elements mostly known to comic book fans from DC's (and indeed Marvel's) long catalogue. The film does, however, incorporate elements of DC comic book storytelling over the previous thirty years and draws in part from the Batman comic book *The Dark Knight Returns* by Frank Miller; the death-and-return-of-Superman story arc from the early 1990s Superman comic books, which featured Doomsday; and 1985's *Crisis on Infinite Earths*. It also has a sly reference to the 2003 graphic novel *Superman: Red Son*. There is even a blink-and-you-will-miss-it, an unacknowledged, reference to Elliot Maggin's "Must There Be a Superman" story in *Superman* #247 (January 1972). For those who are not in the know, a Google search using the film's title and "Easter eggs" will produce several websites detailing the not-immediately-obvious nostalgic features. Such elements are now a de rigueur part of comic book movies and a deliberate part of the marketing, so much so that they have acquired a name (Easter eggs), a fan service, and a small industry of websites devoted to detailing these discoveries, both revealing and building insider fan knowledge.[35]

THE OBJECT OF NOSTALGIA AND NARRATIVES

These efforts at evoking nostalgia for Superman revolved around two key incarnations of the character: the 1950s television series *The Adventures of Superman* and the late 1970s early 1980s Superman films starring Christopher Reeve. These versions of the character offer more fixed referents for nostalgia. The comic book Superman as a character is perhaps too variable or suffers from too much narrative bloat to offer readily remembered instances around which nostalgia can form.

Indeed, in my own case, one of the few stories I can recall as a youth reading Superman comics in Australia in locally produced omnibus black-and-white reprints is a story in which Superman takes a giant US flag to Hawaii as part of the celebration of its becoming the fiftieth state in the union. The key to this memory is the flag and Hawaii. But the part I remember consists of two frames in a nine-page story in a Lois Lane comic book in which she suffers terrible injuries and has to live under the sea with Aquaman, her new "boyfriend," but still pines for Superman.[36] The story and my memory do not lend themselves to nostalgia for Superman, although they do trigger some fond memories of those years in my life. Likewise, when I think of the television series *The Adventures of Superman*, which I watched fairly regularly as a child and would have seen on and off during my teen years, I can recall only two specific instances. I remember an episode in which a scientist invented a means to transport people over telephone lines and the efforts of criminals to take advantage of that invention, and I remember another episode in which the denouement involved walls closing in on Lois Lane, threatening to crush her.[37] Again, this is not exactly material for nostalgia. And indeed, the object of nostalgia is not particularly any received narrative episodes of Superman in any form but sets of catchphrases or visualizations like the chest emblem. Generalizing from my own experience and memories is not necessarily a good idea, but my point here is not about me and my relation to given episodes of Superman but about the ways readers and viewers remember, recall, and respond to the character. My memories are individual ones that I use to mediate my interactions with the character. My argument suggests that most viewers and readers would bring such memories, with different specifics, to any interaction with the character.

Given that much of the potential audience for Superman has their own rich set of narrative meditations on the character, meditations that are constitutive of private memories and personal lives and so all the richer and indeed constitute audiences rather than a single audience, any instance of Superman that wants purchase on these audiences will work these elements into narratives. Television series like *Lois & Clark* and *Smallville* and comic books like *Kingdom Come* and films like *Superman Returns* and *Man of Steel*, even if they had not tried to be vehicles of nostalgia, were inevitably going to be so because of what audiences brought to their interactions. But the creators of these products all engaged with nostalgia, some more successfully than others, to the point that those who were too young to remember what was being presented as nostalgia imbibed with no prior meditation connecting them to the character but, in doing so, drank so deeply of nostalgia that sober assessment required some reckoning with nostalgia and the way it shaped what they read or viewed. The television series and the movies have a larger public profile than the comic books and tend to be reviewed in newspapers and magazines. In my review of thousands of these reports since 1978, I cannot remember a case that did not discuss Superman's past. In general, such mentions were nostalgic rather than analytical.[38]

Two recent works help show the importance of nostalgia and narrative mediation on that nostalgia in shaping coherent understandings of Superman. The journalist Larry Tye's 2012 volume *Superman: The High-Flying History of America's Most Enduring Hero* offers a rich account of the character's long career with plenty of detail on Superman, the writers and artists who contributed to the character's story, and the machinations behind the scenes at DC Comics and on the sets of television series and movies. It is a solid piece of work but never quite manages to account for Superman's popularity across so many years. In a smaller 2010 book, *Our Hero: Superman on Earth*, which is more of an extended essay, the novelist Tom De Haven runs through some of the same issues. At heart, though, De Haven is not trying to account for the character over time in a linear sense but rather for the appeal of the character, and so he turns to his own view of Superman. De Haven says that there are certain immutable things about Superman, but he concludes his book with this summary of his character: "Basically, what he needs, and all he needs, is the freedom to act in ways that are satisfying to him. *That's* why he'll 'never stop doing good.' It makes *him* feel good, dammit. Our hero."[39] There is looseness to De Haven's prose and his argument; but he does manage to convey the way Superman resonates for him, and that narrative goes further to explain Superman's popularity than Tye manages to do. De Haven offers his private memories and his own nostalgia for the character, and the richness of this makes up for what the book lacks as history.

As a character, Superman has been particularly effective in mobilizing people's nostalgia and getting them to meditate on their own private histories, to the extent that they will purchase a ticket to a movie or watch a television series. In other words, DC Comics and Time Warner have a product that people will purchase to access their own memories. It is the willingness of significant numbers of people to do so that helps account for the persistence of Superman as a character and product.

CHAPTER FOUR

PRODUCTION, AUTHORSHIP, AND OWNERSHIP

On March 1, 1938, Jerry Siegel and Joe Shuster signed a contract assigning all rights to Superman to Detective Comics, Inc. for $130. The contract, countersigned by Jack Liebowitz for the company, remained a sore point for Siegel for the remainder of his life. Within a month or so of the contract's signing, Superman first appeared in *Action Comics* #1 (June 1938), which would have appeared on the newsstands sometime in April 1938. Superman's immediate origins lay in a 1933 fanzine story written by Siegel and titled "The Reign of the Superman," which Shuster illustrated.[1] This story had little to do with the later comic book version, save for the name and a notion of incredible powers. Indeed, the Superman in this story used his powers for personal enrichment and was a villain. A five-year gestation period followed before the much-revised heroic Superman's 1938 appearance in comic books. Attributing authorship for Superman is a complex matter. Even the origins of the character and his creation are more intricate than the standard tale of Siegel devising the character after a restless night's sleep and rushing to Shuster's house to work up the idea as a comic.[2] For instance, until 2008, there had been little mention by Siegel, or anyone else, that in 1934 he worked unsuccessfully with the *Buck Rogers* comic strip illustrator Russell Keaton on trying to develop a Superman comic strip.[3]

After Superman's 1938 debut, all the comic book and comic strip adventures appeared over the signatures of Siegel and Shuster until April 1948.[4] This occurred despite a range of other artists and writers working on these productions. Superman's appearance in other media such as animated cartoons, a radio series, and a movie serial also expanded the number of hands at work producing his adventures. Siegel's belief that in Superman he had a sure-fire character, and his dogged determinism in the pursuit of opportunities to bring his creation to print, is undeniably the reason Superman exists. But at the same time, Superman quickly became the product of more people than Siegel and Shuster. Although Siegel in particular regretted signing the contract with Detective Comics, it is fair to say that Superman's success owed something to the confluence of Siegel's drive and the business acumen of Jack Liebowitz and others at DC. And initially that achievement also drew on the distinctive art of Shuster. Superman was not simply the creation of Siegel and Shuster but, as with much serial fiction of this type, a character that relied on writers, artists, editors, and publishers. Superman persists as an icon of American culture not simply because of Siegel's and Shuster's creative genius but because of processes of moving written and drawn work to publication or, indeed, other media appearances.

The relationship between writer and artist is an issue of immediate concern when discussing authorship in comics. At stake are matters of narrative, plot, and character. How these are drawn is often as important, and perhaps more important, than how they are written. When a corporation, which organizes and oversees the creation of other stories in other mediums, owns a character, then clearly the corporation is exercising some form of authorship as well. In the many years of Superman's existence, he has had many authors and forms of authorship. DC's poor treatment of Siegel and Shuster before 1976 and the pair's effort at regaining control of their character through legal action have figured in most tales of Superman's authorship. These accounts focus on Siegel and Shuster or at the very least frame their narratives as a contest between the good creators and the wicked company. To be sure, there was conflict and tension between DC on the one hand and Siegel and Shuster on the other, but it was that very process that shaped Superman. Culture is not produced in a vacuum. Roger Chartier reminds us that authors write and publishers publish and that although both are important in producing a publication, their concerns are not necessarily the same.[5] Although Siegel and Shuster may have been poorly treated, particularly between 1947 and 1976, it is clear that DC played a role in nurturing and developing the character. Certainly that was for commercial gain, but without that role, Superman would not have been the popular character he became as early as 1939. In other words, without the confluence of Siegel and Shuster and DC, Superman as we know him would not have existed. This chapter explores this issue mostly through letters between Siegel and DC executives and editors, particularly Jack Liebowitz and Whitney Ellsworth, and various other legal documents from a series of court cases over the copyright of Superman and Superboy.

Understanding the authorship of Superman requires more than looking at the copyright grievances of Siegel and Shuster. To be sure, the issue of intellectual property is a key factor in the long success of Superman, but so too is the way DC transformed the character from the creation of a writer and an artist into something larger. In the early years of Superman, the clashes between DC and Siegel and Shuster often mirrored the struggles in the garment industry in the late nineteenth century over issues of inside contracting and outside contracting, which were struggles over the control of work processes.[6] DC wanted the pair to relocate from Cleveland and stay in New York, where, as independent contractors still, they would be more readily managed. Siegel and Shuster wanted to remain in Cleveland and sought every opportunity they could to distance themselves from the daily management of DC. Ironically enough, both Harry Donenfeld and Jack Liebowitz at DC had significant connections to the International Ladies' Garment Workers' Union (ILGWU). Donenfeld's family printed material for the union, and Liebowitz's father, Julius, was a union organizer.[7] DC's early quarrels with Siegel were just as much about disciplined work processes as about intellectual property.

WRITER AND ARTIST: SIEGEL AND SHUSTER'S SUPERMAN

The story of Siegel and Shuster's creation of Superman has been told many times, with particularly useful accounts coming from Thomas Andrae, Les Daniels, Gerard Jones, and Brad Ricca.[8] While these authors provide much of the color, sentiment, and memories of Superman's creation, one of the clearest narratives comes from Stephen G. Larson's judgments in the US district court during a suit by Siegel's heirs in 2008 and 2009. Larson unpacked the development from the 1933 fanzine story through to the 1938 publication in *Action Comics*. The first version of the new heroic Superman had the character dressed simply in a tight tee shirt and pants and going by the name the Superman. In August 1933, the Chicago-based publishers of the *Detective Dan* comic book offered to publish this version, but shortly after, the publication folded. As Siegel recalled about a year later, on a hot summer's night he "was up late counting sheep and more and more ideas kept coming to [him]": "I wrote out several weeks of syndicate script for the proposed newspaper strip. When morning came, I dashed over to Joe's place and showed it to him."[9] But in fact, in June 1934, Siegel had written to Keaton suggesting that they collaborate on a comic strip version. In this version, Siegel had "the last man on Earth" send Superman as an infant back in time from the future. The hot summer's night was not until 1935, after Keaton decided not to pursue doing the strip with Siegel. Siegel worked again with Shuster in mid-1935, and the two created four weeks of a proposed Superman strip in which for the first time his origins were extraterrestrial. It was this material that was later repurposed for the comic book format of *Action Comics* #1. Siegel returned to this 1934 material after Superman appeared in print and used a synopsis he had written for Keaton to develop the college-football story that appeared in *Action Comics* #4 (September 1938).[10]

In this history, Siegel emerges as the dominant figure in the Siegel and Shuster partnership. Not simply the writer of the comic, Siegel conceived the character and developed him through a number of permutations between 1933 and 1935. Furthermore, looking at Siegel's 1934 script and comparing it to *Action Comics* #4, it is clear that Siegel scripted Superman in such a way that his words easily translated into panel, complete with dialogue. Judge Larson cited the passage as a near "seamless interweaving" between script and six panels from page 8 of *Action Comics* #4:

> The coach says: "This is going to be good! The sap is running for a goal, with everyone on the field trying to stop him. There goes Martin for him. Watch Burke come down faster than a windowshade!"
>
> Martin is the first to reach Superman. As he dives for a tackle he says: "This is for poking into my locker!" Superman's outthrust arm connects with Martin's face, thrusting off the tackler. "And this," says Superman, "is for busting me on the jaw!"
>
> Three more players close in on Superman, from all sides. The

coach says to his assistant: "He'll have to be a superman to get by them." Superman leaps to the shoulder of one of the three oncoming players, and springs on over the other two. The coach's assistant replies: "There's your superman!"

Superman is already half-way down the field. The coach's assistant says: "I believe he's going to make it!" To which Coach Oliver replies: "Just fool's luck so far. Wait until he meets our 'unbeatables'—Stevens, Burns, and Dennis." The entire remaining team piles onto SUPERMAN. The coach yells: "They've got him!"[11]

Judge Larson reproduced an image from *Action Comics* #4 in his judgment (see figure 17). In Siegel's own account of the early years, in a 1973 affidavit, he notes that in 1938, "upon receiving word from Detective that we could proceed, Joe Shuster, *under my supervision*, inked

FIGURE 17. *Action Comics* #4 (September 1938)

the illustrations, lettering and dialogue balloons in the three weeks of daily strips that had been previously penciled."[12]

Nonetheless, Shuster's art made an important contribution to the initial success of Superman. Verdicts on the quality of Shuster's art vary. Robert Harvey, an early scholar of comics and himself a cartoonist, said, "Shuster's art, often called 'primitive,' was nonetheless entirely adequate to its task. He did not plumb the depth of the medium."[13] Harvey's comment seems to damn with faint praise. The acclaimed playwright, cartoonist, and graphic novelist Jules Feiffer, on the other hand, wrote, "But oh those early drawings Superman running up the sides of dams, leaping over anything that stood in his way. (No one drew skyscrapers like Shuster. Impressionistic shafts. Superman poised over them, his leaping leg tucked under his ass, his landing leg tautly pointed earthward), cleaning and jerking two-ton get-away cars and pounding them into the sides of cliffs—and all this done lightly." Feiffer described Shuster's work as "direct, unprettied—crude and vigorous; as easy to read as a diagram. No creamy lines, no glossy illustrative effects, no touch of that bloodless prefabrication that passes for professionalism these days. Slickness, thank God, was beyond his means."[14] Whatever the merits of Shuster's art, the pressures of producing Superman for both a comic book and, from 1939, a comic strip led him to hire an array of assistants. By 1943, his eyesight had apparently deteriorated to the point that he "could not meet all the demands of his work."[15]

Shuster's exuberant art matched Siegel's conception of Superman. Described condescendingly in a 1941 *Saturday Evening Post* profile as "a highly individual stylist," Siegel made his Superman not only powerful but humorous, in a corny sort of fashion.[16] In *Action Comics* #1, Superman, challenged to "try and knock down *this* door" by a sneering aide to the governor he is trying to reach, accomplishes the task. To the astounded aide, he jokes, with hands on hips, "It was *your* idea." Shuster illustrated the scene in three panels: in the first, the aide perceptively sneers; in the second, speechless panel, Superman rips the door away; and in the third, the aide's shock is registered through his body's deportment, opened-mouthed wonderment, and the comic artist's stock-in-trade shock lines emanating from his head. The scene captured the nature of Superman, who sought to right wrongs legally but was not averse to a little extralegal force. Superman was trying to reach the governor to present evidence to prevent an innocent man from being executed, rather than simply breaking the innocent man out of jail himself. Likewise, Superman was never averse to humor and seemed constantly bemused by his own powers or at least the reaction to them. In *Action Comics* #2, when told, "You can't do this! It's impossible," Superman replies, "Thanks for letting me know." In *Superman* #5 (Summer 1940), when his head bangs against the ground while hiding on the underside of a speeding car, Superman drily notes, "Just a good scalp massage."

The Superman comic had some of the characteristics of science-fiction comic strips like *Buck Rogers* and *Flash Gordon* in that Superman's origins were extraterrestrial and his powers derived from those origins. Siegel's approach in 1934 to Russell Keaton, the Sunday *Buck Rogers* artist, was predicated on these science-fiction connections: "I think it will follow the lines you like," Siegel told Keaton.[17] The Superman comic that eventually appeared also had something in common with action-adventure strips like Milton Caniff's *Terry and the Pirates* and Roy Crane's *Captain Easy*. Whether by design or because of the limits of Shuster's talents, his art did not have the sheen of the science-fiction strips or the draftsmanship of Caniff and Crane. In effect, though, Shuster achieved some of the same feel as Crane's art. Crane's strip evolved from his daily humor strip, *Wash Tubbs*, and retained some of that strip's cartoon style, with some characters having broadly exaggerated features. Shuster's work was not as cartoon-like in its qualities, but the rawness of his work combined with Siegel's humorous efforts to give the Superman comic a distinctive look and feel, beyond just the presence of its superhero character.

SIEGEL AND SHUSTER AS OUTSIDE AND INSIDE CONTRACTORS

The success of Superman in *Action Comics* quickly resulted in the McClure syndicate negotiating for a comic strip version. Siegel and Shuster entered into a revised contract with DC, dated September 22, 1938, that gave detailed page rates for Superman and the other features they produced for DC and an eventual 40 percent of the profits from the new Superman comic strip, with DC taking 10 percent and the McClure syndicate 50 percent. The contract also provided for DC's "right to reasonably supervise the editorial matter of all features."[18] At the same time, Jack Liebowitz, in a separate letter dated

September 28, reminded Siegel, who had been questioning page rates, that DC owned Superman and that he and Shuster could be replaced at any time. Almost immediately, on September 30, Siegel replied in a conciliatory tone. But the die had been cast, and DC increasingly asserted its rights as an owner, and Siegel, in effect reduced to a sub-contractor, bristled.

Syndication brought with it problems for both DC and Siegel and Shuster. Initially the releases for syndicated strip went directly from Siegel and Shuster to McClure, but on April 21, 1939, shortly after the comic strip commenced publication in January 1939, Liebowitz wrote to Siegel expressing McClure's displeasure: "Every morning it seems to me I receive copies of criticisms and complaints sent to you by Miss Baker of McClure." He noted that McClure "definitely do not intend to go on as they are." In this letter, Liebowitz complained that he had written many times to tell Siegel to improve his work practices. At crux, the problem was that Siegel worked in a "haphazard fashion," not submitting continuities in an orderly way. For Liebowitz, the solution was for Siegel and Shuster to move to New York, where the company could be "at a moment's touch" with everything Siegel and Shuster did.[19] At some stage in 1939, around the time DC released the new quarterly comic book *Superman*, Siegel and Shuster did move to New York. Evidentially this move produced some satisfactory results, because although there is no correspondence to reveal how things stood between Siegel and Shuster and DC in his period, a revised contract from December 19, 1939, gave them a 100 percent increase in their page rate to twenty dollars for Superman comics. They also received 5 percent of all net proceeds for ancillary licensing and the like. But by January 1940, Siegel and Shuster were back in Cleveland, and DC again exerted editorial control by mail.

In addition to DC's concerns about Siegel and Shuster's capacity to produce quality work in a timely fashion, the company worried about the tone of the comic. In a January 22, 1940, letter, editor Whitney Ellsworth suggested that Shuster redraw a forthcoming cover so that "the thug is grabbing a string of gems from the gal's neck instead of holding a gun on her." He explained, "We're trying to get away a little from the excessive use of firearms and knives on the covers, at least."[20] By this point, DC was trying to capitalize as much as it could on the popularity of Superman. In addition to the McClure comic strip and the new quarterly comic book, DC was at work developing a radio serial. Indeed, *Action Comics* #24 (May 1940), with the cover in question, carried an advertisement for the new H-O Oats–sponsored radio serial, which had commenced in February 12, 1940, and was broadcast by twelve stations. DC had already begun a campaign to market the comic book Superman more clearly to an audience of children and teenagers. The first issue of the *Superman* comic book in the summer of 1939 announced a Supermen of America club. Members received Superman's special code, which allowed them to decode messages in every issue of *Action Comics*. Radio serials like the *Little Orphan Annie* serial, based on the comic strip of the same name, had used this marketing device earlier. It was a familiar means of drawing audiences into a deeper engagement with a show or character.[21] DC also began a short-lived attempt at promoting literature, imploring *Action Comic* readers to "read a good book every month" in a monthly book-review page that began in #23 with Robert Louis Stevenson's *Treasure Island* and finished in #24 with Mark Twain's *Life on the Mississippi*. Liebowitz explained in a January 29, 1940, letter to Siegel, "At the present time there seems to be a concerted drive against the movies and comic books which parent-teachers groups and women's clubs claim are harmful for children. . . . We must point our editorial policy with a view of obtaining the approval of parents, while not sacrificing the adventure and the thrill Superman has always brought children."[22]

DC's efforts at shaping Superman had a double-pronged focus of trying to make him both respectable and, as a result, highly marketable. Making Superman respectable required reining Siegel in, at least in Liebowitz's view. Much of the correspondence between Liebowitz and Siegel is almost reducible to stereotypes. The methodical NYU-trained accountant Liebowitz, charting a plan to market Superman, is driven to distraction by the immature, hare-brained antics of Siegel, who tended to see opportunities as realized and to dream of larger accomplishments before basic groundwork had been laid—or, in summary, a business temperament versus an artistic disposition. In a January 25, 1940, letter to Siegel, Liebowitz complained to Siegel that in an interview with the *Cleveland Plain Dealer*, he had not given enough acknowledgment to DC for recognizing the worth of Superman and to the satisfactory compensation that Siegel and Shuster received from DC. Liebowitz specifically told Siegel, "we forbid you to grant any interviews relating to Superman and its development." All requests for such were to be directed to the new publicity department at DC. Allen Ducovny, the new publicist, organized a good many events such as a Superman Day at the world's fair on July 3, 1940, appearances for Siegel and Harry Donenfeld on *The Texaco Star Theatre* on October 9, 1940, and a Superman float in Macy's Thanksgiving Day Parade.[23]

DC's concern about respectability proved to be well justified since shortly after Liebowitz outlined this need to Siegel, the Chicago literary critic Sterling North launched an anti-comic-book tirade, in May 1940, that was taken up by some educators. Also in 1941, the New York State legislature introduced a section to the Code of Criminal Procedure that allowed local authorities to act against comic books deemed "obscene, lewd, lascivious, filthy, indecent or disgusting."[24] DC countered these efforts at restricting comic books by setting up an editorial board of academics and social workers and proclaiming itself the better choice of magazine.[25] It is possible that Kobler's June 1941 *Saturday Evening Post* article was in some way part of DC's response to North's diatribe and the New York State Legislature's regulations. Reading the quotes attributed to Siegel and Shuster, it seems DC massaged the piece as much as it could.[26] Certainly DC came out of the piece better than Siegel did. And indeed, at least in the *Saturday Evening Post's* account, the main danger that Superman seemed to represent to the youth of America was to their grammar and syntax.

As Kobler reported, Whitney Ellsworth had "the delicate task of curbing [Siegel's errant] tendencies."[27] From January 1940, when Siegel and Shuster returned from New York to Cleveland, all continuities for the McClure comic strip went first to DC for clearance. For DC, it was more than Siegel's scripts that were of concern. Ellsworth informed Siegel that DC had discussed the daily releases at some considerable length. Liebowitz reminded Siegel that the constant editorial criticism of the scripts should have convinced him that DC would not "accept slipshod work." He continued, "I know . . . that you can influence Joe to do a very good job on this strip."[28] The introduction of assistants because of the expanded production of Superman, combined with the strain on Shuster's eyesight, had led to a falling off of quality in the art. Shuster's art remained a key feature of the comic at this point. As Feiffer put it, "He could not draw well, but he drew single-mindedly— no one could ghost that style. It was the man. When assistants began 'improving' the appearance of the strip it promptly went downhill. It looked like it was being drawn in a bank."[29]

Siegel and Shuster were not simply contractors to DC. They ran their own shop in Cleveland with as many as five assistants for Shuster. Paul Cassidy was the first of these assistants. He commenced work in December 1938 on the *Action Comics* stories. The job came his way after he replied to an advertisement in the May issue of *Professional Art Quarterly* seeking help on "nationally established features." Cassidy worked to a script provided by Siegel. He worked from scratch on the page layouts, starting with the speech balloons and narrative boxes and then filling in the action across his established panels. After completing these in pencil, he then inked the panel frames, the boxes and balloons, and the backgrounds. The figures and faces were left in pencil and sent to Shuster, who completed them.[30] Prior to February 1940, Cassidy did all this work by correspondence. In 1940, he moved to Cleveland and worked full-time in Siegel and Shuster's studio until August that year. During that time, his duties were expanded so that he inked all but the face of Superman. After leaving Cleveland, he still worked on Superman but mostly only penciling layouts that were inked by others.[31] Although Cassidy recalled that he worked on a full-time basis, Jack Liebowitz in a May 2, 1940, letter to Siegel expressed unhappiness with the quality of Cassidy's art and blamed it on Siegel's paying Cassidy on a "piece work basis." His advice to Siegel was, "Your income at present is large enough to warrant your taking a little additional expense which will prove to be a very wise investment, if we are to perpetuate the Superman strip. Pay the man a little more so that he will be able to allow himself a little more time and give it better quality."[32]

Wayne Boring, who had begun working for Siegel and Shuster on a freelance basis sometime in 1938, also came in for criticism. Boring worked on the comic strip. Whitney Ellsworth complained in his January 22, 1940, letter to Siegel that Boring drew the figures too small, that one of his characters looked like Charlie McCarthy (a ventriloquist's doll), and that in one instance "Superman's physique is a bit on the lah-de-dah side": "I like particularly his nice fat bottom."[33] Boring, who was originally from Virginia, moved to Cleveland in February 1940 and worked for a time in Siegel and Shuster's studio at a salary of fifty dollars a week.[34] Boring, who went on to a long career on Superman, seemed to take criticism well, and just a week after Ellsworth's letter, Liebowitz wrote Siegel on January 29, 1940, to note, "In looking over the daily releases by Boring, I must say that there is a decided improvement. If the quality is kept up, I'm inclined to believe that we will not have to worry about the art." But by March 18, Ellsworth complained again in a letter to Siegel, "The last set of dailies, as well as the last Sunday pages which you sent in were not entirely satisfactory. . . . Some of the figures are absolutely too grotesque. . . . The release which you did for 'Look' magazine was pretty good, I understand that was done by Boring and the thing I can't understand is why he can't keep up to the same standard. The thing that you should shoot for, Jerry, is to have all the material look as Joe himself had done it." By May 2, it seems that Liebowitz at least had come to the conclusion that the Siegel and Shuster studio mismanaged its staff. Liebowitz wrote, "While in your last letter you seem to be imbued with a new spirit to raise the standard of the material, I am afraid that you will in a few weeks lapse into your old way of doing things. I hope that you will see to it that this does not happen."[35]

In the first few years of Superman, the issues surrounding authorship were as much to do with the process of production as with ownership. DC wanted Siegel to manage the process as well as write the scripts. Siegel felt DC was taking the lion's share of the money being made. But just as much, he felt harassed by DC's demands. Two days before the *Saturday Evening Post* article by Kobler appeared, a piece ran in the *Cleveland Plain Dealer* in which Siegel complained of "irascible editors."[36] Again and again, DC warned Siegel that things had to improve. On May 2, 1940, Liebowitz asked Siegel, "Please let me hear from you as to what you plan to do to improve the art work." Ellsworth wrote to Siegel on November 4, 1940, to say that he and Liebowitz were planning on visiting Cleveland for a chat about the poor quality of art. The next day, again complaining about the art, he wrote, "Something's going to have to be done, and soon." On February 19, 1941, Ellsworth was exasperated enough with the way artists drew Lois Lane that he sent a sketch outlining the ideal proportions.[37] Siegel probably had read so many complaints that when he received yet another letter from Ellsworth, dated February 21, 1942, suggesting, "Altogether, the situation is serious enough to warrant your doing some real worrying," he probably ignored it. Sometime shortly after this letter, DC finally acted and took some of the production of Superman comics in-house. What caused DC to act is not clear. Of the two long-standing issues raised by DC, Siegel's inability to manage the process and the poor quality of the artwork, what seems to have changed is that Shuster could no longer render Superman's face in the expected manner. Ellsworth noted in the February 21, 1942, letter, "we just can't got away from the fact that Superman's face is incredibly bad in more than fifty percent of its renditions." That Ellsworth went on to write, "I have no complaint about the backgrounds, which are very well handled, but perhaps more attention is paid to backgrounds than to the figure work," suggests that much of the problem lay with Shuster, who by this stage, according to both Cassidy's and Kobler's accounts, was doing only the figure of Superman and sometimes just the face.[38]

The extent that DC took control is not clear, but according to Les Daniels's in-house history of DC, by 1942 Wayne Boring worked directly for DC doing pencils and inks on both *Action Comics* and *Superman*.[39] On November 12, 1942, Ellsworth wrote to Siegel informing him that Winsor McCay Jr. (Bob McCay) might be someone who could help out on Superman. He also noted, "I also have in mind having Citron and Komisarow do Superman releases complete from your scripts. . . . I think they can handle Superman. You, of course, would have to supply the scripts and be paid for them on the same basis as you are now working with Joe, and Joe would be given whatever differential existed between what he would normally get and what we would have to pay Citron and Komisarow."[40] Although McCay did not do any work on Superman, and Don Komisarow seems to have worked mostly directly for Siegel and Shuster, Sam Citron did twelve stories published between 1943 and 1946. By late 1942, then, DC was not just exerting editorial control but beginning to take complete control of the creative process. On June 28, 1943, Jerry Siegel entered the army, having been drafted. After training at Fort Meade, he was posted to Hawaii, where he worked on the army newspaper *Stars and Stripes*. Shortly after, apparently at the insistence of DC, Shuster moved his studio back to New York.[41]

DETECTIVE COMICS, INC.'S SUPERMAN

Until Siegel entered the army, he in effect worked as an outside contractor for DC, providing the company with comic strip and comic book adventures. He was not simply the author of the stories but worked to package them for DC. Indeed, he even bought story plots from other writers.[42] Much of the correspondence between DC and Siegel reflects this status, and in a March 8, 1942, letter to Liebowitz, Siegel detailed his own problems in dealing with Shuster. Siegel noted that he "manages everything": "I helped locate and deliberately had him [Shuster] sign up his artists to long contracts so that he wouldn't have to worry about production for the full length of our contract. I created the character, and outside of the first three of four Superman magazine releases and the first several weeks of the syndicate strip, Joe hasn't drawn up anything complete. In the past he used to ink work penciled by other men, but now he doesn't even do that. Every once in a while now he helps out by making pencil sketches or inking heads." Siegel notes that he "deliberately decided to pay [Shuster] on a 50% partnership basis instead of paying him a flat salary out of the gross earnings." Siegel even had offered Shuster some of the advice he himself received from Liebowitz: "I've told Joe many time that if he's a smart boy he should try to avoid complications of any kind and be content with quietly making a lot of money. That if he does this, after a period of years he will be financially set for life."[43] And indeed Shuster was making money, grossing $15,000 in 1941 after paying the artists in his shop, or approximately $250,000 in 2016 dollars when adjusted for inflation. The total joint earnings from DC in 1941 were $56,573.48, which meant that Shuster paid roughly half his share on costs. Before expenses, then, Siegel took in a little over $28,000 in that year, or about $475,000 in 2016 dollars.[44]

When Siegel entered the army, the payments from DC did not dry up, despite Siegel's production of stories dropping off considerably. Liebowitz reminded Siegel in a February 4, 1947, letter that he had been paid for stories he did not write.[45] DC, then, treated Siegel and Shuster as something more than simply hired hands paid only for what they produced. Nonetheless, DC controlled Superman, and the comic strip and comic book were just part of the Superman enterprise. By 1940, DC had set up Superman Inc. to merchandise Superman products. One of the first licensees was Daisy, which produced a Krypto-Raygun in 1940 that later featured in a tie-in Superman story in *Action Comics* #32 (January 1941) (see figure 18). On August 27, 1938, DC filed to register a stylized version of Superman as a trademark, thereby taking ownership of the very way the name is represented and

FIGURE 18. *Action Comics* #32
(January 1941)

moving its domain of ownership from simply a copyright holding.[46]
DC also created a radio serial in 1940 and in 1941 licensed a series
of animated cartoons by Fleischer Studios (later Famous Studios).
Superman, then, from very early in his existence was more than what
appeared in the comics. This meant that a host of other writers were
involved in producing Superman stories. Indeed, the mantra by which
many people are most familiar with Superman was developed in the
animated series and radio serial before being used in the 1950s television series. Jerry Siegel had nothing to do with these words:

> NARRATOR: Faster than a speeding bullet. More powerful than a
>   locomotive. Able to leap tall buildings in a single bound.
> MAN 1: Look! Up in the sky! It's a bird.
> WOMAN: It's a plane.

MAN 2: It's Superman!

NARRATOR: Yes, it's Superman, strange visitor from another planet who came to earth with powers and abilities far beyond those of mortal men—Superman, who can change the course of mighty rivers, bend steel in his bare hands, and who, disguised as Clark Kent, mild-mannered reporter for a great metropolitan newspaper, fights a never-ending battle for truth, justice, and the American way.

This opening was shaped and reshaped in both the radio serial and the Fleischer animations. Robert Maxwell, the producer/writer of the radio serial, was responsible for much of this, along with Allen Ducovny, and Olga Druce suggested adding "and the American way" shortly after the United States entered World War II. "Truth, justice, and the American way" first opened a broadcast on August 31, 1942.[47]

At times, Siegel was happy enough with all of this, particularly the revenue it produced. In a letter to Liebowitz on January 1, 1944, Siegel thanked him for the recent checks totaling $4,400 and noted that a check from the McClure syndicate for the comic strip was due soon. Later in 1944, on April 4, Siegel wrote to Liebowitz that "it's tough squeezing out time to work on scripts," but he did send along a seventeen-part Superman story for the Sunday comic strip. Whether that story was published is unclear. But on October 1, 1944, Siegel received a letter from Shuster, with whom he had not corresponded for close to a year. Shuster informed him that he had just finished a five-page Superboy story that would appear in *More Fun Comics*. According to Shuster, another artist had worked on the story, with unsatisfactory results. Shuster's concern was that he knew "this feature . . . is one of your original ideas which you tried to get Jack to put out." When Shuster tried to get a copy to send to Siegel, he was told that the story would not appear until after the war. Nonetheless, the story appeared in *More Fun Comics* #101 (January–February 1945), a comic that would have most likely been on the newsstands sometime in November 1944. Moreover, despite the story originating with Siegel and Shuster doing the art, the story carried no byline.[48]

DC's act in running this Superboy story with no byline and no consultation with Siegel eventually brought out all of Siegel's simmering frustrations. In 1975, Siegel remembered it this way:

In July, 1943, I was drafted into the United States Army during World War II. It was at this time that National took over production of the Superman material. When I got out of the Army, National refused to return full production of all Superman material to Joe Shuster and me, though our contract specified we were to supply and furnish all Superman material. Taking the exclusive art and script production away from us against the terms of our agreement, not only injured us economically but caused us great mental distress.[49]

While it was true that the contract with DC as revised in December 1939 called for Siegel and Shuster "to furnish all art and continuity work for Superman," that agreement had clearly been defaulted when Siegel entered the army. The position of that contract, then, would have been open to some question, and by accepting payment from DC in this period for work created by others, Siegel may have left himself open to an argument that he had agreed to this change in status. In particular, Siegel noted that during this time, DC "published Superboy without any notification or compensation to [him], thus precipitating the Westchester action." The "Westchester action" was a 1947 lawsuit in which Siegel and Shuster sought to regain their rights to Superman and assert their right to Superboy. It resulted in Siegel and Shuster accepting compensation for granting DC the rights to Superboy and losing all their other claims. In 1946, though, Siegel had held out hope that he could negotiate with DC. In a September 3 letter of that year to Liebowitz, Siegel wrote that from his recent conversation with Liebowitz he thought DC would offer "a considerably improved set-up, along the lines of the contracts now being prepared for Superboy."[50] By January 1947, Siegel was peppering Liebowitz with "sarcasm and insult" on an "almost daily" basis, at least according to a February 5, 1947, letter from Liebowitz to Siegel. In that same letter, Liebowitz made it clear that DC regarded Superboy as merely an extension of Superman and therefore its property under the terms of the 1938 contract.[51] Sometime in January 1947, Shuster moved to Mount Vernon in Westchester County, New York, and Siegel followed soon after.[52] Shortly after, in March or April, Siegel and Shuster launched their action.[53]

Judge J. Addison Young's decision in the Westchester case declared that the March 1, 1938, release transferred all rights to DC, which consequently "became the absolute owner of the comic strip Superman, including the title, names, characters and concepts." The 1947 case resulted in DC paying $94,000 to Siegel and Shuster as part of a negotiated settlement to ensure all rights to Superman and Superboy, which was formalized in a stipulation signed by the parties May 19, 1948, and issued as a consent judgment by Judge Young on May 21, 1948.[54] That DC did not control the copyright to Superboy before May 21, 1948, is implicit in that case because the court found that DC controlled all rights to Superman and the $94,000 was a sum exchanged in consideration for the rights to Superboy.

BEYOND 1947

The decision in the 1947 case seemed to have settled the issue of Superman's ownership. It did not. Siegel and Shuster and then their heirs launched further action in the 1960s and the early 2000s. But the 1947 case did hand undisputed control of Superman to DC for eighteen years. This control let DC bring the production of Superman in-house and more closely regulate the comic's production. To the comic book, comic strip, and radio appearances of Superman, DC added a movie serial in 1948. The serial was successful enough that it spawned a sequel in 1950. Not only that, but DC launched *The Adventures of Superman* television serial in 1952. Michael Hayde, a fan historian of Superman's radio and television appearances, argues that the radio serial and later the television series ensured the survival of Superman, because these media reached far more people that the comic books did.[55] Broadcast media like radio and television certainly had the potential to reach far-greater audiences, especially if carried in enough markets. For starters, after viewers' initial purchase of a receiver, broadcast radio and television content was freely available.

Hayde may well be right, but perhaps the larger point is that Superman was much, much more than the comic as early as 1940. Whether through conscious decision—and the printing of a Superboy story without Siegel and Shuster's byline suggests some thought—DC separated Superman from Siegel and Shuster, not just as a matter of law but also as a broader cultural notion of ownership and authorship. After 1948, Superman clearly became DC's Superman and not Siegel and Shuster's Superman. A host of talents went on to work on various incarnations of Superman without being thought of as anything more than artists in the broad sense working on a cultural product. These included Robert Maxwell and Whitney Ellsworth of the 1950s television series; Mario Puzo, Tom Mankiewicz, and Leslie and David Newman on the 1980s movies; Debra Joy LeVine on the series *Lois & Clark*; Alfred Gough, Miles Millar, Jeph Loeb, and Geoff Johns on *Smallville*; Bryan Singer on 2006's *Superman Return*; Christopher Nolan and David Goyer on 2013's *Man of Steel*; and Curt Swan, Wayne Boring, Elliot Maggin, John Byrne, Alan Moore, Mark Waid, Alex Ross, and Jerry Siegel on the comic book. Indeed, DC was so confident of its ownership of Superman that Siegel was hired to write Superman stories and returned with an uncredited story in *Superman* #133 (November 1959) and wrote for DC until he tried to reclaim his copyright in the mid-1960s. No single writer or artist would ever again be associated with Superman in the way Siegel and Shuster had been.

FURTHER CHALLENGES TO OWNERSHIP

In the mid-1960s, Siegel and Shuster were able to launch another action against DC because the US Copyright Act of 1909 that granted copyright protection for twenty-eight years on registration also provided that a copyright holder could renew copyright for a further twenty-eight years during the final year of the initial registration. In this action, which was eventually decided in DC's favor in 1974, Siegel and Shuster argued that the 1948 settlement had not transferred the renewal rights to DC. The pair further argued that since the Superman strip they submitted to DC in 1938 was a fully developed work, it could not be, as DC argued, "work for hire" under the terms of the Copyright Act. The Second Circuit Court of Appeals found in its judgment that DC controlled the renewal rights and found in favor of DC. But in doing so, the court reversed a lower court's decision in this case that the 1948 settlement had deemed Siegel and Shuster's initial work in creating Superman as work for hire, on the basis that, regardless of the fact that DC had required the pair to revise the work, Judge Young had found as a matter of fact in 1947 that Siegel and Shuster were "the originators and authors of the cartoon character Superman of the title Superman and first created cartoon material in which the said character and title first appeared in 1934." In 1974, this finding might have been a rather abstract point of law since it gained Siegel and Shuster nothing in legal terms. But ensuing changes in the US Copyright Act gave this decision, along with the 1948 acknowledgment of Siegel's creation of Superboy, an unforeseen legal weight.[56] Shortly after this case was decided, Siegel launched a public attack on DC, and the resulting publicity resulted in DC's granting Siegel and Shuster $20,000 per year "pensions" in an agreement signed December 23, 1975. These pensions staved off any potential bad publicity leading up to the 1978 release of the movie *Superman*. In a letter dated March 15, 1982, DC agreed to pay Joanne Siegel the amount it was paying Jerry if he predeceased her.[57] On August 8, 1988, DC, which had already increased the annual amount several times, pushed it up to $80,000, promised an annual cost-of-living adjustment up to 10 percent, and made a one-time payment of $15,000 each to Siegel and Shuster. Joanne Siegel, who it appears had negotiated increases in 1979, took a 20 percent fee on increases and bonuses granted by DC to Shuster.[58] DC's lawyer revealed in a May 14, 2010, court filing that Joanne Siegel received $135,000 per year in 2010, as well as DC covering all her medical costs. All in all, DC had paid out $4 million in the thirty-four years since the 1975 agreement took effect.[59]

In 1976, Congress passed a new copyright act. The act incorporated some generous protection for the individual creators of intellectual property. Section 203(a)(5) granted authors the right to terminate rights that they had transferred "not withstanding any agreement to the contrary." Because the act excluded work for hire from this termination right, the 1974 decision became particularly important for Siegel and Shuster, as did the 1948 case and the implicit recognition that Siegel created Superboy. Successive copyright acts, cumulating in the Copyright Term Extension Act of 1998, have extended the term of copyright protection so that now it is for the life of the author plus seventy years. This action obviously made the Superman property more valuable; since Siegel died in 1996 and Shuster in 1992, the copyright lasts at least until 2062 under the current law and Siegel's share possibly until 2066. Siegel's wife and daughter set about reclaiming the copyrights of both Superman and Superboy. In their case against DC-Warner, the Siegels at first gained a ruling on March 23, 2006, that they had recaptured the copyright to Superboy due to renewal claims, but a later decision of Judge Stephen G. Larson on July 27, 2007, put this judgment aside and determined that the key to ownership turned on whether Superboy was a work derivative of Superman. Importantly,

Larson provided a detailed legal rationale as to why the decision in the 1948 case that Superman was not a work for hire must apply as a matter of collateral estoppel, which basically means that although the judge's decision was put aside in favor of a settlement between the two parties, the effort expended by the court, and the better factual evidence before it, requires that the decision hold weight in subsequent legal explorations of the nature of Superman's creation.[60]

In these subsequent considerations, the court decided in 2008 and 2009 that Jerry Siegel and Joe Shuster created Superman of their own accord and that subsequently Siegel's heirs were able to recapture copyright in those elements of Superman that appeared in *Action Comics* #1 and the first two weeks of the newspaper comic strip, as well as some other early instances.[61] This aspect of the long-running case turned on evidence of Siegel and Shuster's creation of Superman in the years between 1933 and 1938. Siegel's work with Russell trying to develop a comic strip version of Superman in 1934 was a key point in this decision. The legal significance of this material was that it strengthened the case for Siegel's creation of Superman beyond any involvement of DC and provided hard evidence of another Superman story that preexisted any contract with DC.[62] But all of these decisions were moot because a later court action by DC resulted in a judgment that found the Siegels had already agreed to a new contract with DC in 2001 before launching their action.[63] The long-running saga seemed to end when the Supreme Court declined to hear the appeal of Mark Warren Peary, a nephew of Joseph Shuster, with an interest in his estate and its claims to copyright, against a decision in DC Comics' favor. Peary was left in a similar position as the Siegels: an earlier agreement had been reached, and it remained valid.[64] Nonetheless, Laura Sigel Larson launched yet another appeal, arguing that her mother had rescinded the 2001 assignment of copyrights. The Ninth Circuit of the United States Court of Appeals dismissed this argument in a February 10, 2016, memorandum since it had not been raised earlier and would in effect restart the whole case. At the same time, the court reaffirmed Judge Larson's findings that Superman works were not made for hire, rejecting Warner-DC's attempt to overturn that decision.[65]

The heirs of Siegel and Shuster may seem hard done by in these decisions. But financially the decisions did not leave them with nothing. Mark Warren Peary, Shuster's nephew, will most likely receive

$25,000 per year in accordance with a contract his mother agreed to August 1, 1992.[66] Had he accepted an offer from DC on April 28, 2005, he would have received $2 million up-front and a minimum of $100,000 per year until 2033.[67] Under the terms of the October 19, 2001, agreement, Laura Siegel Larson, who on her mother's death on February 12, 2011, inherited her share of the estate, should receive a little over $15 million plus reimbursement of her medical and dental expenses from November 2000 on and those of her children from that time until they are legally adults. The estate of Michael Siegel, Jerry's son with his first wife, Bella, should receive around $5 million.[68] But for Laura Siegel, the case was not so much about the money but about making her parents' dream of "restoring [her] father's rights to his family" come true.[69]

CONCLUSION

In 2008, as part of the Siegels' case, the legendary comics creator Jim Steranko offered an expert report on Superman. He argued that Siegel and Shuster's initial stories established the essential characteristics of Superman. The Siegels made an argument through their lawyer that in viewing any version of Superman, audiences "bring to bear all of its pre-existing Superman associations which are largely derived from and driven by the iconic core of the Superman mythos established in *Action Comics No. 1*."[70] Siegel and Shuster certainly created an outstanding character. But so much has been derived from that iconic core and by so many hands and from so early in Superman's existence that it is hard to attribute Superman's success and place in American culture, and indeed global culture, let alone its persistence for eighty years, simply to Siegel and Shuster. Superman long ago became something larger than Siegel and Shuster's creation and indeed something larger than DC's intellectual property. No matter what DC's legal possession might entail, it relies on a favorable attitude toward Superman from his potential audience. Siegel and Shuster were able to use this need in 1975 to extract "pensions" from DC and the restoration of their byline.

The 1975 win for Siegel and Shuster created a mythology of its own that privileges their role in making Superman an iconic figure. Like Superman, they have become figures of ideology, myth, and nostalgia. In ideological terms, they have become representatives of suffering artists taken advantage of by large corporations. Without diminishing their role as creators of Superman, their contribution to his popularity has been mythologized; "Siegel and Shuster" has become a single byline for what in many ways was Siegel and artists including Shuster. And the nostalgia is for a time when two young men could pursue a dream and create an American icon. At heart, this seems to be the appeal of the Siegel and Shuster story, particularly when it is written as the naïve artists being cheated by an insidious corporation. Such a version is unreflective nostalgia and ignores the realties of cultural production. Laura Siegel Larson's 2012 response to the court ruling in the case upholding the 2001 contract that she and her mother entered into with DC appealed to that sort of nostalgia and belief. She wrote, "Would Superman, the embodiment of 'truth, justice and the American way,' let Warner Bros., DC Comics, and their gang of attorneys get away with this? Not for an instant!"[71] Perhaps he would not, but as much as the Siegels tried to link Siegel and Shuster with all that is Superman, property and contract law has little space for such sentiment, especially that built on a fictional character. And citing these familiar lines, written as work for hire by Robert Maxwell and Olga Druce, to lay claim to Superman as Jerry Siegel and Joe Shuster's sole creation is ironic.

CHAPTER FIVE

READERS AND AUDIENCES

One of the reasons for Superman's great popularity for over seventy-five years is that he connected with diverse audiences. From his initial 1938 success as a champion of redemptive justice, Superman segued, by 1941, into a character that mostly fought mad-scientist types and what would become supervillains and whose actions were more curtailed by a respect for legal niceties. His audience followed him in this venture, and during World War II, he became a touchstone of the American way and the promise of postwar prosperity. Postwar Superman found fresh success in movie serials and then television. In the late 1970s, the Superman feature film offered a reassuring version of the superhero who, under the slogan "you'll believe a man can fly," also offered renewed belief in the American way after the debacle of the Vietnam War and Watergate. In the early 1990s, Superman almost carried off the task of combining action-drama and romance-comedy in the series *Lois & Clark* and certainly found an audience invested in the latter. Superman could even serve as a fall guy for Jerry Seinfeld's gentle mockery of his powers and character in a series of American Express advertisements. And for ten years in the 2000s, Superman, or the promise of Superman, carried *Smallville*, a series focused on the angst of teenagers and young adults.

At the heart of Superman's persistence is that his audiences have engaged with the character. With Superman, engagement goes beyond comic books to all his media incarnations, which results in multiple variants of engagement. In Superman's case, such engagement has been variegated over the years. Indeed, Superman's origins have much to do with the way Jerry Siegel was engaged with the science-fiction community that developed in the United States in the interwar years.[1] Roger Chartier's distinction between "text" involving authors writing and "print" involving publishers publishing is a useful starting point to understand this community.[2] As John Cheng notes in *Astounding Wonder: Imagining Science and Science Fiction in Interwar America*, such distinctions applied to science fiction, which was at the same time a genre of fiction, several publishing ventures, and activities such as reading and letter writing. He argues, "the pulps gave rise to science fiction's name, its recognition as a genre and category, and to the social character of its overlapping reading, writing, and fan communities and their attendant networks."[3] It is useful to think about superhero comic books, their characters, and their audiences in a similar fashion, seeing the industry and the audiences as social networks, bordering on discursive communities, and with this notion in mind trying to trace the nature of that discourse by looking at the various ways these audiences engage with characters.

"Engagement" is a broad term that I use to designate a set of activities and behaviors that people may employ when they interact with media. What I have in mind here is the way audiences understand Superman by using him in a particular fashion. Using the character in some fashion is not the only way audiences encounter, understand, or engage with media but is a way that has some readily traceable features. There are numerous theories of media reception from social sciences, cultural studies, and linguistics, but the way people receive media, and process it to create meaning, is not my approach here, as fascinating a study as that might be when applied to Superman. Rather, I look at the way Superman's audiences express the meaning they create from their engagement. Those who engage with Superman in this way are often labeled as fans.

In the very useful book *Media Reception Studies*, Janet Staiger describes fan behavior as a "specialized mode of reception" and goes on to enumerate different ways of understanding fan behavior as "an interpretative community, an activism, a production of new material, an extension into the rest of living, and an alternative social grouping."[4] Jean-Paul Gabilliet, on the other hand, in discussing fans and comic books, has noted that there are different levels of engagement with comics. As he remarks, comic book readers may be fans and collectors, but not all readers engage in this level of activity. Likewise, most fans may be collectors, but not all collectors are necessarily fans. And not all fans engage in the same types and array of activities, such as publishing fanzines, writing fan fiction, and attending conferences.[5] I take Gabilliet's comments as a reminder that not all who engage with Superman are necessarily fans or behave at all times in a manner fitting Staiger's helpful categories. That is, for some of the readers and audiences, an instance of Superman may have spoken to them in some form or another and resulted in a response but not necessarily an involvement with the character beyond that immediate response.

From late 1958, DC began printing letters from readers in the pages of *Action Comics* and *Superman*. These letters, which at first mostly concerned questions about Superman's powers or noted inconsistencies or errors in stories, grew into something of a broad forum for all matters related to Superman. The letters pages also helped give rise to fans and organized fan communities. DC published letters in all its Superman comic books until 2002, when in the face of many online bulletin boards with widespread discussion, the company abandoned letters pages. In 2011, the company reintroduced letters without much fanfare. The letters pages show many of the ways readers and audiences have engaged with Superman over the years and are an underused source for scholars wishing to study comics.

Letters pages have certain advantages over web-based sources such as fan sites, fan fiction, and online discussion forums. Letters pages are more direct in the ways they demonstrate readers' and audiences' engagement with Superman than fan fiction is. Fan fiction is an important form of engagement, but analyzing its engagement with Superman requires addressing the way its writers have deployed the characters in their own stories and reflecting on these stories both as literary constructs and as acts of engagement. There is a richness and complexity there that is beyond the scope of this book. The letters pages have a certain fixity, having been printed in comic books that have been collected and preserved by libraries. Fan sites and online discussion boards can disappear. For instance, the Comic Book Resources site reset all its discussion forums at the end of April 2014.[6] The comics creator Brian Bendis also shut his long-running discussion board and deleted all content in September 2014.[7] The disappearance of these sites would make it largely impossible for anyone to check and verify the accuracy of any presentation of the discussion that took place. Moreover, such sites often have a very low signal-to-noise ratio. Letters pages, on the other hand, were mediated, which has both obvious advantages and disadvantages, in that there is less to read (but still more than ample for the sole researcher) and that editors stand between the researcher and the readers. Reading the pages, though, it quickly becomes clear that they are not univocal, and while some voices may have been excluded, many voices are present. To engage with readers, DC needed to represent on the letters pages the array of opinions it received. But even before DC introduced letters pages, it sought to engage with its readers.

EARLY READERS AND AUDIENCES

In the summer of 1939, DC announced a Supermen of America club in the pages of *Action Comics* and *Superman*.[8] Readers wishing to join had to send in a coupon with their name and address and ten cents. For their dime, they received a membership certificate and button and Superman's secret code. Thereafter, issues of both comic books carried coded messages from Superman, and these ran at least until May 1965 (*Action Comics* #325), even after DC, looking for different ways to engage readers, introduced letters pages to the comic books. DC was building bonds with readers and seeking to get them to engage with Superman beyond the stories. Coupons had been used as a tactic by advertisers since at least 1905 as a means of gauging consumer interest.[9] Setting up a club with a secret code was nothing new either, and as noted in chapter 4, the producers of the *Little Orphan Annie* radio serial had used this technique earlier in the 1930s to lock in its audience.[10] After the Superman radio serial commenced, Radio KGKO in Forth Worth, Texas, established a Superman Club in 1941, trying for similar connections with its audience.[11] These actions sought to encourage engagement, but there are no ready records of that engagement.

There is some evidence that during World War II service men and women wrote to Superman for help with their problems. Certainly the Superman comic strip carried many episodes in which Superman responded to calls for help.[12] The flight crew of one B-17 bomber in VIII Bomber Command decorated their plane's nose cone with a Superman image that was captured in Margaret Bourke-White's 1942 photo for *Life*. Use of imagery in this manner was similar to the ways soldiers affirmed their private obligation to the war by using combinations of pinups and personal photos, as Robert Westbrook has described.[13] There were no doubt other instances of such engagement, given the widespread distribution of Superman to troops through comic books and most likely in some locations the radio serial.[14] But these examples are partial and fragmentary and hint more at ways of engagement than allowing for a full examination.

THE CONCERNS OF READERS

The letters pages in DC comic books commenced in *Superman* #124 (September 1958), and the following month *Action Comics* #245 (October 1958) also began carrying letters. The editors responsible for their introduction, Mort Weisinger, and his associate Julius Schwartz had, like Siegel, been teenage science-fiction fans. Weisinger borrowed the concept of letters to the editor—or letters of comment, as they were sometimes called—from the science-fiction magazines. At first, the letters pages were rather basic affairs with queries from readers, mistake spotting, and the like. But over time, the letters pages developed into something larger. The pages were a place where readers could communicate with a like-minded community interested in Superman. *Superman* and *Action Comics* were not the only comic books with letters pages, and most DC and Marvel titles carried such letters pages by the early 1960s. The letters pages allowed DC to engage with readers in a number of fashions. In *Superman* #145 (May 1961), DC published a story full of errors and asked readers to spot those errors. The response was so great that, three years later in *Superman* #169 (May 1964), DC ran another contest for readers in which a story contained only one *D* and one *C*; hence, the contest was named "The Great DC Contest" (see figure 19). The letters pages provided DC a way to interact with readers, and they gave readers the ability to interact not only with DC but also with each other.

From the beginning, the letters to the Superman comics reflected readers' interest in his powers and abilities. Asking, as Mary Anne Riccardi did in *Superman* #126 (January 1959), where Superman hid his Clark Kent clothes after changing may seem unsophisticated, but this sort of information was basic to an understanding of how Superman functioned. Likewise questions in *Action Comics* #245 (October 1958),

FIGURE 19.
Superman
#169 (May
1964)

#247 (December 1958), and #249 (February 1959) about why Superman did not do more to rid Earth of the Kryptonite that was so deadly to him, or at least better protect himself from it, had the basic logic that a powerful being ought to be able to do something about such threats. And Mary Ellis's question also in *Superman* #126 about why Clark Kent's glasses do not melt when he uses his x-ray vision seems eminently reasonable. DC understood readers' needs for basic information and from time to time provided them with guides such as the list of different Kryptonite colors and their effect on Superman, contained in *Superman* #169 (May 1964).

Other early letters from readers requested such things as the return of favorite characters. In *Action* #251 (April 1959), the self-described longtime reader Jeff Gerard asked for the return of Mxyzptlk, the fifth-dimension trickster against whose magic Superman had no defense and who could only be dispatched by making him say his name backward. Readers made such appeals on a fairly regular basis, such as John Hitchen's request for the return of the Superman villain the Toyman in *Superman* #224 (February 1970). Many letters, like that of Tony Edwards in *Superman* #328 (October 1978), expressed pleasure at the return of various characters from the long history of Superman. At one level, then, readers' engagement with Superman involved acquiring and displaying knowledge of the character and his history.

A key concern of readers was the place of various characters in the larger Superman tale. Supergirl's debut in *Action Comics* #252 in May 1959 set off a debate on the letters pages about her place in the Superman mythos. In *Action Comics* #255 (August 1959), Neal Flomenbaum and Lawrence Miller welcomed her appearance, although Miller wondered if she would have someone trying to find out her secret identity. Herbert Linsey, though, wrote, "I protest against this addition of Supergirl to the magazine. I'm sure most of us boys would prefer the book much better with something else. So how about moving Supergirl to Lois Lane Comics or some other comic and make everybody happy?" DC let this letter pass without comment. Linsey shaped the question in gender terms. For him, girls had no place in the masculine world of Superman—Superboy and Krypto the Superdog, yes, but girls, no thank you. Linsey was most likely, from his tone, a young adolescent at best when he wrote this letter, but the idea that girls and women do not belong in a certain space is expressed by some male readers across age groups. To be sure, not all males responded with such a gendered reading. In the period immediately following Supergirl's debut, male readers wrote to *Action Comics* (#256, #257, #261, and #262) saying they enjoyed the stories and the character. Other male readers, like Robert Morgan (in #256) and Brian Cutler (in #260), suggested that Supergirl needed a super pet. Since Superboy had a dog, Krypto, they suggested that Supergirl should have a cat. Streaky the supercat debuted in *Action Comics* #261 (February 1960). When

Supergirl acquired another pet, Superhorse, aka Comet, in *Action Comics* #292 (September 1962), it may well have been because it fit the stereotype of every girl wanting a pony.

Beyond these concerns, and the identification of minor errors, readers began to develop more critical sensibilities aimed not so much at the structures of storytelling but at the artifice of the tales. Some readers also began to look for stories that they could relate to, in that the characters moved beyond stock representations and had foibles and the like. Guy Lillian's letter, published in *Superman* #272 (February 1974), displays some of those sorts of concerns.

> So Clark Kent betrayed a national secret in "Wild Week-End in Washington" (*Superman* #268) because he was under the influence of some weird gem called the Golden Eye. huh? Bunk! The reason Kent let his big mouth flap once too often was simply because he was out with a redheaded girl, Barbara (Batgirl) Gordon, and he was so overcome with the hope of impressing her that he let his senses lapse. I know exactly how he feels! That situation and mine in the past (and probably future) correspond very closely, and you are to be commended on making Kent a truly human being, despite his super-powers. I've grown up with Superman a part of my life, as I suppose most Americans have. . . . I always found Kent a little too phony . . . too much the secret identity, too much the suit of blue clothes thrown on to conceal the uniform and super-self underneath. Well, the Schwartz editorship of Superman has changed all that. I recognize Kent now as a person I could know, or could be, and, heck, have been. When I think of all the redheads (and brunettes and blondes and so on) that I have bored into a stupor trying to make small talk. . . . yech, the memory pains. But this entertaining, human story in an increasingly entertaining, human series brings a laugh to the memory . . . and thanks, as Bob Hope said, for it.

Over the course of the forty-four years from 1958 to 2002, Superman and the cast of characters underwent many changes. From time to time, these changes and developments caused concern for some readers. Beth Dierauer's letter, published in *Superman* #410 (August 1985), complained that a story in #406 confirmed her suspicion that

Superman stories were regressing to the sort of shallow, characterless stories of the 1960s. She thought that during the 1970s DC was "working on making him more human": "We got to see the human side of him, something that I really feel has been rather lacking recently. Even the supporting characters seemed more alive and real. Now it seems that Superman is just sort of there, almost a demi-god." Dierauer, who identified herself as a *Superman* reader since #200 (October 1967), was most likely somewhat rare for a reader, having read the comic continuously for almost twenty years.

Over the years, readers questioned and challenged each other and DC on a number of issues. Kryptonite and its uses and effects were a favorite topic. After many years of overuse in stories, it was retired for several years, but in the late 1970s, it began to creep back into use. Beppe Sabatini wrote two letters to *Superman* in October and November 1978 on the use of Kryptonite (#328 and #329). He then suggested in a letter published in *Action Comics* #490 (December 1978) that it was "the most convenient device for a writer to abuse." Other perennials were whether Clark/Superman was a single identity or an unnecessary duality and whether Clark/Superman should marry Lois.

On numerous occasions, DC explored the nature of Clark/Superman. In *Superman* #301 (July 1976), readers responded positively to the presentation of a more virile Clark in issues #296–299. Kevin L. Callahan found that Clark Kent's efforts at living without Superman and becoming more assertive showed that "Superman-and Clark cannot exist independently" because the personas bled into each other. In 1986, Alexander J. L. Bouchard and Kiril Kundurazieff responded to the John Byrne reboot of Superman, writing in letters published in *Superman*, vol. 2, #2 (February 1987) that they welcomed the greater focus on Superman's humanity. When Superman temporarily lost his powers in 1996–1997, Dann Lees wrote a letter published in *Adventures of Superman* #546 (May 1997) comparing it to an athlete's fading prowess. In a series of stories across Superman titles in early 1999, Superman abandoned his existence as Clark Kent and set himself up as a global vigilante. James Hanifen wrote a letter published in *Superman*, vol. 2, #147 (August 1999) criticizing the story as tarnishing Superman's character. Readers cared about the fate of Superman.

As for Lois and Clark's relationship, Gary Koehler asked in January 1959 (*Action Comics* #248) why Superman had not married Lois. DC replied, "Your solution to Superman's dilemma sounds simple. But, since Lois is impulsive, impetuous and sometimes reckless, Superman feels that she may inadvertently reveal his secret." DC constantly presented Lois in this manner. In *Superman* #327 (September 1978), in response to the by-then-old question of whether Lois Lane and Superman should marry, Tommy Krasker took DC to task for the manner in which its writers portrayed Lois Lane.

> Nobody seemed to agree on just who Lois is. Jerry Siegel seemed to think she'd have a mental fit if Superman forgot their anniversary. Len Wein spoke of her "constant snooping" and "loving bitchiness," which Gerry Conway magnified into her being "too suspicious, pushy and critical." Uh-uh. I haven't seen Lois running around snooping in a long time, unless you call being a serious reporter for a great metropolitan newspaper (when's the last time you heard that phrase?) "snooping." Suspicious? Who wouldn't be? If you were in love with somebody who might be in disguise, wouldn't you be anxious to know the truth? And her "pushiness" is merely impatience with a man who insulted her intelligence with pathetic excuses to cover up his secret identity.

When DC finally had Superman and Lois wed, all the letters, and all but one from men, published in the various Superman titles at that time were positive, except in one instance. Nick Pitcher wrote about the wedding in a letter published in *Adventures of Superman* #545 (April 1997), "[It] touched me—no moved me, more than any other story I've read." Jonathan Reid wrote in a letter published in *Adventures of Superman* #546 (May 1997) that he almost cried. In *Action Comics* #732 (April 1997), Jonathan Clark Petersen responded with pleasure and related that his father had proposed to his mother while wearing a Superman costume and that he and his fiancée could enjoy their own forthcoming wedding now that Lois and Clark had wed. Christina Bennett in a letter published in *Superman*, vol. 2, #123 (May 1997) said, "[I] thought it was the best Superman comic I ever read." But in the same issue, Bill D. Middleton thought the representation of Lois Lane was unfortunate. He suggested that she came off as a "psycho nutcase," and he labeled her behavior akin to a "feminazi," the right-wing talk-show host Rush Limbaugh's favorite term of disparagement for feminists. DC had actively sought letters from readers about the wedding, so the one negative response is curious, given many readers' long antipathy to Lois Lane. In a letter that appeared in *Superman: Man of Steel* #63 (December 1996), Ross Fastfinder wrote of Lois, "You sorry state of affairs. . . . Just leave! Get out! Take your 'foreign correspondent' position and retreat with your tail between your legs. And watch as the Man of Steel slowly recovers his life and fills the void you left with someone more worthwhile, like Lori or Wonder Woman. Good riddance!" To be sure, the eventual wedding of Superman and Lois had been a long time coming and endlessly foreshadowed, but this major narrative shift, breaking a key tension that had furnished years of story lines, caused nary a ripple of opposition in letters save from what appears to be two misogynists. A few issues later, DC experimented with a new costume for Superman, and the letters opposing the change poured in. The passion engendered by this costume change is captured in Jeff Brenner's threat, published in *Adventures of Superman* #547 (June 1997), never to buy another DC comic with what he regarded as a faux Superman.

LETTER WRITERS, FANS, AND PROFESSIONAL

The letters pages gave rise to a broader community of fans. Although not directly linked to Superman specifically, the rise of comic book fans in the early 1960s as something of an organized force, often referred to as "fandom," shaped some of the interactions of readers with comics. A version of the history of fandom goes something like this: In November 1960, discovering a shared interest in the work of Gardner Fox on the 1940s *All-Star Comics*, Roy Thomas wrote a letter to Jerry Bails, a professor at Wayne State University in Detroit who had earlier expressed a similar interest, inquiring about copies of the comic. Shortly after, in February 1961, Bails visited Julius Schwartz in DC's offices in New York. Schwartz showed him *Xero*, the science-fiction fanzine edited by Dick Lupoff. Fanzines were mimeographed (or some other form of cheap reproduction) magazines produced by fans. They carried articles and art by fans. They varied in quality greatly. Bails, on return to Detroit, produced a comic book fanzine, *Alter-Ego*, which he had ready for mailing by late March.[15] In a short space of time, Bail spun off two other fanzines from *Alter-Ego*, established the Alley Awards for comics, and developed several other initiatives such as microfilming a series of 1940s comic books. By 1963–1964, he moved on to establishing *Capa-Alpha*, a cooperatively produced fanzine, an effort directed at producing a higher standard of fanzine without developing an overreliance on any one central figure.[16]

Out of this milieu came a host of later comic book writers and artists. Roy Thomas was one of the first, as was Stephen King, who published in the fanzine *Comics Review* in 1964. Gabilliet notes that the fanzines let "a profound interest in genre . . . be expressed" alongside a developmental space and that many fans moved into writing comics as the industry underwent a generational change in the 1970s.[17] Other fans translated their fan activities into businesses like comic book shops and prozines, professionally produced magazines that replicated the focus and concerns of fanzines, and some fans entered the convention business.[18] Although most fans did not go on to careers, of one sort or another, in comics, those who did from this period created a sense that the letters pages offered a path to a professional career.

The letters pages helped develop fandom, but not all letter writers were necessarily fans. Paul Levitz, a longtime DC employee and one-time publisher, estimated that in the 1960s and 1970s, DC published between 10 and 25 percent of letters to the editor of superhero titles like *Superman*. This slightly contradicts Mort Weisinger's statement, in response to a reader's letter published in *Action Comics* #319 (December 1964), that DC received some ten thousand letters each month. But of the two, Levitz is probably a more reliable guide, since Weisinger was renown for hyperbole. As Levitz tells it, selection depended on volume of mail and the quality of letters, and writing regularly was no guarantee of publication.[19]

I sampled and indexed 2,043 letters from 1958 to 1978, which constitutes the bulk of the letters to *Action Comics* and *Superman* in that period. I chose this period because it was the time when fan activity developed and when the industry was undergoing a renewal of writers and artists. I found that of these 2,043 letters, the writers of two or more letters wrote 523, or 25 percent, of them; 140 people wrote these letters. That is to say, 8 percent of writers wrote 25 percent of the letters. The average number of letters published from this group of writers who had two or more letters published was almost four letters. Richard H. Morrissey, with twenty-six letters over almost nine years, wrote the most letters and over the longest time. Guy Lillian III wrote two letters over seven years, for the fewest number of letters published over the longest time. Lillian was more of a Flash fan. Ninety of these writers had their letters published in the space of a year. Twenty people had letters published over a space of more than two years. Eleven wrote letters published over a time of more than five years. Fifty-eight people had more than two letters published, and ten individuals had more than ten published. The average number of years over which this group wrote letters to these two comics was 1.8 years. Of these 2,043, 262, or almost 13 percent, were from women and girls.

What these figures suggest is that the comic book fan letter writers were highly variegated. Most often, letter writing was a singular event, or at least, once one letter was published, it was unlikely that another letter would be published. On the evidence of published fan letters, it would seem that writing such letters was also a short-lived exercise for many fans, since the average time span of letters appearing is under two years. This tells us something of the letter writing/publishing experience as a fan activity, but it does not necessarily mean that fan activity was limited to such a time span, since it is hard to establish any extended correlation between writing letters and reading and/or collecting comic books. Even so, it is clear that for some of these comic book readers, writing letters was part of a much broader engagement with comics.

My survey of published letters revealed a good number of names that comic book fans would recognize instantly. For instance, in January 1968, the future creator of Cerebus, the then-eleven-year-old Dave Sim, wrote from Kitchner, Ontario, in Canada to *Superman* thanking DC on behalf of "all Canadian readers" for the images of the 1967 Montreal Expo as a fine tribute by DC to the Canadian centennial. A year earlier, in January 1967, Mike Benton, then around seventeen years old, had a letter published commenting on a more action-oriented story in *Superman* #190 (October 1966), which unbeknown to him had been written by the fifteen-year-old wunderkind of comics Jim Shooter, who some years later became editor in chief at Marvel. Benton may not be a name that is instantly familiar even to comic book fans. His *The Comic Book in America: An Illustrated History*, published in 1989, and *Superhero Comics of the Golden Age*, in 1992, are nonetheless reference sources for a range of authors including Gerard Jones in his *Men of Tomorrow*, David Hajdu in *The Ten-Cent Plague*, and

Bradford Wright in *Comic Book Nation*. Benton currently runs a company called Custom Comic Services that provides propaganda comics to businesses and social causes.[20] Both Sim and Benton developed a professional life in comics, albeit at different ends of the spectrum, with Sim acclaimed by his peers as one of the greatest comics creators and Benton running a small publishing company.

Issue #359 of *Action Comics* in February 1968 contained letters from Dave Cockrum from San Diego, Tony Isabella from Cleveland, and Martin Pasko from Clifton, New Jersey. Although I have only found two letters from Cockrum and one from Isabella in *Action Comics* and *Superman*, all three were regular letter writers to comics. For instance, Cockrum and Isabella both wrote letters to Marvel's *Fantastic Four*, and Pasko and Isabella wrote to *Daredevil*.[21] In their letters to *Action Comics*, Pasko asked who the new cover artist was (Neal Adams), Cockrum complained about Supergirl's hair style, and Isabella welcomed the array of new foes for Superman and enjoyed an instance in which Superman thought before using his fists. There is nothing particularly startling about these letters. Such letters probably helped DC gauge the appeal of different artists and story lines. These letters would have helped letter writers and readers begin to get a sense of each other and to locate each other in a community of letter writers. For instance, Isabella's letter evoked a response from Jimmy Taylor in *Action Comics* #366 (August 1968), disagreeing about Superman's perceived lack of good foes. Pasko and Isabella became comic book writers, and Cockrum became an artist, best known for his work on *X-Men*.

The letters pages, then, were a way into the profession. Others who appeared in the letters pages and went on to become writers and editors at DC include Mark Evanier (three letters), Bob Rodi (ten), Bob Rozakis (ten), and Peter Sanderson (three). Evanier is widely known for crafting the letters page in *Groo the Wanderer*, which he cowrites, to the point where it is an inherent part of reading the comic. Elliot S. Maggin, on the other hand, wrote one letter to *Superman* #238 (June 1971) and, six months later in January 1972, had a Superman story published and went on to be one of the key writers of the comic book throughout the 1970s and into the 1980s. Letter writing was not a particular hallmark of talent. As a sixteen-year-old in 1973, Frank Miller wrote one letter to the third issue of an obscure Marvel title, *The Cat*, and only broke into comics in 1978.[22] Not everyone who wrote to comics entered the profession. George Oldziey, who went on to work as a composer and orchestrator, mentioned in his July 1967 letter to *Action Comics* that he and four friends planned to name their group after a DC superhero. Although Oldziey never worked in comics, he worked on films such as *Spy Kids*, *Once upon a Time in Mexico*, *Kill Bill*, and *Sin City*, all of which, and most notably the last, have strong comic book influences and links. Beppe Sabatini, another member of the letter-writing community who aspired to work in comics, wrote several letters to both DC and Marvel. His letter in *Superman* #328 (October 1978) criticized the aforementioned Martin Pasko's use of Kryptonite as a plot device in Superman stories. Sabatini worked at a comic book store, the Curious Bookshop in East Lansing, while attending Michigan State University. He wrote a story that appeared in *Action Comics* #572 (October 1985). The key plot point was Superman's compassion. In 1986, he moved to California, where he wrote for several semiprofessional fanzines and worked for Eclipse Comics. He now works as a software engineer.[23] The critic Douglas Wolk, a writer who frequently does pieces on comics in the quality press, reported to Sabatini when, as a high school student, he worked at the Curious Bookshop stocking shelves and the like.[24]

LETTER WRITING AND FAN COMMUNITIES

The networks and communities shaped by writing letters were part of a broader array of comic book readers and did not exist in isolation from them but rather as a set of practices that some readers engaged in. Figures like Richard Morrissey and Irene Vartanoff allow us to see some of the broader dimensions of those who wrote letters to Superman comics and the ways in which being part of the letter-writing fan community shaped their lives. Morrissey was the most prolific of the letter writers to *Superman* and *Action Comics* for which I have data. The first letter I found from Morrissey was in the June 1968 issue of *Action Comics*; the last was in the February 1977 issue of *Superman*. I found twenty-six letters in all. He was born January 23, 1954, and died May 22, 2001, aged forty-seven. In his many letters to *Action* and *Superman*, he took issue with misleading covers, poor inking of pencils, lazy plot devices, and recycled stories. He criticized hack writing and praised innovative stories that surprised him. That these were sometimes by the same writer mattered little to Morrissey, whose interest was in the character and his representation, not in star writers and artists. On the other hand, he worked long and hard to discover who these anonymous writers and artists were, and in his letter published in *Action Comics* #422 (March 1973), he wrote, "Leo Dorfman—along with Otto Binder, Robert Bernstein, Edward Hamilton and the other writers of the Weisinger era—deserve appreciation for their many years on anonymous, but sometimes brilliant efforts."

As well as comic books, Morrissey had an interest in *The Wizard of Oz* and participated in an online listserv fan community on Oz in the 1990s. In 1985, he had a letter published in the *New York Times* on Disney's adaption of one of the Frank Baum's other Oz works. He studied law but did not practice, save to file a 1982 trademark registration for his friend Robert Jennings's fanzine *Comic World*.[25] Mostly he worked as a circuit designer, according to the information he provided on the *Oz Digest*. There Morrissey described his reading and collecting of Frank Baum's Oz stories. But even in that forum, fellow comic book readers and fans cropped up. On January 27, 1997, Morrissey wrote in reply to several posts and asked a question of a poster: "Are you the same Dwayne Best who used to subscribe to *Batmania* when I published it? (Talk about fandom crossovers!)." And Best replied two days later that indeed he was one and the same.[26] In October 1996, Morrissey corrected a fellow *Oz Digest* member's account of a rhyming character that appeared in *Action Comics*. Morrissey also said he was working on a book about Superman and believed he had "talked to . . . all his living editors and most of his living writers and artists." And Morrissey drew these comic book connections out further, relating a Supergirl story from *Adventure Comics* #394 (June 1970) that clearly drew inspiration from *The Wizard of Oz* and pointed to the Oz connection in Alan Moore's *Lost Girls*, which included a grown-up Dorothy.[27]

Fellow letter writers Mark Evanier and Tony Isabella wrote obituaries of Morrissey. Both noted that he did a lot of work in giving credit to earlier writers of comic books whose stories were uncredited. Evanier noted that despite selling a story or two to comic book publishers, Morrissey realized his talents lay elsewhere. Morrissey wanted a life in comics, and when he could not get that as a writer of comic books, he found other ways to make his life in comics. For Morrissey, much of that life was discovering who had written the anonymous stories he enjoyed in his youth and connecting those writers with fans. This process involved using social networks of fans that went as far on one occasion as to raise funds from fans for an airfare for the early DC writer John Broome to attend a comics convention.[28]

Irene Vartanoff wrote many letters to different comic books during the 1960s, and my research only captured a part of her letter-writing career. The first I found was a letter in the March 1965 issue of *Action Comics* (#322), and the last I found was in the October 1970 issue of *Action Comics* (#393). Around the time her first letter was published in 1965, she submitted a Lois Lane story to Mort Weisinger. Indeed, she had also been invited to the DC office in New York and had a VIP tour when still in high school. But when she asked Julius Schwartz for a job as a writer, he told her to go home and get married—advice that did not sit well. Vartanoff sold some stories to DC, but only one seems to have been published, in *Young Romance* in May 1972.[29] From 1974 to 1980, she worked for Marvel in editorial and then left for DC, where she worked until 1982, leaving to work as an editor on romance novels.[30] She now writes romance novels.

In June 1970, *Action Comics* (#389) published a letter from the fourteen-year-old Alvin Yellon of Highland Park, Illinois, complaining that the letters page was "monopolized" by Vartanoff and others because the editor had a bias for "intellectual" letters. Yellon had previously had one letter published, in *Superman* #220 (October 1969). In a letter in *Action Comics* #393 (October 1970), Vartanoff took Yellon to task for this assertion. She informed him, and the collective readership, why her and other letters were chosen: "We *work* on them. We take the time to be legible, coherent, polite, humorous, and, hopefully, intelligent. All that isn't enough, though. Plenty of 'intellectual' letters never make the columns. If someone else happens to write a more thought-provoking letter that month, ours are rejected with the same indifference, as would be a smudgily penciled, unsigned 'I hate your mag' card. Those are the breaks." What Yellon may have thought of this takedown is unknown, since he never seems to have written to a comic again, rather shifting his attention to *Sports Illustrated*, where he had a letter published on May 20, 1974.[31] But the exchange led to further letters and showed something of the letter writers' awareness of each other and their engagement with the letters page that I think is fair to call a discursive community.

In *Action Comics* #395 (December 1970), Arlene Lo dedicated a poem to Yellon and his ilk, who, she suggested, if they are "not a master of the written word, or a great literary critic who can point out obscure parallels or do detailed character analysis," then they might try some doggerel verse such as hers that began,

> A pox on Martin Pasko
> A plague on Irene V.
> And fie to all the other fans
> More fortunate than me

Action Comics #397 (February 1971) printed a letter from John Krzyston, who praised Vartanoff as "a legend in the comic world" and whose letters he always enjoyed, with the October 1970 letter being no exception. The April 1971 issue of *Action Comics* contained a letter from Martin Pasko, who responded with his own poem, name checking creators like Denny O'Neil, Mike Friedrich, Gardner Fox, and John Broome, thanking Arlene Lo, and saying it was time for a change of subject before someone like Yellon wrote again. But the last word went to William Blau, who in the August issue used this chain of letters to suggest that DC should try to improve on the four-month lag in publishing letters of comment on a particular issue. His complaint was that unless "you save back issues," such matters were hard to follow. This exchange of letters shows a community of readers and letter writers highly aware of each other and at the very least able to identify the frequency of letters published and the qualities of those letters. Moreover, Blau's letter raises the issue of a reader and letter writer who may not have been a collector.

The career of letter writers beyond their letter-writing days is varied. Of those I can find, Guy Lillian III is now a defense attorney in Shreveport, Louisiana. He moved from being a letter writer from Walnut, California, to an editorial assistant in New York and then, like so many others, on to something else. He publishes the science-fiction fanzine *Challenger* and writes about comics there from time to time.[32] Other earlier letters writers such as Gerard Triano, who wrote fifteen letters between 1970 and 1973, maintain an interest in some form of publishing. Triano works as an accountant for a publisher and reviews books on Amazon. Gary Skinner, who wrote thirteen letters between

1968 and 1972, seems to still be an active comic book fan in his local community. And Clint Thomas, who wrote twelve letters between 1973 and 1975, is a journalist in West Virginia, where he grew up.[33]

In a 2009 interview, Vartanoff reflected on this period:

> My generation of comic book fans had no comic book stores to go to, so we met each other through letter columns, fanzines, and conventions, which started quite small and thus were great breeding grounds for friendships. My first convention was in 1966, and I made lifelong friendships there. I also corresponded regularly with lots of comics fans, mostly male of course. Many of my comics friends were determined to break into the business, and they lived in the New York metro area. We kept in touch with each other and invited others into our circle. And we made connections with editors, whom we besieged with story ideas and samples while we were still in college.[34]

Not all the letter writers were part of this circle, but it certainly shaped a community. Peter Sanderson offers much evidence of this. The October 1976 issue of *Superman* (#304) carried Sanderson's letter complimenting the "Imaginary Story" that appeared in issue #300. For Sanderson, part of the appeal of this story by Elliot S. Maggin and Cary Bates was that it "presented an argument against people being dependent on heroes." Twenty-three years old at the time of writing the letter, Sanderson noted that he gave up reading Superman comics "many years ago," which suggests as much precociousness as many of the other letter writers exhibited. Nonetheless, he displays a good deal of familiarity with the character and must have recommenced reading it sometime in between, especially since he had a letter published in *Superman* #291 (September 1975) and another letter in *Action Comics* #448 (June 1975). In addition to writing to Superman, Sanderson wrote to numerous other DC comics and also had over twenty letters published in various Marvel comics.[35] Sanderson used the knowledge gathered through these activities to gain positions with both DC and Marvel Comics in the early to mid-1980s, when he worked on producing guides to the characters of the two comics universes. Sanderson studied at Columbia University, earning his BA and an MA and a MPhil in English literature. In May 2010, Chronicle Books published his book *Obsessed with Marvel*, which covers Marvel Comics' entire history from 1939.

Sanderson wrote some nine thousand words on his blog about the memorial service held for Julius Schwartz in Manhattan on March 18, 2004. He noted that along with the many writers and editors of comics who paid tribute, so too did fans. Toward the end of the memorial, there "came another message from an absent mourner, a surprising voice from the past. In the 1960s there was a small, prolific cadre of writers who regularly turned up in Julie Schwartz's letter columns, the fan critics with the most incisive and stylishly written LOCs (Letters of Comment). The foremost of these writers, the dean of LOC correspondents, was the erudite and aristocratically named Guy H. Lillian III. I've never met him, and he was not there, but he had sent in a LOC, by e-mail." And after the memorial, Sanderson was part of "a group that decamped to a nearby restaurant for lunch, and ended up sitting across from, and meeting for the first time, Irene Vartanoff, another of the leading lights of the Silver Age Schwartz lettercols":

> As a fan, I greatly admired Irene's work as I did Lillian's and others, and was thrilled when Julie began printing my letters regularly, too, elevating me into this honorable circle. . . . It is at once strange and very appropriate that I should finally meet Irene, finally put a face and voice to the name, at the memorial for the man we both wrote letters to decades ago. Irene made the point that Julie was our editor, too: that we knew we had to meet his high standards, to do our best work writing these reviews of his books, in order that he would print them in his letter columns. She's right, and those letters were not just my first published work, but my first works of comics criticism. I went on to do more such work, in those oxymoronic entities, professional fanzines, which led in large part to my many years of work chronicling continuity for the Big Two, Marvel and DC, a satisfying way to make a living until recent years.[36]

VARIETY OF LETTER WRITERS

This group of letter writers belongs mostly to the late 1960s through to the mid-1970s. Before this group, letters from Jerry Bails in *Action Com-*

ics #287 (April 1962), E. Nelson Bridwell in *Action Comics* #284 (January 1962) and *Superman* #167 (February 1964), and Cary Bates in *Action Comics* #324 (May 1965) and *Superman* #195 (April 1967) are reminders that there was not one single group of readers who coalesced around the letters pages and became fans or professionals. Both Bates and Bridwell went on to careers at DC. These three were but part of an earlier group of letter writers, which overlapped with and eventually gave way to Vartanoff, Morrissey, Evanier, and others in the late 1960s. This group wrote well into the mid-1970s, when another group of writers, Tom Mitchell, Mike White, Beth Montelone, and Thomas Krasker, came to the fore. By the late 1970s, this group too was fading, and new names like Ed Via, Zohar Rom, and the aforementioned Beppe Sabatini took up more space on the letters pages. Although Sabatini aspired to work in comics, most of this latter group appeared to have other interests in addition to comics. For instance, although Beth Montelone participated in fan activities beyond her letter writing years, she regarded it as a hobby.[37] She earned a PhD from the University of Rochester and went on to a highly successful academic career doing DNA research. Tommy Krasker operates a specialty record label and on reflection noted that he felt most connected to stories that came after his letter-writing days.[38] Zohar Rom works in media production. Indeed, most letter writers ended up in occupations well outside comics, and the experience of those who transformed their experience writing letters to careers in or associated with comics was an exception.

Shelley Van Geffen wrote letters published in *Action Comics* #368 (October 1968) and *Superman* #214 (February 1969). She was a contemporary of Vartanoff and that group of letter writers. She went on to earn a bachelor of science from the University of New Orleans and a Juris Doctor from Tulane University. She married in 1976 and, although she passed the Louisiana bar exam, pursued a career as a middle-school teacher. While other letter writers have left a footprint on the web, Van Geffen left none, save for her obituary. Tragically, she died in September, 2014, at age sixty-one.[39]

Not being directly or indirectly involved with comics beyond the original letters to the editor did not necessarily mean an abandonment of some engagement with comics. Matt Huber, who had a letter in the February 1968 issue of *Action Comics*, which also contained letters from Martin Pasko, Tony Isabella, and Dave Cockrum, taught in public schools for thirty-three years in Brazil, Indiana. His father, a Popeye fan, got him started on comics as a preschooler. He bought comics weekly through high school but ceased in 1971, when he commenced college. Around the time he wrote the letter to *Action Comics*, Huber and a friend between them purchased the bulk of another older student's collection. Huber keeps his comics in acid-proof covers in acid-proof boxes, and the friend who sold him some of the collection still wishes he had not done so. Although he long ago stopped reading comic books, he purchased a replacement copy of *Superman Annual* #1 from August 1960 because his existing copy had lost its cover. He continues to read comic strips and likes older strips like *Beetle Bailey* but also enjoys *Mutts* and *Zits*. Although he stopped reading comic books, Huber remains connected to them through his collection.[40] Huber took the time to reply to an inquiry about a letter written over forty years ago. His willingness to do so seems to me a hallmark of community and discourse. To return to Gabilliet's reminder about the variegated experience of comic book readers, Huber was a reader, is a collector, and remains a member of a social network engaged in discussions about comics.

Although I do not have a group of letters as representative as I have for 1958 to 1978, my review of letters from 1979 to 2002 reveals similar patterns in letter-writing activity as in my earlier sample. Most letter writers after 1979 had similar practices and trajectories as the late-1970s writers, with short spans of letter writing being a constant. For instance, Mic McConnell wrote four letters between March 1987 and December 1988 and then moved on to other pursuits after this short period of writing. In *Superman*, vol. 2, #32 (March 1987), he commented on the representation of Batman's physique, noting that "a man who moves and performs like our cowled acro-Batman should be built like a gymnast, not a bodybuilder." In this, he brought his own knowledge as a bodybuilder to his interaction with the comic. In 2012, as a fifty-year-old medical-malpractice attorney, McConnell returned to competitive bodybuilding.[41] Some letter writers wrote a large number in a relatively short space of time. Jason Crase wrote ten letters between May 1991 and September 1992 but thereafter disappeared from the letters page. David Pulleyblank had thirteen letters published between May 1985 and August 1986, and Rick (LA) Steel had six letters published between April 1985 and June 1986. Both Pulleyblank and Steel then apparently moved on from letter writing, since I have found no more letters from them. Other letter writers wrote regularly over several years. Neil Ahlquist wrote twelve letters over ten years between June 1982 and September 1992. Charles D. Brown averaged a letter a year over fifteen years from November 1983 to July 1998. Joe Frank managed thirty-five letters between May 1987 and March 1999.

At the same time, many letter writers, sometimes called "letter hacks," sought to compete with each other for the highest number of letters published. Augie De Blieck allegedly wrote some four hundred letters to comic books, but he had only seven published, between August 1992 and January 2001 in the various Superman titles I have reviewed.[42] Another prolific letter writer, T. M. Maple (a pseudonym for Jim Burke, aka The Mad Maple), wrote some three thousand letters to comic books before he died in 1994.[43] Burke had twenty-seven letters published in various Superman titles between September 1979 and June 1987. Dale Coe published over three hundred letters in DC comics and at least fifty-one in various Superman titles between November 1983 and September 1995.[44]

One notable change between the group of letter writers from 1958–1978 and those from 1979–2002 was the drop in the number of women and girls writing to the Superman comic books. As mentioned previously, of the 2,043 letters I have from 1958 to 1978, 262, or almost 13 percent were from women and girls. By contrast, the percentage of letters from women in the period 1979–2002 seems to have dropped to 3 percent, on the basis of my sample of 435 letters, which I compiled using a slice approach, gathering letters from Superman titles in three periods from April to March in 1985–1986, 1992–1993, and 1999–2000. This occurred despite the presence of more women in the industry, from DC president and publisher Jenette Kahn down. It is difficult to account for this drop in women letter writers in definitive terms. Supergirl's presence in *Action Comics* in the 1960s may account for some of the engagement of women letter writers during that time. For instance, 35 of 134, or 26 percent, of women's letters to *Action Comics* between issue #250 (March 1959) and #349 (April 1967) mentioned Supergirl. There were 660 letters in this period. Of the 526 letters that men wrote, 160, or 30.5 percent, mentioned Supergirl. All this suggests that Supergirl gathered equal attention from the genders, but it does not help explain the drop in women letter writers. The figures suggest that women readers were less engaged with Superman after 1970 than earlier. The drop in women writing letters started in the 1970s. For instance, between January 1962 and December 1968, women accounted for 127 letters. Between January 1972 and December 1978, this number fell to 28. Of the 127 letters between 1962 and 1968, 106 were to *Action Comics*. This number would suggest that Supergirl in *Action Comics* was the reason for women's engagement with the broader Superman ur-text at least in the 1960s. When Supergirl moved from *Action Comics* to *Adventure Comics* in June 1969, the letters from women to the main Superman titles decreased rapidly.[45]

LETTER WRITERS AND THE AUDIENCES FOR SUPERMAN BEYOND COMICS

Despite the respectable ratings for *The Adventures of Superman* on radio from February 12, 1940, to March 1, 1951, which, while not as high as evening dramas, were on par with similar daytime serials, at around three to four million listeners, there is little evidence of the way audiences interacted with the serial and its version of Superman.[46] Likewise, the 1950s television series of the same name that originally aired from September 19, 1952, to April 21, 1958, has not left much evidence of audience engagement with it at that time. In both cases, however, since the advent of the Internet, significant groups of people have displayed keen interest in both shows. As I argued earlier, both these shows were important in coloring the way readers interacted with Superman. And, unlike the radio serial, there is evidence of the impact of the 1950s television series. The comic book letters pages show us some of the ways audiences integrated the television show into their understanding of Superman.

In *Superman* #132 (October 1959), Charles Dellinger asked, "Why is Inspector Henderson of the Superman television program never seen in the comic books?" The editor replied that the character had been in the comic books and would be again soon. He did indeed appear in a single panel of *Action Comics* #252 (May 1959) but was unnamed. He cropped up again from time to time, such as in *Action Comics* #440 (October 1974) and in *Superman* #289 (July 1975). If he appeared beforehand, I have not been able to locate him in my research. But in any case, this instance demonstrates that both readers and DC understood the connection between the comic book version and the television show. Other instances of the comic book letters page being the site for a discussion of the television series include a January 1966 letter from Dwayne Calvert to *Superman* (#182) to ask the editor if he knew "that Robert Shayne, who plays Inspector Henderson in the Superman TV films, was a District Attorney in an Abbott and Costello movie and a police lieutenant on NBC's *Hazel*?" And from DC's side, when Oscar Schwartz from Washington, D.C., asked in a letter published in *Action Comics* #249 (February 1949) if Perry White would ever gain his own comic book series, given that both Lois Lane and Jimmy Olsen had such series, DC referred him to the television series, where White played a prominent role. When audiences of the television show sought more information about the series, they turned to the comic book letters page. Mary Lou Sims wrote a letter published in *Superman* #132 (September 1959) asking for more information about George Reeves, who played the television Superman. Francis Baker wrote a letter published in *Superman* #146 (July 1961) to inquire about what stations were televising the show. Nancy Heller wrote a letter published in *Superman* #151 (February 1962) to ask why other aspects of Superman from the comics were not incorporated in the show. The answer was that the shows were all repeats. In May 1967, Stephen Harrell wrote a letter published in *Superman* #196 praising an earlier story focused on Clark Kent because "ever since the days of George Reeves' TV portrayal," he had favored Clark Kent. And writers published in *Action Comics* #418 (November 1972) and #449 (July 1975) criticized the use of names that were too similar to George Reeves in stories.

The television series continued to resonate with readers long after its original broadcast. Mic McConnell wrote a letter published in *Adventures of Superman* #437 (February 1988) to say that in a recent story, he "could have sworn [he] was hearing the voice of George Reeves, a friendly, warm voice, with a sense of humor even in times of seriousness." The editors replied, "Comparing [us] with the George Reeves classic is the highest praise for everyone connected with this title, Mic—and that specific version of the Man of Steel is exactly where we've all derived our inspiration for the general mood here every month." Nelson Jimenez wrote a letter published in *Superman*, vol. 2, #43 (May 1990) suggesting "a photo cover tribute to the late, great George Reeves. His portrayal of Superman in the 1950s show lives on in syndication, and is probably bringing new fans to DC to this day." And in reply to a letter published in *Action* #648 (December 1989), the writers and artist of the Superman story in *Action* #644 (August 1989) acknowledged they had deliberately paid tribute to George Reeves and the 1950s series in their choice of costume color for a doppelganger of Superman. Reeves was in evidence again on the cover of the March 1991 issue of *Superman* (vol. 2, #53), which replicated his stance at the end of the television series's opening credits, with a billowing American flag and the words "truth, justice, and the American way." In a letter published in the May issue (vol. 2, #55) of that year, Septimus O'Donnor wrote, "I don't think I could tell you how peculiarly sweet the memories were that you people revived with that one silly comic book cover."

By contrast with George Reeves, two later Supermans, Christopher Reeve from the first series of feature films and Dean Cain from the television series *Lois & Clark*, seldom received a mention in the letters pages. In my review of almost all the letters pages in the various Superman comics from 1978 to 2002, which spans the time of the two actors' Superman appearances, I found few mentions of Reeve and Cain and only two substantial mentions of either. In September 1982, Eric Baker wrote a letter published in *Superman* #375 praising a story in the April issue (#370). In the dialogue of Clark Kent in that issue, he "could have sworn [he] heard Christopher Reeve speaking. The naïveté and meek politeness combined with the fact that he still got the upper hand—this is the way Clark should be portrayed." Raymond Chuang wrote a letter published in *Action Comics* #585 (February 1987) praising the writer John Byrne for "magnificently . . . capturing the true spirit of Superman, especially the convincing use of tongue-in-cheek humor." He went on to note about Byrne's Superman, "[He] reminds me so much of the first Superman movie that I could see Christopher Reeve in those situations." Other than these letters, there was no substantial engagement with Reeve's and Cain's portrayals of Superman in the comic books. In the case of Cain, that may well be because the broadcast of the television series coincided with the rise of the web, and there is a large amount of web-based material on that series that was generated more or less concurrently with the broadcast.

CONCLUSION

The letters pages show that readers were actively engaged in a process of creating Superman. Whether or not DC paid attention to their particular interpretation of the character, readers had strong views as to what constituted Superman and how he should be represented. Readers brought their experience with other incarnations of Superman to their reading of the comic book and, from the evidence available, most likely took their reading of the comic book to their own interactions with Superman on television or in film. For instance, in June 1972, Robert Ablenas wrote a letter published in *Superman* #252 asking whether a discrepancy existed in a story about Superman's foe Brainiac. He remembered a different origin story from that presented in the comic book. The letters page editor E. Nelson Bridwell replied that the story in the comic book was correct and that the other version that Ablenas recalled had been done for an animated television series. Bridwell continued, "we don't accept the later TV version." Just who the "we" Bridwell refers to might have been is unclear, perhaps DC's in-house version of canonical scholars deciding on apocrypha. Despite such declarations, readers brought their own meanings to Superman, sometimes regardless of the various creators' intentions. Readers and audiences sometimes came together as a community and other times not so much so. Some readers stayed with the character for long periods of time and others for a short, sharp, focused encounter. The variety of experience, the different takes on Superman, and the richness of the corpus with which readers and audiences engaged suggest that Superman is and was a process of individual interpretation. Whatever certainty DC tried to bring and fix to the character of Superman often dissipated under the responses of those readers and audiences who brought other incarnations of the character to the moment of their engagement.

CHAPTER SIX

SUPERMAN THE BRAND AND BEYOND

A letter from Paul Emmett from Westport, Connecticut, in *Superman* #178 (July 1965) read, "I am a great Superman fan, I have seen several Superman products, such as the Aurora model kit, which I built; but I'm interested in other Superman products." On first glance, the letter seems a wonderful example of Superman's readers understanding him as something more than a comic book character and as an array of products. The editors helpfully supplied a list of products in reply to this letter. "We featured a page listing Superman products in some of our recent magazines. However in case you missed them, here they are again: Ben Cooper, Inc.—costumes and masks; Colorforms—boxed activity sets; Hassenfeld—board games, coloring set and paint sets; Kenner Products—color slide film strips; Pressman Toy—kites; Roalex Company—plastic puzzles; Whitman Publishing Co.—coloring books and jigsaw puzzles; Colgate Palmolive—Soaky; M. Polaner & Son—jams, jellies and preserves. All these besides the Aurora Plastics Superman and Superboy Model Kits." But this smoking gun, showing readers' deep engagement with the character, is a little too good to be true, and, alas, Paul Emmett was the son of Jay Emmett, who ran the Licensing Corporation of America, an arm of DC, and who later became the president of Warner Communications Inc.[1] The letter suggests that DC understood the value of the letters page as a way of connecting with its readers, even surreptitiously as in this example. This instance, both the letter and the response, demonstrates that DC at least saw Superman as something broader than simply a comic book character, wanted its readers to connect to the character in such a manner, and took every opportunity to sell him beyond those pages. An array of goods and services featuring Superman meant that the character was understood in part through acts of consumption. These acts and this dimension of Superman contributed to his persistence.

After writing a science-fiction story with an evil character called "the Superman," Jerry Siegel reconceived his idea and developed Superman as a hero in the form of a comic strip. He worked at shaping this concept with the artist Joe Shuster and for a short time another artist, Russell Keaton. The potential strip failed to sell to any syndicates. In 1935, Siegel and Shuster as partners did manage to sell other features to the comic book company National Allied Publications, a forerunner of DC, run by Major Malcolm Wheeler-Nicholson, but they held back Superman, perhaps still hoping to develop the character as a comic strip.[2] Only when they were unable to attract a comic strip deal did they sell the feature to DC. In the instance of Superman's creation, then, he already moved from one format to another. Superman's appearance in *Action Comics* did not cease Siegel's desire to see him as a comic strip feature. Both DC and Siegel pursued such an opportunity. The success of Superman in comic books opened the door to a syndicated comic strip, licensing, and other marketing opportunities.

Superman was not the first comic feature to be licensed. At the time, Disney had already licensed a large number of Mickey Mouse products. After dissatisfaction with a New York–based licensing agent, George Borgfeldt & Company, Disney turned to Herman "Kay" Kamen, a former hat salesman, in 1932. By early 1934, Kamen's efforts had made the licensing operations more profitable than the animation.[3] Some later licensing executives, such as Allan Stone, thought of Kamen as the originator of such licensing.[4] But licensing comics characters had been common since the days of Richard Outcault's the Yellow Kid, and indeed the cartoon figures the Brownies were used in the marketing for, and gave their name to, the Kodak Brownie Box camera. Kamen's efforts at generating more profit for Disney through licensing than through original animation was impressive, but again Richard Outcault had achieved that with his Buster Brown character as early as 1904.[5] Nonetheless, Kamen's efforts gave DC a ready example of what they might achieve with Superman. Once Superman's popularity became clear, DC hastened to market him as widely as possible.

The first addition to the Superman comic book was the Superman comic strip. In September 1938, DC, the McClure's syndicate, and Siegel and Shuster entered into a contract for the strip, and it ran for the first time on January 16, 1939. The comic strip was just the beginning of the expansion of Superman. In early 1939, DC engaged the George Evans publicity organization to promote Superman. The agency assigned Allen B. Ducovny to this work.[6] Ducovny organized publicity and press items for Superman, such as John Kobler's *Saturday Evening Post* article in June 1941. In 1939, alongside Robert Maxwell, who had earlier written for Harry Donenfeld's pulp magazines, Ducovny set about creating sample episodes for a radio serial. Over the next year, Ducovny and Maxwell managed to sell the concept to Hecker's Oat Cereal. Unable to interest one of the broadcast networks in the serial, Hecker's paid for the production and bought airtime on ten East Coast stations. The serial debuted February 12, 1940.[7] The show aired three times a week and slowly added more stations. Issues of *Action Comics*, *Superman*, and other comic books from DC, such as *Detective Comics* and *More Fun Comics*, carried listings of stations broadcasting the serial and suggested that readers ask their local stations for the show if it was not available in their area. Broadcast three times a week, the radio serial was very popular but hampered in its success by not having five episodes a week. Unfortunately for DC, Hecker's, the only sponsor initially willing to take a chance on the show, was not a firm with a national market. Hecker's held an option that it exercised, and this limited the show's potential audience. DC was able to sell the show to sponsors in areas where Hecker's did not have an interest, but this situation limited distribution.[8]

Sometime in late 1939 or early 1940, DC formed a separate business, Superman Inc., to handle the emerging Superman brand. From #4 (Spring 1940), the *Superman* comic book carried Superman Inc. as publisher, although *Action Comics* remained unaffected by the change. In May 1940, Ducovny left his position with the Evans organization and joined Superman Inc. directly to work on extending sponsorship of the radio serial in other markets.[9] DC also trademarked a Superman logo in August 1938 to enhance his brand name and further protect it from imitation. From 1940 on, DC sold Superman as a brand and one that brought synergy to the marketing of sponsors' products. DC looked to drum up business through trade advertisements in the *Radio Daily* and *Variety* during July 1941. The advertisements, seeking new regional sponsors for the serial, boasted of its ratings success in other markets and noted that Superman's comic books had a combined circulation of 2.2 million, that his comic strip appeared in 385 newspapers with a circulation of 20 million, and that he would feature in twenty-four animated screen shorts from Paramount. Not only that, but "key city department stores" had scheduled promotions, and the company's "Superman promotion staff" was building publicity.[10] Superman Inc. worked hard at selling the program, but the ultimate goal was a network broadcast deal. By August 1942, the Mutual Broadcasting System, a national network, picked up Superman, and by year's end, Kellogg's had come on board as a national sponsor.[11]

DC sought to profit as much as it could from Superman's popularity and used Superman Inc. to license a variety of products. In August 1940, DC ran an advertisement in *Playthings*, the trade journal of the toy industry, seeking Superman licensees. By 1941, DC had licensed thirty-three Superman products, including a doll, a toy ray gun, two wind-up mechanical toys, and a wristwatch.[12] One of the first Superman products licensed by DC, the Superman Krypto-Raygun produced by Daisy, received strong marketing support from both companies. The September 1940 issue of *Playthings* carried an advertisement placed by Daisy that promised a special campaign by Daisy that would help retailers "cash in." *Superman* #5 (Summer 1940) and *Action Comics* #30 (November 1940) carried advertisements for the toy, as did other DC titles. *Action Comics* #32 (January 1941) carried not only an advertisement for the toy but also a story in which Superman invents just such a gun to help establish proof against a club conducting illegal gambling. The toy had a battery-operated small light that could project a set of images. Superman's invention in the comic book differed in that he could take, develop, and project photographs with it. Not all Superman-licensed products received the same treatment as Daisy's, but ads for Superman chewing gum, a Superman toy plane, and Superman moccasins also appeared in *Action Comics* #32, with a note from DC explaining, "Each manufacturer is a definite leader in his own field, so we believe any of the products advertised may be purchased with absolute confidence that the product is of high quality and honest value" (see figure 20). In this manner, DC tied the popularity and the standing of Superman not just to selling a set of products but, by associating Superman with them so closely, to linking the value of one with the other. Superman, then, has to be understood through the

FIGURE 20. *Action Comics* #32 (January 1941)

manner of his consumption not just as a comic book character, not just as a media figure, but as a series of iterations in different forms.

FROM TROPES TO PRODUCTS: CROSS-PROMOTION OF THE SUPERMAN BRAND

Although DC sold the radio serial to sponsors as a cross-promotional opportunity, it made more of a push to cross-promote the Paramount animated features produced by the Fleischer brothers. The Fleischer animated cartoons came about because Paramount Studios, to which the Fleischers were indebted, asked the brothers to produce the features. To fob off Paramount, the Fleischers suggested a much-inflated figure, but when Paramount agreed to meet them halfway, the brothers accepted. The Fleischer animations replaced an earlier deal for a movie serial that DC was negotiating with the small Republic studio.[13] According to the comics historian Gerard Jones, when Paramount came calling with a better offer, DC took that deal.[14] The first animated Superman adventure debuted September 26, 1941. The November 1941 issue of *Action Comics* (#42) carried a full-page advertisement for the feature and asked readers to inquire with their "favorite theatre" about when they could expect the film (see figure 21). A little later, Jerry

FIGURE 21.
Action Comics
#42 (November
1941)

FIGURE 22.
Superman #19
(November–
December
1942)

Siegel wrote a tie-in story for the series, "Superman, Matinee Idol," which appeared in *Superman* #19 (November–December 1942) (see figure 22). The story has Clark Kent and Lois Lane attend the movies and see one of the Fleischer animations. The story shows scenes from the cartoon that Lois and Clark are viewing and uses film-sprocket panel borders to distinguish these "animation" panels from the regular panels. The story within the story does not match any of the Fleischer cartoons, although there is a gesture toward *The Mechanical Monsters*, the second in the series that Paramount released November 28, 1941. When Clark changes into Superman on-screen, the comic book Clark tries to distract Lois so she will not witness the transformation. This disconnect to any internal logic in the comic book seems odd, and when DC reprinted the story, it labeled it "Our Very First Imaginary Story." But at the time, it was simply one more tale in a *Superman* comic.[15] In this instance, it seems that cross-promoting a Superman product outweighed the need for an internal logic to the comic book.

In addition to shaping the opening narration of both the radio serial and the 1950s television series, as discussed in chapter 4, the Fleischer animated features also contributed two tropes of the Superman mythos. At the end of the first Fleischer cartoon, Lois Lane's editor congratulates her on a great scoop. Lois replies, "Yes, Chief. Thanks to Superman." The camera then pans to Clark Kent, who winks at the audience. In Siegel's "Superman, Matinee Idol" story, he concludes with the on-screen Superman winking at the comic book Clark Kent, who winks back, as he ushers Lois from the cinema. This knowing wink exchanged with the audience became a hallmark of the 1950s television series *The Adventures of Superman*. In episode 18 of the first season, Clark winked directly at the camera, at the show's end, to indicate that he and the audience were in on him being Superman, to the exclusion of the other characters in the show. Thereafter, Clark or Superman often winked at the camera at the end of the shows, and if he did not actually wink, it was at least implied in the form of a joke. Writing a letter published in *Superman* #264 (June 1973), Joe Cohen suggested that the ending of a story in *Superman* #260 (January 1973) was similar to the television series with its friendly wink. The story itself does not have a wink but rather has a last panel in which Clark seems to address the reading audience with the same message of the reader and Clark/Superman being bonded in the knowledge of what really happened (see figure 23). In the two-part story "Whatever Happened to the Man of Tomorrow?," which provided a wrap of sorts to Superman to that point before DC's first reboot of the character in 1986, Alan Moore wrote in the prologue in *Superman* #423 (September 1986), "it ends with a wink." In the second part of the story in *Action Comics* #583 (September 1986), the story does indeed conclude with that wink to indicate that yes, the reader was in on Superman's secret (see figure 24). In using the wink, Moore deftly

FIGURE 23. *Superman* #260 (January 1973)

linked the 1950s television series, where he most likely encountered its use, with the comic book at the close of the original comic book iteration of Superman. In this instance, a small moment from the Fleischer cartoon grew to be an important trope of the 1950s television series. The television series colored many people's interactions with Superman, clearly including Alan Moore, and shaped perceptions of the character. The wink was not always present in Superman, but it did unite different incarnations of the character across time and format and helped create the broader brand.

Another feature first seen in the Fleischer animations was Clark's use of a phone booth to change to Superman. *The Mechanical Monsters* had the first occurrence of Clark using a phone booth. DC itself lost track of the origins of this small part of the Superman mythos. Mort Weisinger related a possible origin of the story in the letters column of *Action Comics* #349 (May 1967). Apparently the television show *Candid Camera* set up a gag in which "Superman" asked people coming out of a phone booth if they had found his civilian suit in there. In the letters column of *Superman* #228 (July 1970), George Brooks, a reader, inquired, "when did Superman start (as Maxwell Smart would say) 'the old switching to

FIGURE 24. *Action Comics* #583 (September 1986)

the super-costume in the phone booth trick'"?—to which the editors mistakenly replied that he only started changing that way after the quip was made on *Get Smart*. A fan, Mark Woldt, hastily corrected this error in the November 1970 issue (#231), noting Superman's use of a phone booth in *Superman* #69 (March–April 1951). In April 1971 (#236), Nick Van Hoogstraten and Robert Leardo both pointed out a September–October 1949 (#60) occurrence. In the meantime, in the January 1971 issue (#233), Denny O'Neil had Clark Kent, in his new role as a television

FIGURE 25.
Action Comics
#421 (February
1973)

reporter, joke that he could use a dust cloud as cover to change rather
than "ducking into a phone booth." From December 1972 (#419), *Action
Comics'* letter page used a splash panel showing Clark changing into
Superman in rapid motion but with a phone booth as the location of
the shift from Clark to Superman. The February 1973 (#421) cover had
Captain Strong, a figure very similar to Popeye, trapping Superman in
a phone booth while changing and making a quip about the unlikeli-
hood of such a scenario (see figure 25). By 1978, Superman changing

in a phone booth had become part of Superman's shtick. In the 1978 feature film *Superman*, it became a sight gag. Christopher Reeve as Clark Kent had trouble finding a place to change into Superman because telephone booths no longer existed, having been replaced by nonenclosed pay phones. Along the way, the phone booth as changing venue had been used in a late 1942 comic strip and in the 1966 Broadway musical *It's a Bird, It's a Plane, It's Superman!* The Superman phone-booth motif is so well known that since the 1990s, it has been licensed as a watch theme, a salt and pepper shaker set, a bonus toy from both Burger King and Jack in the Box, a Hallmark Christmas tree ornament, a money box, and a light switch plate.[16] Perhaps most ironic of all is the Superman Phone Booth iPhone cover, which nicely brings this small piece of Superman's history to an item of technology that ensures its redundancy (see

FIGURE 26. Superman Cell Phone Cover

figure 26).[17] In this way, something as minor to the Superman mythos as where Superman changed his costume could be not only monetized but also used as a means of building the brand. DC thinks some readers or some section of Superman's audience will connect with the phone-booth section of Superman's history enough to consume such an item. It scarcely matters whether those who are making such purchases are doing so for their iconic status or for some ironic effect.

SUPERMAN AS PUBLIC SERVICE ANNOUNCEMENT

America's entry into World War II resulted in Superman lending his vast popularity to the war effort. Superman himself did not serve in the war, explaining in one instance that his interfering would be presumptuous and instead having faith in America's ability to overcome its foes.[18] Instead, Superman and DC lent their help to selling war bonds. In the radio series, Superman fought Japanese and German saboteurs (although, as with so much of the war effort, the Germans were called Nazis and the Japanese labeled racially).[19] Episodes of the radio serial often encouraged listeners to spend spare dimes on war bonds. Likewise, rather than advertising Kellogg's, the national sponsor, many of the Mutual Broadcast System's episodes during the war opened with an appeal for the youthful listeners to contribute to the war effort. For instance, the October 15, 1942, episode opened with an announcement thanking listeners for collecting metal and rubber scrap. The announcer continued, "the work you're doing is very important in Uncle Sam's war effort because it makes up for the shortage in raw materials and rubber needed in the stepped up manufacture of guns and bullets, and tanks and planes, and all other much needed war material."[20] The next day, after the usual opening, the announcer asked listeners too young to join the armed forces or assist in civilian defense groups to buy war savings stamps regularly. Explaining how buying a ten-cent stamp would help, the announcer points out that it would buy "five 45 caliber bullets that can be used by our soldiers, sailors, or marines to knock five Japs or five Nazis out of commission."[21]

Action Comics and *Superman* carried messages urging readers to buy war bonds, both on covers and inside the comic. In *Superman* #19 (November–December 1942), a page-long message from Clark Kent urged boys and girls to join salvage efforts because in doing so they would contribute "to the steady stream of mammoth bombers and army transport vehicles that flow off the assembly line!" These scrap drives, as the economist Hugh Rockoff has noted, "had a limited impact on the economy" and were more important for civilian morale than any other purpose.[22] Nonetheless, by involving Superman in the campaigns to sell both war bonds and stamps and to collect scrap to aid the war effort, DC established Superman as a way and means of delivering messages to children. DC had certainly taken steps to present Superman as a friend of children, particularly those in need. In 1940, Superman Inc. donated $250 to the *New York Times'* Neediest Cases fund. Its covering letter noted, "Superman, feeling that he is indebted to the children of America, would like to share his success in some small measure by contributing the enclosed check to the 100 Neediest Cases. He hopes that it will find its way to those families where children are in need of some comfort and joy." The company repeated the gesture in at least several of the following years.[23]

Beginning in August 1949, Superman comics started carrying a series of public service announcements (PSAs). These were generally page-length, comics-style stories aimed at delivering a point. A range of characters delivered these messages, including "Binky" and "Buzzy," but more often than not, Superman or Superboy made the point. As a supporter of national causes and a figure with an established concern for children, Superman was a useful deliverer of PSAs. The PSAs were also useful for the Superman brand and DC comics in general. In 1948, the psychiatrist Fredric Wertham published an article "The Comics . . . Very Funny!," in the *Saturday Review of Literature*. This piece was then reprinted in condensed form in *Reader's Digest* in August 1948.[24] This piece, in conjunction with a moral panic over juvenile delinquency and some crime and horror comic books best suited to older audiences, whipped up a campaign against comic books that resulted in Wertham's 1954 book *The Seduction of the Innocent* and the comic industry's response in establishing a Comic Code Authority. In 1949, DC, which had seen similar anti-comic-book efforts just before World War II, seemed to have moved to shield itself as much as possible from a coming attack.[25] Or perhaps the advent of PSAs in DC comics was simply a fortuitous occurrence. Superman's concerns in the PSAs certainly had merit. As early as *Action Comics* #70 (March 1944), Superman had asked readers to support the March of Dimes campaign to defeat infant paralysis in a full-page advertisement in which he punched out an amorphous green mass. In *Action Comics* #135 (August 1949), DC, in conjunction with the Advertising Council, had Superman warn readers about the need for traffic safety. He warned against the dangers of jaywalking and noted that 32,200 people had been killed in traffic accidents in the previous year. In other issues of the comic, he spoke of the values of volunteer work, sang the praises of vocational guidance, touted basic education as a hard-won privilege, reminded readers of the need to preserve people's dignity when dispensing charity, lent his voice to the concept of free speech, and urged citizens to "hop on the welfare wagon," by which he meant contributing to community welfare programs.

Running these PSAs allowed DC to tie Superman to the sort of consensus politics of 1950s America. The advertisements added one more dimension to the Superman brand and, in the language of

FIGURE 27.
Action Comics
#143 (April
1950)

marketing, leveraged his position as a social do-gooder. As discussed
in chapter 2, this brand strategy tied in to a particular postwar version
of the American way in which consensus was key. If DC commenced
the PSAs as a means of heading off trouble, as comic books came under
increasing criticism, the company also carried the torch, sometimes,
for the struggle for equality inasmuch as consensus politics allowed a

space for such a struggle. Jack Schiff, a senior editor at DC, wrote all the PSAs in the 1950s and 1960s, and Al Pastino, a regular Superman artist, did the art. Superman's name, then, was not simply lent to PSAs created outside the company, but rather he appeared as part of in-house creations, which implies a degree of editorial control. In *Action Comics* #143 (April 1950), Superman intervenes when one of a group of boys, much to his older brother's shock, suggests excluding Sam Levy, a new and obviously Jewish boy. He flies the boys and the older brother to Iwo Jima, where the older brother points out to his wayward sibling that a Joe Rubin had died to save him. Apologies ensue, and Superman rams home the point: "It should never matter what a person is—Protestant, Jew, or Catholic. Nor should it matter what the color of a person's skin is, or where his parents were born" (see figure 27). In a later PSA, in *Action Comics* #179 (April 1953), Superman points out unconscious racial bias and reminds readers, "People are People and should be judged as such regardless of color or beliefs." By this stage, the Advertising Council no longer lent its name to these advertisements, and instead DC said they were published "in cooperation with leading national social welfare and youth-serving organizations."

By the mid-1950s, DC had established Superman as a superhero character across media forms, from comic books to television. He was a supporter of America's national causes and a friend to children, particularly those in need. He was also a pair of moccasins, a tee shirt, and numerous other licensed products. And in public service announcements, he supported notions of universal brotherhood. Not all these variants of Superman held to a single unitary vision of the character. To a certain extent, the success of popular characters relies on creating stories that give readers and audiences an ability to fill them with their own meaning and interpretation. DC certainly carefully calibrated Superman over the years to avoid confrontations with parents' groups and censorious authorities. PSAs against anti-Semitism and racial bias were not that big a stretch for his character, and the parties he confronted about such bias immediately saw the error of their ways. Superman officially may have seen racial bias as a bad thing, but even in an issue where he denounced it, writers still resorted to racial characterizations as plot devices. For instance, in *Action Comics* #143

FIGURE 28.
Action Comics
#143 (April
1950)

(April 1950), writer Dorothy Woolfolk refers to two turban-wearing South Asian men as "swarthy strangers," which is clearly at odds with the PSA in the issue that denounces bias based on skin color (see figure 28). These PSAs culminated in a story in *Superman* #170 (June 1964) in which Superman, at President John F. Kennedy's request, promotes

FIGURE 29.
Superman #170
(June 1964)

the president's national physical-fitness program (see figure 29). That PSA, as a Superman story, has its own history, since after Kennedy's assassination, DC pulled the story before eventually running it after encouragement from President Lyndon Johnson.

The high point of Superman's PSAs was from the 1950s until the mid-1960s. The announcements still appeared from time to time in the comic books until the late 1970s. In 1980, DC authorized a Superman-animated PSA in which he warns children of the dangers of smoking. This PSA tied in with the 1978 film *Superman*, in which he tells Lois Lane that she really should not smoke. The PSAs were an extension of

Superman's basic shtick in the 1950s and 1960s, as Eco says, of limiting his actions to small acts of charity.[26] They strengthened the Superman brand by making explicit Superman's activities in promoting social good through volunteerism and charity. This part of the Superman brand did not lend itself directly to commodification in items for purchase. Nonetheless, Superman's willingness, or DC's, to lend his name to the broad social goal probably increased the value of the brand by making him acceptable as a figure of civic virtue.

SUPERMAN AND COMICS BEYOND THE PAGE

The sheer amount of Superman merchandise would make any list take on the properties of a telephone book. In 2015, for instance, in addition to the usual tee shirts, action figures, and coffee mugs, one could purchase Superman-logo stepping stones, dog activity blankets, chess pieces, and pool cues. Paul Emmett's 1965 letter, cited at the beginning of this chapter, makes clear that a plethora of Superman products is not a recent phenomenon. Nonetheless, the release of the 1978 film *Superman* somewhat altered the scale of Superman-licensed material and the way DC regarded the process of licensing.

The father-and-son team of Alexander and Ilya Salkind produced the 1978 film version of Superman, having acquired the rights in 1974. The Salkinds raised money to produce the film through a strategy of signing headliner actors such as Marlon Brando and Gene Hackman to major supporting roles and widely publicizing this fact to further promote the film and raise funds. Ranya Denison has described the many innovative ways the Salkinds promoted and produced the film and its sequel. Matthew P. McAllister et al. have argued that the film was instrumental in reshaping the summer blockbuster.[27] Although the film was produced outside of the Warner company, DC's parent corporation, the company bought 80 percent of world distribution rights for $10 million. This move resulted in $140 million in film rentals revenue. Film distribution was but part of the revenue stream. Warner published an account of the film, *The Making of Superman*, "a Superman novel, a Superman encyclopedia, a quiz book, blueprints of . . . the Fortress of Solitude, a calendar, a scrapbook and a portfolio." In addition, Warner Records released the soundtrack album with John Williams's score. Through another subsidiary, the Licensing Corporation of America (formerly Superman Inc.), Warner derived 6 percent on the wholesale price from over one thousand licensed products produced by two hundred licensees.[28]

DC established Superman Inc. with the hope of marketing the character as broadly as possible across media and product. Licensing grew to be an even more important part of the business after Superman Inc. merged with the organization that mechanized the children's television show puppet character Howdy Doody. The newly named Licensing Corporation of America (LCA) became a major source of revenue. Indeed, the revenue generated by LCA from the 1960s Batman television series and the James Bond material that it also held the rights to license were part of the reason DC and its associated companies became part of the new minted Warner Communications corporation in the late 1960s.[29] Prior to the 1978 film, though, most of the licensed products were for children's goods. As part of the marketing associated with the film, DC developed a new Supermobile for Superman in association with Corgi Toys. Corgi had enjoyed good success with a Batmobile in the 1960s and even more so with a toy Aston Martin modeled after James Bond's car in the film *Goldfinger* (1964), selling millions of both.[30] Both of these were licensed products from LCA. Even more so than with the 1940 Daisy Krypto-Raygun, DC turned over the story line in *Action Comics* to provide an origin and rationale for Superman, an invulnerable being who can fly, having such a craft. In *Action Comics* #481 (March 1978), Superman, weakened by Red Kryptonite and unable to get help from other superheroes, deploys his Supermobile. Helpfully, although trapped in another dimension, a chorus of heroes, including Batman and Wonder Woman, are able to see Superman and his Supermobile in action and describe its abilities as replicating all of Superman's powers. The Supermobile appeared in the continuing story line in the next two issues of *Action Comics*. Corgi ran advertisements in DC comics in late 1978 for the new Supermobile toy, which was part of a series of Superman-related vehicles including a *Daily Planet* helicopter. In the 1978 *Superman* film, Superman saves Lois from a helicopter accident, so the toy was clearly linked to the film. The Corgi toys tied the comic book and the movie together. It also showed the way that ancillary elements of the Superman mythos, such as the *Daily Planet* newspaper, formed part of the broader construction of the Superman brand. Indeed, in late 1978, DC sued Jerry Powers, the publisher of a 1960s underground newspaper titled *Daily*

Planet, who set out to resurrect his own publication to profit from the film. DC, which had ignored the earlier use of its title, sued and won an injunction preventing Powers from proceeding. In a hearing, Joseph Grant, the president of LCA, testified that DC and LCA always licensed Superman as a package, granting license holders rights to all characters.[31]

Although LCA sold licenses mostly to manufacturers of children and young-adult products, some other companies like General Electric and Gillette explored options to take a license, and in Japan, Toshiba marketed a coffee maker in 1978 using Superman.[32] DC and LCA tried to market Superman and the whole DC line of characters as far and as wide as they could on the back of the film. LCA certainly saw all incarnations of characters as united in one purpose: selling licensed products. The 1979 LCA marketing booklet, used to sell licenses to merchandisers, trumpeted the publicity for the *Superman* film and the way linking to that publicity and exposure could increase sales. As the booklet put it, "Everything is stage center when your product is identified with the Super Heroes characters of DC Comics. Because DC Super Heroes are up front with the public. In movies, comics, department stores and on TV."[33] DC had planned to use the *Superman* film as a means to reinvigorate the company as a whole in an announced "DC Explosion." The DC publisher Jenette Kahn planned to increase story page counts from seventeen to twenty-five and raise the price of comics from thirty-five cents to fifty cents. Although this was a raise in price, it represented a slightly better value for money in terms of story page count. Kahn also planned to increase the number of titles DC published. Originally Kahn planned the Explosion for June 1978 to coincide with the release of *Superman*, but the schedule was not changed when production issues caused the film's release to be delayed until December. Kahn announced the Explosion formally in her "Onwards and Upwards" column that appeared in DC comics with September 1978 cover dates. These comics were distributed in the first week of June. But on June 22, 1978, DC's corporate owner, Warner Communications, gave directions to DC to scale back on the number of comic books and the story page counts. The DC Explosion became the DC Implosion.[34] The explosion collapsed before it even had a chance in part because of extremely low distribution of comics to the West Coast in the blizzard of 1978, which caused sales to collapse both on newsstands and through the emerging special-ist comic book stores. Those poor sales from earlier in the year were the cause of Warner's decision and not the planned campaign itself.[35] These setbacks for the comic books, coupled with the success of the *Superman* film, not only in box office sales but also in merchandising, were early signs that the center of the Superman business, and indeed of superhero characters in general, was shifting.

The reasons for this shift were many. In part, the business of comic book distribution had considerable problems. DC distributed its com-ics through another Warner company, Independent News. This com-pany then worked with various other distributors, supplying them with comics on a sale-or-return basis, except that comics were not actually returned but rather destroyed, with the lower-level distributors filing affidavits to that effect. These distributors supplied newsstands and other outlets with comics and other magazines. Some of these distrib-utors held onto comics as a speculative investment, expecting to reap profit from comics by popular creators by creating artificial shortages and selling at inflated prices. Nonetheless, they filed affidavits swear-ing they had destroyed them, thus acquiring their stock free of charge. Comic books on the whole were not such a great business for distribu-tors because they offered a low return for the effort compared to other magazines. DC and other comic book companies eventually shifted to a system of direct distribution to specialty comic book shops. In this model, the companies received payment up-front and so could tailor print runs to fit orders. This not only saved money on printing but also gave them a firmer set of data on what audiences were buying.[36] But this system was not without its disadvantages. Without newsstand distribution and the like, younger, which is to say new, audiences were less likely to encounter comics serendipitously and rather had to seek them out. As a result, audiences skewed older, and comic books focused on that older audience.

DC had weathered many changes in the shifting comic book mar-ket, including the mid-1950s controversy. Moreover, the company adapted quite readily to changing circumstances and sought new directions. A 1962 *New York Times* feature on DC reported that the company derived 60 percent of its annual sales of $36 million from fifty-five comic book magazines. DC had seen a serious decline in the revenue it derived from advertising in its comics, from $1 million to only $176,000 a year between 1952 and 1962. The article also reported that DC believed its audience to be the children of parents who had read its comics when they were young.[37] The *Times* did not report on the sources of the other 40 percent of revenue, but this most certainly included monies from the television series and licensed merchandise. DC continued its efforts at finding audiences for its products through the 1960s and had particular success with a Batman television series that resulted in a craze for all things Batman related, but this lasted only three years or so before the audience moved on. Finding a way to make the adult former readers of Superman return to the character themselves, and not just provide their children with the comic books, might well have been a goal for DC. The marketing effort around the 1978 *Superman* film suggested a deliberate attempt to cultivate such an audience. Marlon Brando and Gene Hackman were not actors known for appearing in children's fare. The film, with its appeal to nostalgia and an older audience ready to be nostalgic, expanded that potential adult market for Superman. The availability of products like Superman car-seat covers, eau de cologne, and soap on a rope are indicators of an older purchasing audience.[38]

THE TRADEMARK TIES THE BRAND TOGETHER

If in 1962 DC earned 60 percent of its revenue from comic book sales, then twenty years later, in 1982, this situation had almost certainly deteriorated. Reported sales for DC sales dropped dramatically in this period. For instance, in 1962, the *Superman* comic book sold 740,000 copies a month on average. In 1982, it sold 136,931.[39] Revenue in 1962 on the *Superman* comic book alone amounted to over $1 million. In 1982, even with a price increase from twelve cents in 1962 to sixty cents in 1982, DC's revenue on this book was less than a million. When adjusted for inflation, that means DC's revenue from its most popular comic book in 1962 had dropped by two-thirds by 1982.[40] The revenue from the comic book paled in comparison, then, with the $140 million in film rentals alone Warner-DC took in for the 1978 *Superman* film. These figures show that the market had clearly shifted, and DC was no longer in the comic book business so much as in the superhero entertainment business. A key component of this business was selling nonmedia products or, rather, seeing a character like Superman as a revenue generator for which every iteration requires a particular strategy to sell. Such a business plan may not have found articulation—certainly synergy fell out of favor at Warner—but when holding corporations talk of their comic book divisions as research and development, even metaphorically, then the import of a character like Superman for the company lies in his ability to generate profit no matter what the venue.[41]

In this shift, Superman's value to DC was more as a trademark that could be used to brand an array of different products. While it is clear that by 1982 the business model DC had in 1962 needed to shift—and indeed by 1962 it must have been clear that the model for 1952 needed to change—DC and its parent corporation took some years to realize the full ramifications of these changes and adjust their corporate structure to maximize their ability to market Superman and other DC superheroes. Some of the steps DC took to reinvigorate its business included the dramatic reboot of Superman and many other characters in 1986 through the wide-ranging reordering of DC's character universes in the miniseries *Crisis on Infinite Earths*. In that same year, DC published both *Watchmen* and *The Dark Knight Returns*, two comic book miniseries that have since racked up enormous sales. For instance, a *Watchmen* trade paperback sold one hundred thousand copies in 2007 and, on the back of a film version, one million copies in 2008.[42] These efforts and the added sales from trade paperback collections of stories previously published in the traditional comic book format helped DC increase its revenue. Various series of hardback and softbound compendiums reprinting classic comic books including *Action Comics* and *Superman* also generated more revenue, and probably both fed nostalgia and created new audiences for Superman and other characters. Much of this effort helped cross-promotional strategies even if the initial impetus was to improve DC's publishing sales.

These publishing successes were important and speak to the innovative leadership of both Jenette Kahn and Paul Levitz as DC publishers in finding new ways to publish superhero comics. The belief in the comics industry is that for many years Warner wanted to move DC from its somewhat-independent position in New York closer to other entertainment divisions in Los Angeles. Levitz as publisher apparently managed to resist this move; but after 2009, Levitz had gone, and by April 2015, so had DC from New York.[43] The strength of Superman as a brand had outstripped comic books. The success of the television series *Smallville* is indicative of the way in which the brand and its trademarked elements brought together different incarnations of the character, generating revenue across media forms.

Smallville debuted on October 16, 2001, on The WB, a network owned by the Time Warner Corporation, DC's parent company. The WB aimed at a teen audience with series such as *Dawson's Creek*, *Roswell*, *Buffy the Vampire Slayer*, and *Gilmore Girls*. *Smallville* underplayed the superhero aspect of Superman, focusing on Clark Kent's teenage years in the eponymous Smallville. Critics, though, understood the series as part of the Superman mythos, describing it variously as "Superboy redux," a "teenage Superman series," and "a teen friendly update of the Superboy saga." As the latter article suggested, it was a series with teen-themes similar to *Dawson's Creek*. The series then was both a teen "angst-filled" drama and part of the Superman mythology.[44] The series in effect was one long wink at its audience, who knew that Clark was in the throes of becoming Superman. Indeed, in the tenth season in 2011, as Clark's emergence as Superman came close to fruition, he used a phone booth to change from his work clothes to the outfit he wore for superhero deeds.[45] That a phone booth of the sort he used would have been next to impossible to find anywhere in America, or indeed most of the world, mattered little compared to the symbolism of this action, which firmly tied this version of Superman to earlier iterations. The knowledge of the ultimate destiny of Clark Kent meant the series could have a "no flights, no tights" rule, that is, not use the iconic Superman suit with its distinctive crest symbol on the chest or the fully realized superpowers of the character. Warner released the first season of the series on DVD shortly before the third season commenced in 2003 and released the second season during the third season's run. Thereafter, Warner timed the release of the previous year's season to coincide with the start date of the new season. Significantly, despite the absence of Superman's costume and developed powers from the series, the DVD boxes contained prominent use of the Superman chest symbol to brand the series. The series generated extensive revenue for Warner. Information on the revenues generated by *Smallville* is available in a series of documents related to the Siegels' intellectual property case against Warner/DC. Available evidence shows that "gross receipts after accounts receivable" by June 30, 2006, were at least $353,696,456.00, but this amount excluded 50 percent of "merchandising revenue earned by the Series and likely only reports 20% on home video sales." Indeed, another $64.4 million worth of television sales remained uncollected at the time these figures were calculated.[46]

This some $400 million in revenue was spread across the Warner corporation and its subsidiaries. The Smallville Television Agreement between DC and Warner Bros. Television Production licensed Superman to Warner for an up-front fee of $10,000 and a provision for $45,000 per episode produced. The agreement also provided for DC to receive "3% of the first dollar distributor gross from the first $1.5 million garnered, and then 5% thereafter." The agreement also provided for a fifty-fifty split between DC and Warner for net proceeds form merchandising related to the series. In this production deal, Warner was able to minimize development costs for a television series by using one of its own well-established characters and developing a concept that told a backstory, or prequel, to the more familiar aspects of that character. More importantly, the series not only contributed to The WB network but also derived revenue from sales to overseas television networks. Beyond this, the DVD sales of the series, at a time when marketing DVD releases of television series was in its infancy, not only produced revenue for *Smallville* but also led to further revenue through the release of the two earlier Superman television series, *Lois & Clark* and *The Adventures of Superman*, both of which were released beginning in 2005 following the success of *Smallville's* DVD sales.[47] Quantifying how *Smallville* contributed to more generic Superman merchandizing, beyond the immediate products for the series, is next to impossible, but the series gave Superman a fresh currency and helped raise the character's profile with a younger generation.

The long gestation of new Superman movies in the 2000s led to calls for the star of *Smallville*, Tom Welling, to play Superman on the big screen in both *Superman Returns* (2006) and *Man of Steel* (2013), which came to naught.[48] Nonetheless, these calls, mostly by fans, touched off many web-based discussions on who best represented Superman, Welling or the eventual stars of the Superman movies, Brandon Routh and Henry Cavill, respectively. Although such disputes might seem damaging to the brand, since they divide fans, they most likely increase the brand value by involving fans in a discussion centered on the character and creating deeper affective ties to

Superman, albeit through some particular representation. Moreover, by having several incarnations of Superman at any given time, DC can increase the number of licensed products it sells. So, for instance, in 2007, DC licensed a series of *Smallville*-themed action figures at the same time as the *Superman Returns* series of figures.[49]

In addition to strengthening the Superman brand, *Smallville* also gave DC and Warner an opportunity to introduce other characters from their superhero stable and to attempt spin-off series. Characters such as Aquaman, Green Arrow, and the Flash made guest appearances on *Smallville*. After the ratings success of a 2005 episode featuring Aquaman, the series producers, Alfred Gough and Miles Millar, developed a pilot for an Aquaman series, but nothing came of this effort when The WB merged with rival network UPN to form The CW and the new network passed on the pilot. With reportedly $7 million invested in the pilot's production, the producers released it on the then newly minted iTunes platform, but despite some positive buzz, the tale ended there.[50] Green Arrow fared better, with a series developed based on the character and picked up by The CW in 2012. Although not directly derivative of the *Smallville* take on the character, the new *Arrow* series did have a similar emphasis on nonsuper aspects of the character. Two other series, following much the same model as *Smallville*, debuted in 2014: *The Flash* and *Gotham*. *Gotham* focused on the development of Batman and his nemeses, while *The Flash* fleshed out the nonsuper aspects of that character. *Smallville*, then, not only demonstrated how the Superman brand offered synergy across media forms but also provided a model for moving other DC properties to more media incarnations.

BRANDS AND BEYOND

If Superman functions in one register primarily as a brand, then all the forms in which he appears are perhaps forms of media because they circulate the character. Matthew Freeman coined the term "narrative-fronted promotional content" to describe the sort of "interaction between texts and advertisements" that shaped a form of storytelling in Frank Baum's Land of Oz story world, of which *The Wizard of Oz* is the best-known component, that stretched beyond not just beyond a particular work but across forms and genres of media and beyond into products and services.[51] Superman, with his many forms, seems very similar to Freeman's concept, although to talk about "narrative-fronted" and "promotional content" seems to offer an explanatory binary similar to a cultural superstructure and an economic base. Nonetheless, there is an idea at play here that takes the relationship beyond simply saying that Superman is a brand. This concept too captures some of the way narratives can create brands, which is distinct from the sort of brand narrative strategies favored by some marketers.[52] It is the available narratives of Superman that make the character so effective in selling goods and services. Superman has a multiplicity of narratives but also a select set of trademarks and visual representations. These are mutually reinforcing: for instance, a Superman movie can generate tee-shirt sales, and these tee shirts in turn act as reminders of the movie and other instances of Superman. The link between these two Superman products might be as minimal as a representation of the familiar stylized S chest emblem. Given the circulation and visibility of Superman tee shirts, they might well be thought of as a form of media, particularly since they probably have a greater circulation and visibility than the Superman comic books.

Most superhero comic books are no longer a form of mass media. In July 2014, the most popular Superman title, *Superman Unchained*, sold 69,523 copies, which suggests something less than mass. Even at $3.99 a copy, total yearly revenues generated by this comic would be just $3,328,761.24, which is a little more than 1 percent of the $291 million domestic gross of the latest Superman film, *Man of Steel*.[53] On the other hand, there are over four thousand different listings for Superman tee shirts at Amazon; no doubt many are duplicate listings, but this number gives some indication of the sheer range of Superman tee shirts and suggest some widespread availability and, by extension, circulation. There is no ready measure publicly available for the circulation of these tee shirts. The business structure of Time Warner, which owns DC Comics and hence Superman, means that tee shirts are licensed products and the revenues received are buried in corporate reports under broader licensing fees. In May 2014, the industry magazine *Global License* reported that DC's parent, Warner, did $6 billion in sales of licensed products through its Warner Bros. Consumer Products arm. How much profit Warner derives from these sales is unclear, as is the amount that derived from Superman products.[54] In 2008, as part of the Siegel family's attempt to claim copyright

FIGURE 30. Superman tee shirt on sale in Kuala Lumpur, April 2010

termination of Superman, lawyers asked for an accounting of receipts from numerous Superman products, but this matter was one of several awaiting determination as submatters when a judge ruled in 2013 that DC Comics–Warner retained the rights to Superman.[55] Anecdotally, though, seeing Superman-branded tee shirts on sale in official DC shops in Singapore, Malacca, and Kuala Lumpur, branches of the Primark department store in London and Vienna, the Chocoolate fashion boutique in Tseung Kwan O in Hong Kong's New Territories, the Jay Jay's chain of youth outfitters in Australia, department stores like Target and Macy's in the United States, and in many other venues suggests a reach and circulation far beyond that of the comic book. Indeed, in Kuala Lumpur, in the space of a mile, it is possible to buy a rather-staid Superman tee shirt in the DC store and in the less upscale market nearby a shirt on which a self-satisfied Superman says, "I can see your underwear" (see figure 30). Both of these tee shirts are licensed products. Although the DC stores in Singapore and in the

Malaysian cities of Malacca and Kuala Lumpur are official stores, they do not sell comic books and only offer the various licensed products like tee shirts and action figures.

CONCLUSION

Superman has transcended his origins in comic books and become something far larger both as a product and as an icon of American culture. Referring to Superman as a brand is somewhat redundant—he is clearly more than just a brand—but since he is so often marketed in this manner, including his media incarnations, which increasingly seem product driven, "brand" captures more fully and concisely what Superman has become. Just as Superman caused the advent of a host of superhero characters in the 1930s and 1940s, and just as Superman Inc. created a wave of Superman products, the brand in the twenty-first century relies on a host of incarnations in media and beyond for its strength and marketability. In turn, the strength of the brand, and the strategies DC and Warner use to ensure that strength, are transferable to other superhero marques in the DC portfolio.

EPILOGUE

Superman is an icon of American culture and a figure recognized across the globe. Understanding the popularity of the character and just what he represents is a complex process that I have addressed by analyzing the vast Superman corpus across media forms through registers of myth and history, ideology, and nostalgia. I have also addressed the processes that create Superman: authorship, reception, and brand creation and consumption. These factors all come together to make Superman and explain his persistence. But just who or what Superman is tends to be situational, both in his production and in his reception. The American writer Adam Gopnik, in the context of a discussion about Jesus, has suggested that a search for "the historical Superman" would reveal that "there's nothing there but a hopeful story and a girlfriend with an alliterative name."[1] It is a great line that contains a grain of truth, but he needed to add a modifier that there is nothing *stable* there. Superman does have a history, both as a character and as a piece of intellectual property. He also has a history in the memories of his audiences.

It is this history that producers of Superman stories must struggle with whenever they create a new Superman adventure or product. The greater the need to attract broad audiences, such as with a film, the greater the struggle to find the connection to the memories that such audiences expect to be evoked or triggered by the story or the product. On the other hand, a product like a tee shirt, which simply carries the stylized S Superman logo, lets audiences bring whatever memories or expectations they have to fill the meaning behind the symbol. The importance of the Superman logo is, then, manifold. It is a piece of intellectual property from which DC derives profit. It is the site of, or trigger for, a vast array of memories that potentially stretch back almost eighty years and through which people engage with the character. The meaning behind the symbol, or the meaning of Superman, is a dynamic process in which the value attached to the property is accorded through audience engagement, where engagement is measured as a desire or willingness to purchase and the company's ability to transform that desire into actuality. The bottom line, then, is that Superman's history is determined by which product will put behinds on seats or tee shirts on bodies.

Although generally regarded as a comic book character, Superman has been more than that for almost the entirety of his history. The numerous media appearances in print, radio, animation, television, and film made him a multimedia phenomenon before the word was coined. His transcendence to an American icon during World War II, and beyond, made him a national symbol—but a privately owned one. Moreover, his regular appearance in comic books since 1938, with at least one story a month and often a good many more, means that he is an icon with a far-greater narrative history than, say, the Statute of Liberty or Uncle Sam. When the numerous stories from the radio serial, the three television series, and the various films are added, there is a certain amount of narrative bloat. In some ways, this makes the character easier to market to audiences since there are numerous hallmark moments of Superman that various media producers can include or allude to, in order to catch an audience's attention and expectations. On the other hand, leaving out an expected touchstone can cause discord among those who expect certain things of Superman. Witness Bill O'Reilly and other conservatives' displeasure at the lack of "the American way" in *Superman Returns*. In comic books, DC has since 1986 tried to remove this narrative bloat several times by rebooting the character, reboots in which much of that which has gone before is said never to have happened. While DC can decree this to be the case within the internal world occupied by Superman, the memory of Superman's audience, and particularly the readers of these comic books, cannot so easily be wiped clean and the slate started afresh. The same can be said for a Superman movie, since so many reviewers of the 2006 *Superman Returns* and the 2013 *Man of Steel* used 1978's *Superman* as the reference point against which to judge a Superman film.

Superman, then, may arrive as a product in the form of a comic book, a television series, a movie, or a tee shirt, but in doing so, the product has to contend with its audience's memories. Two processes of narrative bricolage—choosing from available versions, perhaps adding new twists, and assembling a version of Superman—occur here. First, the producers of a given Superman item must think through which of the many versions of Superman they may care to reference and how explicit they will make such references. Second, audiences receiving said products work at integrating them, or not, into their preexisting concept of Superman. In films, this bricolage approach has become a marketing strategy in which directors hide "Easter eggs" in the background of films, but not so carefully that they cannot be discovered by those who are looking for them.[2] Part of the pleasure for audiences is spotting these moments and recognizing their meaning.

This process of bricolage extends beyond already mediated and constructed narratives into the realm of the wearable. While a product like a Superman tee shirt with the stylized *S* symbol might seem to offer few moments for bricolage or interpretive nuances, it really depends on just how that symbol is depicted. There are a range of tees shirts with this symbol that run from bright and shiny versions that approximate the symbol as depicted on Christopher Reeve's costume in the 1978 film, through to the muted, darker hues of Henry Cavill's in 2013's *Man of Steel*. There are also prewashed, distressed tee shirts in which the logo is fading and worn. This range of tee shirts, then, offers their wearers a range of options. Exactly what it means when someone wears one or the other is not clear and would take an ethnographical study to determine with any authority. And that is just the point: far from being immutable, Superman, and the response he invokes, is fluid and a process.

NOTES

INTRODUCTION: THE PERSISTENCE OF AN AMERICAN ICON

1 John Kobler, "Up, Up and Away! The Rise of Superman Inc.," *Saturday Evening Post*, June 21, 1941, 14–15, 70–78.

2 Herbert Corey, "Your Son's a Better Soldier than You Were," *Nation's Business*, September 1942, 42–44.

3 "Superman's Dilemma," *Time*, April 13, 1942, 78.

4 Ian Gordon, *Comic Strips and Consumer Culture, 1890–1945* (Washington, DC: Smithsonian Institution Press, 1998), 140.

5 Jerry Siegel, Jack Schiff, Wayne Boring, Jack Burnley, and Whitney Ellsworth, *Superman: The Golden Age Sundays, 1943–1946* (San Diego: Idea and Design Works, 2013).

6 John Morton Blum, *V Was for Victory: Politics and American Culture during World War II* (New York: Harcourt Brace Jovanovich, 1976), 17.

7 Harrison B. Summers, ed., *A Thirty-Year History of Programs Carried on National Radio Networks in the United States, 1926–1956* (Salem, NH: Ayer, 1986).

8 Leslie Cabarga, *The Fleischer Story* (Boston: Da Capo, 1988), 174–180.

9 Peter Bart, "Superman Faces New Hurdles: Publishers of Comic Books Showing Decline," *New York Times*, September 23, 1962.

10 "Kinney Plans to Acquire National Periodical in Exchange of Stock," *Wall Street Journal*, July 24, 1967; "Kinney's Acquisition of National," *Wall Street Journal*, August 25, 1967; "Kinney National Acquisition," *Wall Street Journal*, March 27, 1968.

11 Eric Nash, "Jack Liebowitz, Comics Publisher, Dies at 100," *New York Times*, December 13, 2000; Roger Cohen, "The Creator of Time Warner, Steven J. Ross, Is Dead at 65," *New York Times*, December 21, 1992; Connie Bruck, *Master of the Game* (New York: Simon and Schuster, 1994).

12 Time Warner, Warner Bros. Entertainment, home page, accessed March 31,

2015, http://www.timewarner.com/company/operating-divisions/warner-bros-entertainment.

13 Martin Kemp, *Christ to Coke: How Image Becomes Icon* (New York: Oxford University Press, 2011), 3.

14 Umberto Eco, "The Myth of Superman," trans. Natalie Chilton, *Diacritics* 2 (1972): 14–22. Originally published as "Il mito di Superman e la dissoluzione del tempo," in *Demitizzazione e imagine*, ed. E. Castelli (Padua: Cedam, 1962).

15 Fredric Wertham, *The World of Fanzines* (Carbondale: Southern Illinois University Press, 1973); Constance Penley, "Feminism, Psychoanalysis, and the Study of Popular Culture," in *Cultural Studies*, ed. Lawrence Grossberg, Cary Nelson, and Paula A. Treichler (New York: Routledge, 1992), 479–500; Henry Jenkins, *Convergence Culture: Where Old and New Media Collide* (New York: NYU Press, 2006).

16 Tom Engelhardt, "The Strawberry Shortcake Strategy," in *Watching Television: A Pantheon Guide to Popular Culture*, ed. Todd Gitlin (New York: Pantheon, 1986), 68–110.

CHAPTER ONE: SUPERMAN MYTHOS AND HISTORY

1 Umberto Eco, "The Myth of Superman," trans. Natalie Chilton, *Diacritics* 2 (1972): 15. Originally published as "Il mito di Superman e la dissoluzione del tempo," in *Demitizzazione e imagine*, ed. E. Castelli (Padua: Cedam, 1962).

2 Eco, "Myth," 22, 19.

3 Umberto Eco, "Apocalittici e integrati: La cultura italiana e le comunicazioni di massa" (Apocalyptic and integrated: Italian culture and mass communications), in *Apocalittici e integrati: Comunicazioni di massa e teorie della cultura di massa* (Apocalyptic and integrated: Mass communications and theories of mass culture) (1964; repr., Milan: RCS, 1996), xxi. See also Jean-Paul Gabilliet, *Of Comics and Men: A Cultural History of American Comic Books* (Jackson: University Press of Mississippi, 2010), xx.

4 Frederic Wertham, "Comics . . . Very Funny!," *Saturday Review of Literature*, May 29, 1948, 6–7, 27–29; Frederic Wertham, *The Seduction of the Innocent* (New York: Holt, Rinehart and Winston, 1954).

5 William Appleman Williams, *The Tragedy of American Diplomacy*, 2nd ed. (New York: Dell, 1972).

6 John Cheng, *Astounding Wonder: Imagining Science and Science Fiction in Interwar America* (Philadelphia: University of Pennsylvania Press, 2012), 179–210.

7 Giambattista Vico, *Selected Writings* (New York: Cambridge University Press, 1982), 102–138.

8 Larry Tye's *Superman: The High-Flying History of America's Most Enduring Hero* (New York: Random House, 2012) is a useful overview of Superman's

history as a character; Glen Wheldon's *Superman: The Unauthorized Biography* (Hoboken, NJ: Wiley, 2013) is a somewhat less successful effort to deal with Superman's many twists and turns in comic books and other media.

9 Claude Lévi-Strauss, *Structural Anthropology* (London: Allen Lane, 1968).

10 Thomas Andrae, "From Menace to Messiah: The History and Historicity of Superman," in *American Media and Mass Culture: Left Perspectives*, ed. Donald Lazure (Berkeley: University of California Press, 1987), 124–138; Ian Gordon, *Comic Strips and Consumer Culture, 1890–1945* (Washington, DC: Smithsonian Institution Press, 1998). See also Tye, *Superman*, 45–46, which draws from both the preceding pieces.

11 Joseph Liebowitz to Jerry Siegel, September 28, 1938; Siegel to Liebowitz, September 30, 1938; Liebowitz to Siegel, April 21, 1939. These letters can be found in *Siegel v. Warner Bros. Entm't, Inc.*, No. 2:04-cv-08400-SGL-RZ (C.D. Cal. 2009), Document 353-3, filed August 5, 2008. Unless otherwise stated, letters cited are from this source.

12 Roger Chartier, "Texts, Printing, Readings," in *The New Cultural History*, ed. Lynn Hunt (Berkeley: University of California Press 1989), 161.

13 Liebowitz to Siegel, April 21, 1939; Whitney Ellsworth to Siegel, January 22, 1940; Liebowitz to Siegel, January 29, 1940.

14 Liebowitz to Siegel, January 25 and 29, 1940.

15 Liebowitz to Siegel, February 8, 1940.

16 Jerry Siegel (w) and Joe Shuster (p, i,) "Superman's Phony Manager," *Action Comics* #6 (November 1938); the interview appeared in the August 1983 issue of the fanzine *Nemo* and has since been republished in Thomas Andrae, *Creators of the Superheroes* (Neshannock, PA: Hermes, 2011), 34; Gordon, *Comic Strips and Consumer Culture*, 135.

17 Agreement of December 19, 1939, between Detective Comics and Siegel and Shuster, reproduced in *Siegel v. Warner Bros. Entm't, Inc.*, No. CV 04-8400-RSWL (RZx), Declaration of Michael Bergman in Support of Defendants' Brief on Additional Issues, July 21, 2008.

18 *Action Comics* #32 (January1941).

19 John Kobler, "Up, Up and Away! The Rise of Superman Inc.," *Saturday Evening Post*, June 21, 1941, 76; Liebowitz to Siegel, May 2, 1940.

20 Gordon, *Comic Strips and Consumer Culture*, 149.

21 Gerard Jones, *Men of Tomorrow: Geeks, Gangsters, and the Birth of the Comic Book* (New York: Basic Books, 2005), 242.

22 Martin Barker, *A Haunt of Fear* (London: Pluto, 1984); John Lent, *Pulp Demons: International Dimensions of the Postwar Anti-Comics Campaign* (Madison NJ: Fairleigh Dickinson University Press, 1999).

23 Eco, "Myth," 19.

24 Otto Binder (w) and Al Plastino (p, i), "The Super Duel in Space," *Action*

Comics #242 (July 1958); Otto Binder (w) and Al Plastino (p, i), "The Bride of Bizarro," *Action Comics* #255 (August 1959); both reprinted in *Superman in the Fifties* (New York: DC Comics, 2002); Jerry Siegel (w), Wayne Boring (p), John Forte (i), "The Shame of the Bizarro Family," *Adventure Comics* #285 (June 1961).

25 Edmond Hamilton (w), Curt Swan (p), and George Klein (i), "The Showdown between Luthor and Superman," *Superman* #164 (October 1963); Len Wein (w), Curt Swan (p), and Murphy Anderson (i), "The Man Who Murdered the Earth," *Superman* #248 (February 1972); reprinted in *Superman in the Sixties* (New York: DC Comics, 1999) and *Superman in the Seventies* (New York: DC Comics, 2000), respectively.

26 Leo Dorfman (w) and Kurt Schaffenberger (p, i), "The Romance of Superbaby and Baby Lois," *Superman's Girl Friend Lois Lane* #42 (July 1963); reprinted in *Superman in the Sixties.*

27 Robert Kanigher (w), Curt Swan (p), and George Roussos (i), "Beware the Super-Genius Baby!," *Superman* #224 (February 1970). Sales figures were filed in October and generally reported in the March or April issues of the comic books, as required by US act: Statement of Ownership, Management, and Circulation (Act of October 23, 1962; § 4369, Title 39, U.S. Code).

28 Jones, *Men of Tomorrow*, 312, links the departure of Weisinger to the takeover of National by Kinney, but Kinney's takeover (more of a merger) was completed in early 1968. "Kinney National Acquisition," *Wall Street Journal*, March 27, 1968, 14.

29 Robert Kanigher (w), Werner Roth (p), and Vince Colletta (i), "I Am Curious (Black)," *Superman's Girl Friend Lois Lane* #106 (November 1970), reprinted in *Superman in the Seventies*; John Howard Griffin, *Black Like Me* (Boston: Houghton Mifflin, 1961); Robert Bonazzi, *Man in the Mirror: John Howard Griffin and the Story of "Black Like Me"* (Maryknoll, NY: Orbis Books, 1997).

30 Jack Kirby (w, i) and Vince Colletta (i), "Jimmy Olsen Brings Back the Newsboy Legion," *Superman's Pal Jimmy Olsen* #133 (October 1970), reprinted in *Superman in the Seventies* and also in *Jack Kirby's Fourth World Omnibus: Volume 1* (New York: DC Comics, 2007).

31 Elliot S! Maggin (w) and Murphy Anderson (p, i), "I Can't Go Home Again," *Superman* #270 (December 1973), reprinted in *Superman in the Seventies.*

32 Henry Jenkins, "'Just Men in Tights': Rewriting Silver Age Comics in an Era of Multiplicity," in *Men in Tights: Comic Book Superheroes*, ed. Angela Ndalianis (New York: Routledge, 2009), 20.

33 For instance, Joseph McCabe, in "Speeding Bullets and Changing Lanes," in *The Man from Krypton: A Closer Look at Superman*, ed. Glenn Yeffeth (Dallas: BenBella Books, 2006), 168, states that Lois and Clark slept together. In *Superman* #322 (April 1978), Superman goes to Lois Lane's apartment, and

although he enters through the window, he takes the time in the last panel to lock her front door securely, which to my mind hints that his intention is to stay for more than dinner.

34 Alan Moore (w), Curt Swan (p), and George Perez (i), "Whatever Happened to the Man of Tomorrow?," *Superman* #423 (September 1986).

35 Jerry Siegel (w), Curt Swan (p), and Sheldon Moldoff (i), "The Night of March 31st!," *Superman* #145 (May 1961).

36 Angela Ndalianis, "Enter the Aleph—Superhero Worlds and Hypertime Realities," in Ndalianis, *Men in Tights*, 273, 285.

37 Eco, "Myth," 19.

38 Janet Horowitz Murray, *Hamlet on the Holodeck: The Future of Narrative in Cyberspace* (New York: Free Press, 1997), 40, cited by Felan Parker, "Official Apocrypha: *Elseworlds, What If . . . ?* and the Transmedia Franchise," paper presented at New Narrative Conference, Toronto, May 2010.

39 John Byrne (w, i) and Dick Giordano (i), "The Haunting," *Man of Steel* #6 (December 1986).

40 John Byrne, "Superman: A Personal View," in *Superman: The Man of Steel* (New York: Ballantine Books, 1988), vi–viii.

CHAPTER TWO: IDEOLOGY AND MORALITY

1 Clifford Geertz, "Ideology as Cultural System," in *Interpretation of Cultures: Selected Essays* (New York: Basic Books, 1973), 207.

2 Arthur M. Schlesinger Jr., "Its My Vital Center," *Slate*, January 10, 1997, http://www.slate.com/articles/briefing/articles/1997/01/its_my_vital_center.html.

3 Wendy Wall, *Inventing the "American Way": The Politics of Consensus from the New Deal to the Civil Rights Movement* (New York: Oxford University Press, 2008), 16–17, 35, 42.

4 Ibid., 6–8, 65.

5 In January 2015, the series appeared on the MeTV cable network from four to five p.m. MeTV, "MeTV Schedule," accessed January 26, 2015, http://metvnetwork.com/schedule/.

6 Michael J. Hayde, *Flights of Fantasy: The Unauthorized but True Story of Radio & TV's Adventures of Superman* (Albany, GA: BearManor Media, 2009), 53–54; Bill O'Reilly, "Superman and the Culture War," BillOReilly.com, July 6, 2006, http://www.billoreilly.com/column?pid=20177.

7 I discuss the specifics of Superman's World War II comic book adventures and their relationship to wartime advertising and the American way in *Comic Strips and Consumer Culture* (Washington, DC: Smithsonian Institution Press, 1998), 128–151; Bullock's advertisement, *Los Angeles Times*, January 1, 1945.

8 Robert Maxwell to George Zachary, April 12, 1943, quoted in Wall, *Inventing the "American Way*," 115; ibid., 149–150.

9   Umberto Eco, "The Myth of Superman," trans. Natalie Chilton, *Diacritics* 2 (1972): 22. Originally published as "Il mito di Superman e la dissoluzione del tempo," in *Demitizzazione e imagine*, ed. E. Castelli (Padua: Cedam, 1962).

10 "South End Eagles Capture Civitan Air Rifle Club," *Hagerstown Morning Herald*, April 28, 1952.

11 Steven D. Levitt and Stephen J. Dubner, *Freakonomics: A Rogue Economist Explores the Hidden Side of Everything* (New York: William Morrow, 2005).

12 "The Clan of the Fiery Cross," *The Adventures of Superman*, radio show, originally broadcast June 10 and July 1, 1946, https://archive.org/details/Superman_page09.

13 Ruth Schwartz Cowan, *More Work for Mother: The Ironies of Household Technology from the Open Hearth to the Microwave* (New York: Basic Books, 1983); Ruth Schwartz Cowan, "Ambivalent Dreams: Women and the Home after World War II," *Journal of Women's History* 13, no. 3 (2001): 151–152; Elaine Tyler May, *Homeward Bound: American Families in the Cold War Era* (New York: Basic Books, 1988).

14 Robert Zieger, *American Workers, American Unions, 1920–1985* (Baltimore: Johns Hopkins University, 1986), 104.

15 Jack Knight and Jean Ensminger, "Conflict over Changing Social Norms: Bargaining, Ideology, and Enforcement," in *The New Institutionalism in Sociology*, ed. Mary C. Brinton and Victor Nee (Stanford, CA: Stanford University Press, 1998), 105–126.

16 Tom Wolfe, "The 'Me' Decade and the Third Great Awakening," *New York*, August 23, 1976, http://nymag.com/news/features/45938/.

17 Jason Deparle, "Harder for Americans to Rise from Lower Rungs," *New York Times*, January 5, 2012.

18 Jules Feiffer, *The Great Comic Book Heroes* (New York: Doubleday, 1965), 18–19.

19 *Kill Bill: Volume 2*, directed by Quentin Tarantino (2004; Santa Monica, CA: Miramax Lionsgate, 2011), DVD.

20 *Superman*, directed by Richard Donner (1978; Burbank, CA: Warner Home Video, 2001), DVD.

21 Ibid.

22 *Superman* #161 (May 1963); Jerry Siegel (w) and Al Plastino (p, i), "Superman's Greatest Feats," *Superman* #146 (July 1961); Jerry Siegel (w) and George Papp (p, i), "The Impossible Mission," *Superboy* #85 (December 1960).

23 Cary Bates (w), Elliot S! Maggin (w), Curt Swan (p), and Bob Oksner (i), "Superman 2001," *Superman* #300 (June 1976). Maggin in 2007 announced a run for Congress in California's Twenty-Fourth District as a Democrat in the 2008 election but dropped out before he even started campaigning. His intention was to campaign for "Truth, Justice, and the American Way." He previously entered the Democratic primary in 1984 for a seat in Connecticut.

Elliot Maggin, "Elliot S! Maggin: Democrat for Congress California—24th CD," accessed October 1, 2007, http://www.maggin.com/.

24 Heidi MacDonald, "DC Retailer Survey Results: Older, Male, Middle-Class, Avid," *The Beat* (blog), February 10, 2012, http://comicsbeat.com/dc-retailer-survey-results-older-male-middle-class-avid/.

25 "Interview: Grant Morrison, Comic Book Writer," *Scotsman*, July 24, 2011, http://www.scotsman.com/news/interview-grant-morrison-comic-book-writer-1-1778295.

26 Tom DeSanto, introduction to *Superman: Red Son*, by Mark Millar (New York: DC Comics, 2004), 7.

27 Benjamin Franklin, "Pennsylvania Assembly: Reply to the Governor, November 11, 1755," in *The Papers of Benjamin Franklin*, ed. Leonard W. Labaroo, vol. 6 (New Haven, CT: Yale University Press, 1963), 242.

28 Benjamin Wittes, "What Ben Franklin Really Said," *Lawfare* (blog), July 15, 2011, http://www.lawfareblog.com/2011/07/what-ben-franklin-really-said/.

29 Adam Smith, *The Wealth of Nations: An Inquiry into the Nature and Causes of the Wealth of Nations* (1776; repr., Petersfield, UK: Harriman House, 2007), 293.

30 Dan Jurgens (w), Georges Jeanty (p), and Joe Rubinstein (i), "Clark Kent No More," *Superman*, vol. 2, #142 (February 1999).

31 See, for instance, the following stories: Joe Kelly (w), Doug Mahnke and Lee Bermejo (p), and Tom Nguyen, Dexter Vines, Jim Royal, Jose Marzan, Wade Von Grawbadger, and Wayne Faucher (i), "What's So Funny about Truth, Justice & the American Way?," *Action Comics* #775 (March 2001); Steven T. Seagle (w), Scott McDaniel (p), and Andy Owens (i), "The American Way," *Superman*, vol. 2, #191 (May 2003); Geoff Johns and Kurt Busiek (w) and Pete Woods (p, i), "Up, Up, and Away, Chapter Two: Mild-Mannered Reporter," *Action Comics* #837 (May 2006).

32 Benjamin Saunders, *Do the Gods Wear Capes? Spirituality, Fantasy, and Superheroes* (New York: Continuum, 2011), 31, 29.

CHAPTER THREE: SUPERMAN: THE OBJECT OF NOSTALGIA

1 Otto Friedrich, "Up, Up and Away!!!," *Time*, March 14, 1988, 72, 74.

2 Fredric Jameson, "Postmodernism and Consumer Society," in *The Anti-aesthetic: Essays on Postmodern Culture*, ed. Hal Foster (Port Townsend, WA: Bay, 1983), 117.

3 Christopher Lasch, "The Politics of Nostalgia," *Harper's*, November 1984, 65–70.

4 Susan Stewart, *On Longing: Narratives of the Miniature, the Gigantic, the Souvenir, the Collection* (Baltimore: Johns Hopkins University Press, 1984), xiii.

5 Svetlana Boym, *The Future of Nostalgia* (New York: Basic Books, 2001), 41, 49–50.

6   Christopher Lasch, *The True and Only Heaven* (New York: Norton, 1991).

7   *OED Online*, s.v. "nostalgia, n.," accessed October 8, 2012, http://www.oed.
com.libproxy1.nus.edu.sg/view/Entry/128472?redirectedFrom=nostalgia.
Unbeknown to Banks, it seems, the term originated with the Swiss Johannes
Hofer. See Boym, *Future of Nostalgia*, 3.

8   Stewart, *On Longing*, 137.

9   Susan Heller Anderson, "It's a Bird! It's a Plane! It's a Movie!," *New York Times*,
June 26, 1977.

10   Mark Waid and Alex Ross, *Kingdom Come* (New York: DC Comics, 2006), 4.

11   Jenette Kahn, the president of DC Comics, in 1983 described Superman as
"the first god of a new mythology." Quoted in Neil Harris, "Who Owns Our
Myths? Heroism and Copyright in an Age of Mass Culture," in *Cultural
Excursions: Marketing Appetites and Cultural Tastes in Modern America*
(Chicago: University of Chicago Press, 1990), 236.

12   Elliot S. Maggin, introduction to Waid and Ross, *Kingdom Come*, 6–7.

13   Jameson, "Postmodernism and Consumer Society," 116.

14   Bruce Westbrook, "A Romance for Superman," *Houston Chronicle*, September
12, 1993.

15   Daniel Cerone, "TV's Superman Undergoing a Planetary Shift," *Los Angeles
Times*, September 17, 1994; Westbrook, "Romance for Superman"; Zoomway,
"How It All Began," Superman Homepage, accessed November 26, 2012,
http://www.supermanhomepage.com/other/krypton'ian-cybernet/kc39.txt.

16   "I've Got A Crush On You," October 24, 1993, *Lois & Clark*, season 1, episode
6, written by Deborah Joy LeVine and Thania St. John, directed by Gene
Reynolds; "The Man of Steel Bars," November 21, 1993, *Lois & Clark*, season
1, episode 9, written by Paris Qualles, directed by Robert Butler; "The House
of Luthor," May 8, 1994, *Lois & Clark*, season 1, episode 21, written by Dan
Levine and Deborah Joy LeVine, directed by Alan J. Levi; "Brutal Youth,"
October 26, 1996, *Lois & Clark*, season 4, episode 5, written by Tom Minear,
directed by David Grossman.

17   "I'm Looking Through You," October 10, 1993, *Lois & Clark*, season 1, episode
3, written by Deborah Joy LeVine, directed by Mark Sobel; Jerry Siegel
(w), Joe Shuster (p, i), and Paul Lauretta (i), "Superman's Phony Manager,"
Action Comics #6 (November 1938); Ian Gordon, *Comic Strips and Consumer
Culture, 1890–1945* (Washington, DC: Smithsonian Institution Press, 1998);
Ian Gordon, "Nostalgia, Myth, and Ideology: Visions of Superman at the End
of the American Century," in *Comics and Ideology*, ed. Matthew McAllister,
Edward Sewell, and Ian Gordon (New York: Peter Lang, 2001), 177–193.

18   Lois & Clark Fanfic Archive, accessed April 10, 2016, http://www.lcfanfic.
com/.

19   "Season 5," Lois & Clark Fanfic Archive, accessed November 26, 2012, http://

www.lcfanfic.com/thm-s5.htm; "The Unaired Fifth Season," The Lois &
Clark Krypton Club, accessed November 26, 2012, http://web.archive.org/
web/20030814012459/http://members.aol.com/thenando/eps.htm.

20 Lois and Clark Message Board, accessed November 26, 2012, http://www.
zoomway.net/ubbthreads/ubbthreads.php.

21 Fredric Wertham, The World of Fanzines (Carbondale: Southern Illinois
University Press, 1973), 132; Constance Penley, "Feminism, Psychoanalysis, and
the Study of Popular Culture," in Cultural Studies, ed. Lawrence Grossberg,
Cary Nelson, and Paula Treichler (New York: Routledge, 1992), 479–500.

22 TNT, "Lois & Clark," accessed November 26, 2012, http://web.archive.org/
web/20020201191019/http://alt.tnt.tv/scifi/loisandclark/.

23 Sara Gwenllian-Jones, "Web Wars: Online TV Fandom and Studio
Censorship," in Must See TV: Designing Schedules, Finding Audiences,
Transforming Technologies, ed. Mark Jancovich and James Lyons (London:
BFI, 2002), 163–177.

24 The WB, "Smallville," accessed February 8, 2015, https://web.archive.org/
web/20010520164435/http://thewb.com/fallseason2001/smallville/.

25 Charlie McCollum, "ABC, WB Schedules Get Major Retooling," San Jose
Mercury News, May 16, 2001.

26 Smallville, season 4, episode 1; season 4, episode 5; season 4, episode 17;
season 5, episode 5; season 5, episode 19; and season 6, episode 13 (Burbank,
CA: Warner Home Video, 2005–2007), DVD.

27 Smallville, season 4, episode 2; season 4, episode 8; season 5, episode 12;
season 6, episode 1.

28 Angela Ndalianis, "Enter the Aleph: Superhero Worlds and Hypertime
Realities," in The Contemporary Comic Book Superhero, ed. Angela Ndalianis
(New York: Routledge, 2009), 286.

29 Matthew P. McAllister, Ian Gordon, and Mark Jancovich, "Blockbuster Meets
Superhero Comic, or Art House Meets Graphic Novel? The Contradictory
Relationship between Film and Comic Art," Journal of Popular Film and
Television 34, no. 3 (2006): 108–114.

30 Umberto Eco, "The Myth of Superman," Diacritics, translated by Natalie
Chilton, 2 (1972): 14–22; Harris, "Who Owns Our Myths?," 236.

31 Matt Yockey, "Somewhere in Time: Utopia and the Return of Superman,"
Velvet Light Trap 61 (2008): 26.

32 Joe Williams, "Crash and Burn Superman Reboot 'Man of Steel' Lacks
Everything We Love about the Comic-Book Legend," St. Louis Post-Dispatch,
June 14, 2013. Others who called the film humorless include Laurence Phelan,
"Superman Goes Up, Up and Way over the Top," Independent, June 15, 2013;
Steven Rea, "In 'Man of Steel,' the Same Old Same Old," Philadelphia Inquirer,
June 14, 2013.

33 Dylan Tan, "Man of Steel Weighed Down by Furious Action," *Business Times Singapore*, June 14, 2013; Ben Child, "*Man of Steel* Reviews: What the Critics Say," *Guardian*, June 12, 2013, http://www.theguardian.com/film/2013/jun/11/man-of-steel-reviews-what-critics-say; Gavin Burke, "A Serious Superhero Fights On," *Irish Independent*, June 14, 2013; Reagan Gavin Rasquinha, "Man of Steel," *Times of India*, June 14, 2013, http://www.indiatimes.com/entertainment/hollywood/review-man-of-steel-83171.html.

34 Manohla Dargis, "Part Man, Part God, All Hunk," *New York Times*, June 14, 2013.

35 Joshua Yehl, "10 Coolest Batman v. Superman: Dawn of Justice Easter Eggs," IGN, March 31, 2016, http://www.ign.com/articles/2016/03/31/10-coolest-batman-v-superman-dawn-of-justice-easter-eggs-references-and-trivia; Bart Beaty, "Superhero Fan Service: Audience Strategies in the Contemporary Interlinked Hollywood Blockbuster," *Information Society* 32, no. 25, (2016): 318–325.

36 Steven M. Bergson, in an email on March 30, 2011, gave me the reference to the original American comic book. The story appeared in *Superman's Girlfriend Lois Lane* #12 (October 1959), and the panels I remember are on page 7.

37 The two episodes of *The Adventures of Superman* that I remember are "Phony Alibi" from season 5, originally aired May 3, 1957, and "The Magic Secret" from season 6, originally aired February 10, 1958. I cannot state with any certainty when I saw them, but most likely it was sometime before 1972.

38 I used the Lexis and Factiva newspaper databases to search for all mentions of "Superman" and read several thousand newspaper reviews and reports.

39 Tom De Haven, *Our Hero: Superman on Earth* (New Haven, CT: Yale University Press, 2010), 206.

CHAPTER FOUR: PRODUCTION, AUTHORSHIP, AND OWNERSHIP

1 Jerry Siegel, "The Reign of the Superman," *Science Fiction: The Vanguard of Future Civilization*, January 1933, available at https://archive.org/details/ReignOfTheSuperman (accessed December 26, 2014).

2 Gerard Jones, *Men of Tomorrow: Geeks, Gangsters, and the Birth of the Comic Book* (New York: Basic Books, 2005), 34–37, 78, 346.

3 *Siegel v. Warner Bros. Entm't, Inc.*, 658 F. Supp. 2d 1036 (C.D. Cal. 2009), 2009 U.S. Dist. LEXIS 78193, a version of this judgment, complete with the panels, can be found at the American Bar Association, accessed January 24, 2015, http://www.americanbar.org/content/dam/aba/events/entertainment_sports/2012/10/forum_on_the_entertainmentsportsindustries2012annualmeeting/tv_cable_radiomusic_publishing/siegel_v_warner_bros_658.authcheckdam.pdf; Jeff Trexler, "Superman's Hidden History: The Other 'First' Artist," Newsarama, August

20, 2008, http://www.newsarama.com/825-superman-s-hidden-history-the-other-first-artist.html.

4 Their byline was absent from *Action* #119 (April 1948) and reappeared in *Action* #461 (July 1976).

5 Roger Chartier, "Texts, Printing, Readings," in *The New Cultural History*, ed. Lynn Hunt (Berkeley: University of California Press 1989), 161.

6 David Montgomery, *The Fall of the House of Labor: The Workplace, the State, and American Labor Activism, 1865–1925* (New York: Cambridge University Press, 1987), 116–125.

7 Jones, *Men of Tomorrow*, 13–22.

8 Thomas Andrae, *Creators of the Superheroes* (Neshannock, PA: Hermes, 2011); Les Daniels, *Superman: The Complete History: The Life and Times of the Man of Steel* (San Francisco: Chronicle Books, 1998); Jones, *Men of Tomorrow*; Brad Ricca, *Super Boys: The Amazing Adventures of Jerry Siegel and Joe Shuster* (New York: St. Martin's, 2013).

9 *Siegel v. Warner Bros. Entm't, Inc.*, 542 F. Supp. 2d 1098 (C.D. Cal. 2008), LEXIS 27217, 4.

10 *Siegel*, 658 F. Supp. 2d, LEXIS 78193, 3–5.

11 Ibid., 5.

12 *Siegel v. Warner Bros. Entm't, Inc.*, No. 2:04-cv-08400-SGL-RZ (C.D. Cal. 2009), Document 347, emphasis added.

13 Robert Harvey, *The Art of the Comic Book: An Aesthetic History* (Jackson: University Press of Mississippi, 1996), 16.

14 Jules Feiffer, *The Great Comic Book Heroes* (New York: Doubleday, 1965), 19–20.

15 *Siegel*, No. 2:04-cv-08400-SGL-RZ, Document 347.

16 John Kobler, "Up, Up and Away! The Rise of Superman Inc.," *Saturday Evening Post*, June 21, 1941, 74.

17 *Siegel*, No. 2:04-cv-08400-SGL-RZ, Document 347.

18 Ibid., Document 353-3.

19 Ibid.

20 Ibid.

21 Jean Shepherd, "The Counterfeit Secret Circle Member Gets the Message or: The Asp Strikes Again," *Chicago Tribune*, March 5, 1967.

22 *Siegel*, No. 2:04-cv-08400-SGL-RZ, Document 353-3.

23 Ibid.; Ricca, *Super Boys*, 187, 193–194.

24 Sterling North, "A National Disgrace (and a Challenge to American Parents)," *Chicago Daily News*, May 8, 1940, reprinted in *Childhood Education* 17 (1940): 56. See also New York State Joint Legislative Committee to Study the Publication of Comics, *Report of the New York State Joint Legislative Committee to Study the Publication of Comics*, legislative document

no. 37 (1954), 33; Edward DeGrazia, *Censorship Landmarks* (New York: R. R. Bowker, 1969), 265; both cited in Steven E. Mitchell, "Evil Harvest: Investigating the Comic Book, 1948–1955" (master's thesis, Arkansas State University, 1982), 10.

25   *Action Comics* #41 (October 1941).

26   That DC managed Siegel and Shuster in this process is supported by an article in the *Cleveland Plain Dealer* on June 18, 1941, three days before the *Post* piece, that gave a more negative take on DC's treatment of the pair. J. A. Wadovick, "Superman 'Dads' Learn the Hard Way."

27   Kobler, "Up, Up and Away!" 74.

28   *Siegel*, No. 2:04-cv-08400-SGL-RZ, Document 353-3.

29   Feiffer, *Great Comic Book*, 20.

30   Paul Cassidy, "An Approach to the Profession of the Comic Strip Cartooning Based upon an Analytical Survey of Current Trends and Personal Experiences" (master's thesis, University of Wisconsin, 1942), 36–37.

31   Ibid., 38.

32   *Siegel*, No. 2:04-cv-08400-SGL-RZ, Document 353-3.

33   Ibid. Ellsworth did not name Boring, but in a January 22, 1940, letter, Liebowitz does so, referencing Ellsworth's letter.

34   Ibid., Document 347-9.

35   ibid., Document 353-3.

36   Wadovick, "Superman 'Dads' Learn the Hard Way," cited by Ricca, *Super Boys*, 197.

37   *Siegel*, No. 2:04-cv-08400-SGL-RZ, Document 353-3.

38   Ibid., Document 353-4; Cassidy, "Approach to the Profession," 38; Kobler, "Up, Up and Away!," 74.

39   Les Daniels, *DC Comics: Sixty Years of the World's Favorite Comic Book Heroes* (Boston: Bulfinch, 1995), 28.

40   *Siegel*, No. 2:04-cv-08400-SGL-RZ, Document 353-3.

41   Ricca, *Super Boys*, 211–212, 223.

42   Ibid., 259; Robert Beerbohm, "The Big Bang Theory of Comic Book History," *Comic Book Marketplace*, August 1977, 50–60.

43   This letter was part of a 1997 find by Lauren Agostino in the trash when a lawyer cleared an office and threw away a file of the 1947 Superman case. The letters are reproduced in Lauren Agostino and A. L. Newberg, *Holding Kryptonite: Truth, Justice and America's First Superhero* (New York: Holmes and Watson, 2014). Kindle edition. Many of these letters have appeared in court documents, but some of Siegel's letters have not been available before.

44   Statement of payments made to Siegel and Shuster by DC from 1947 copyright case, reproduced in *Siegel*, No. 2:04-cv-08400-SGL-RZ, Document 353-4.

45   Ibid.

46 See the registration record at the US Patent Office, accessed March 7, 2015, http://tmsearch.uspto.gov/bin/showfield?f=doc&state=4805:295w3v.4.89.

47 Michael J. Hayde, *Flights of Fantasy: The Unauthorized but True Story of Radio & TV's Adventures of Superman* (Albany, GA: BearManor Media, 2009), 53–54; Anthony Tollin, *Superman on Radio* (Schiller Park, IL: Radio Spirits, 1997), 8.

48 Letters reproduced in Agostino and Newberg, *Holding Kryptonite*.

49 Jerry Siegel, "Superman's Originator Puts 'Curse' on Superman Movie," press release, October 1975, reproduced at *20th Century Danny Boy* (blog), July 8, 2012, http://ohdannyboy.blogspot.sg/2012/07/curse-on-superman-movie-look-back-at.html.

50 Letter reproduced in Agostino and Newberg, *Holding Kryptonite*.

51 *Siegel*, No. 2:04-cv-08400-SGL-RZ, Document 353-4.

52 *Daily Argus* (Mount Vernon), January 20, 1947, cited in Agostino and Newberg, *Holding Kryptonite*.

53 Agostino and Newberg, *Holding Kryptonite*, cite March 5, 1947. See also Les Daniels, *Superman: The Complete History: The Life and Times of the Man of Steel* (San Francisco: Chronicle Books, 1998), 70.

54 *Siegel v. National Periodical Publications, Inc.*, 364 F. Supp. 1032 (1973), gives details of the 1948 action.

55 Hayde, *Flights of Fantasy*, 15.

56 *Siegel v. National Periodical Publications, Inc.*, 508 F.2d 909 (1974).

57 *Siegel*, 542 F. Supp. 2d 1098, LEXIS 27217, 10.

58 Court documents reproduced at *20th Century Danny Boy* (blog), July 20, 2012, http://ohdannyboy.blogspot.com/2012/07/the-history-behind-dc-comics-joe.html.

59 *DC Comics v. Pacific Pictures Corporation IP Worldwide, LLC; IPW, LLC; Marc Toberoff, an individual; Mark Warren Peary, as personal representative of the Estate of Joseph Shuster; Jean Adele Peavy, an individual; Laura Siegel Larson, individually and as personal representative of the Estate of Joanne Siegel*, No. 2:10-cv-03633-ODW-RZ (C.D. Cal. 2010), Document 1, Demand for Jury Trial, May 10, 2010.

60 Dave McNary, "Super Snit in 'Smallville': Skein Faces Copyright Infringement Charges," *Daily Variety*, April 4, 2006; *Siegel v. Warner Bros. Entm't, Inc.*, 496 F. Supp. 2d 1111 (C.D. Cal. 2007).

61 *Siegel*, 542 F. Supp. 2d 1098; *Siegel*, 658 F. Supp. 2d 1036.

62 *Siegel*, No. 2:04-cv-08400-SGL-RZ, Document 368, filed September 23, 2008.

63 Eriq Gardner, "Warner Bros. Wins Blockbuster Victory in Legal Battle for Superman," *Hollywood Reporter*, January 10, 2013, http://www.hollywoodreporter.com/thr-esq/warner-bros-wins-blockbuster-victory-410871. See also *Larson v. Warner*, 504 Fed. Appx. 586 (9th Cir. 2013); 2013 U.S. App. LEXIS 671.

64 Mark Warren Peary, as Personal Representative of the Estate of Joseph Shuster, Petitioner v. DC Comics, 135 S. Ct. 144 (2014); 190 L. Ed. 2d 231; 2014 U.S. LEXIS 5678; 83 U.S.L.W. 3194.

65 Laura Siegel Larson v. Warner Bros. Entm't, Inc., No. 13-56243 (9th Cir. 2016), ID: 9860534, DktEntry: 61-1.

66 DC Comics, No. 2:10-cv-03633-ODW-RZ, Document 578-1.

67 Court documents reproduced at 20th Century Danny Boy (blog), July 20, 2012, http://ohdannyboy.blogspot.com/2012/07/the-history-behind-dc-comics-joe.html.

68 Siegel, No. 2:04-cv-08400-ODW-RZ, Document 709-2.

69 Eriq Gardner, "Superman Heir Pens Letter to Fans about Fight with Warner Bros," Hollywood Reporter, October 12, 2012, http://www.hollywoodreporter.com/heat-vision/superman-heir-pens-letter-fans-378793.

70 Siegel, No. 2:04-cv-08400-SGL-RZ, Plaintiffs Submission, July 21, 2008, 23–24; Steranko's expert report, ibid., Declaration of Keith Adams in support of Plaintiffs' Memorandum, July 3, 2008, 63–64.

71 Gardner, "Superman Heir Pens Letter to Fans."

CHAPTER FIVE: READERS AND AUDIENCES

1 Aldo J. Regalado, Bending Steel: Modernity and the American Superhero (Jackson: University Press of Mississippi, 2015).

2 Roger Chartier, "Texts, Printing, Readings," in The New Cultural History, ed. Lynn Hunt (Berkeley: University of California Press 1989), 161.

3 John Cheng, Astounding Wonder: Imagining Science and Science Fiction in Interwar America (Philadelphia: University of Pennsylvania Press, 2012), pp. 12–16.

4 Janet Staiger, Media Reception Studies (New York: NYU Press, 2005), 95, 114.

5 Jean-Paul Gabilliet, Of Comics and Men: A Cultural History of American Comic Books (Jackson: University Press of Mississippi, 2010), 256.

6 Comic Book Resources Forum, accessed February 20, 2015, http://community.comicbookresources.com/.

7 Albert Ching, "Brian Bendis Shuts Down His Long-Running Message Board," Comic Book Resources Forum, September 14, 2014, http://robot6.comicbookresources.com/2014/09/brian-bendis-shuts-down-his-long-running-message-board/.

8 Action Comics #14 (July 1939); Superman #1 (Summer 1939).

9 Susan Strasser, Satisfaction Guaranteed: The Making of the American Mass Market (New York: Pantheon, 1989), 146–147.

10 "Radio Orphan Annie's Secret Society," Scottish Rite Masonic Museum & Library, March 2, 2010, http://nationalheritagemuseum.typepad.com/library_and_archives/2010/03/radio-orphan-annies-secret-society.

11 "Superman on KGKO," *Radio Daily*, August 25, 1941, cited in Michael J. Hayde, *Flights of Fantasy: The Unauthorized but True Story of Radio & TV's Adventures of Superman* (Albany, GA: BearManor Media, 2009), 45.

12 Jerry Siegel, Jack Schiff, Wayne Boring, Jack Burnley and Whitney Ellsworth, *Superman: The Golden Age Sundays, 1943–1946* (San Diego: Idea and Design Works, 2013).

13 *B-17 Flying Fortress "Superman,"* photograph, Getty Images, accessed April 29, 2016, http://www.gettyimages.com/license/71716541; Robert B. Westbrook, "'I Want a Girl, Just Like the Girl That Married Harry James': American Women and the Problem of Political Obligation in World War II," *American Quarterly* 42, no. 4 (1990): 599, 611–612.

14 The historian of Superman on radio and early television Michael Hyde notes, "the sole surviving episode of 'Mr. Prim and the Dragonfly Adventure' from 1943 is at the Library of Congress, on a reel-to-reel tape with a notation on the box that it derives from an AFRS disc. . . . Whether it aired during wartime or not, I cannot say . . . but the show apparently DID air on AFRS at some point." Email to author, October 24, 2011.

15 Roy Thomas, "Jerry, You're the Bestest!," *Alter Ego* 3, no. 25 (2003): 2; Julius Schwartz, "With a Little Help from His Friends," *Alter Ego* 3, no. 25 (2003): 14.

16 Billy Schelly, "Jerry Bails' Ten Building Blocks of Fandom," *Alter Ego* 3, no. 25 (2003): 5–8.

17 Gabilliet, *Of Comics and Men*, 264.

18 For a more complete history of this period of fan activity, see Billy Schelly, *The Golden Age of Comic Fandom* (Seattle: Hamster, 2003).

19 Paul Levitz, email to author, August 27, 2011.

20 Robert G. Weiland, "Comic Books Seen as Expression of American Values," *Free Lance-Star* (Fredericksburg, NY), February 20, 1990, http://news.google.com/newspapers?nid=1298&dat=19900220&id=seUPAAAAIBAJ&sjid=AowDAAAAIBAJ&pg=2562,1496737; Jerry Bails, *Who's Who of American Comic Books, 1928–1999*, accessed July 23, 2012, http://www.bailsprojects.com/.

21 Stephen Scott Beau Smith, "The LOCsmiths," *Amazing Heroes* 23 (1983): 54–56.

22 Ibid., 56.

23 Beppe Sabitini CV, accessed July 17, 2012, http://home.earthlink.net/~bsabatini/cv/; Bails, *Who's Who of American Comic Books*.

24 Douglas Wolk, email to author, April 7, 2010.

25 United States Patent and Trademark Office, accessed June 23, 2016, http://tmsearch.uspto.gov/bin/showfield?f=doc&state=4809:nazgae.2.17.

26 Rich Morrissey, "Recent Ozzy Digests," *Oz Digest*, January 27, 1997, http://www.put.com/oz/ozdi/199701.TXT.

27 Rich Morrissey, "Recent Ozzy Digests," *Oz Digest*, October 2, 1996;

Morrissey, "Recent Ozzy Digests," *Oz Digest*, October 11, 1996; and Morrissey, "Oz Writers et al," *Oz Digest*, October 27, 1996, http://www.put.com/oz/ozdi/199610.TXT.

28 Tony Isabella, "Rich Morrissey," *Alvin Schwartz's Round Table*, June 23, 2016, http://web.archive.org/web/20100701132938/http://www.comicscommunity.com/boards/alvin/?frames=n;read=325&expand=1; Mark Evanier, "Rich Morrissey," *News from Me*, June 23, 2016, http://www.newsfromme.com/2001/05/23/richard-morrissey-r-i-p/.

29 Irene Vartanoff interview, *The Silver Age Sage* (blog), accessed May 10, 2011, http://www.wtv-zone.com/silverager/interviews/vartanoff.shtml.

30 Irene Vartanoff interview, *Sequential Crush* (blog), October 20, 2009, http://sequentialcrush.blogspot.com/2009/10/interview-with-irene-vartanoff.html.

31 Alvin Yellon, letter to the editor, *Sports Illustrated*, May 20, 1974, http://sportsillustrated.cnn.com/vault/article/magazine/MAG1088589/3/index.htm. Yellon continues to offer his views on baseball on the web.

32 Vartanoff interview, *The Silver Age Sage*.

33 Lillian information: "About Us," *Challenger*, accessed June 23, 2011, http://www.challzine.net/aboutus.html; Triano profile: Amazon, accessed June 23, 2011, http://www.amazon.com/gp/pdp/profile/A3C5VCUFJTBL16; mention of Skinner: The Official Michael Rhodes Website, accessed June 23, 2011, http://www.freewebs.com/mikerhodes1/fandom.htm; "My CV," *Clint Thomas* (blog), accessed June 23, 2011, http://writintitan.blogspot.com/.

34 Vartanoff interview, *Sequential Crush*.

35 Smith, "LOCsmiths," 54–56.

36 Peter Sanderson, *Comics in Context*, accessed July 19, 2012, http://www.asitecalledfred.com/2004/04/02/comics-in-context-32-the-living-legend/.

37 Beth Montelone, email to author, February 23, 2015.

38 Tommy Krasker, email to author, February 26, 2015.

39 "Shelley Adrienne Van Geffen Poole Obituary," *NOLA.com*, accessed February 25, 2015, http://obits.nola.com/obituaries/nola/obituary.aspx?pid=172567005.

40 Matthew Huber, email to author, July 21, 2012.

41 See Mic McConnell's blog at Allen, Allen, Allen and Allen, accessed February 18, 2015, http://www.allenandallen.com/blog/?tag=Mic%2BMcConnell; and "Success Stories," *Vegan Muscle and Fitness*, accessed February 18, 2015, http://www.veganmuscleandfitness.com/success-stories/.

42 Augie De Blieck, "A Decade of Siren," Pipeline, Comic Book Resources, September 23, 2008, http://www.comicbookresources.com/?page=article&id=18169.

43 Brian Cronin, "Comic Book Urban Legends Revealed," Comic Book Resources, March 1, 2007, http://goodcomics.comicbookresources.com/2007/03/01/comic-book-urban-legends-revealed-92/.

44 *Adventures of Superman* #464 (March 1990).

45 For a discussion of girls' and women's relationship with superhero comics and fans, see Karen Healey, "When Fangirls Perform: The Gendered Fan Identity in Superhero Comics Fandom," in *The Contemporary Comic Book Superhero*, ed. Angela Ndalianis (New York: Routledge, 2009), 144–163.

46 Harrison B. Summers, ed., *A Thirty-Year History of Programs Carried on National Radio Networks in the United States, 1926–1956* (Salem, NH: Ayer, 1986).

CHAPTER SIX: SUPERMAN THE BRAND AND BEYOND

1 "Paul Emmett Obituary," *Westport Now*, February 15, 2015, http://www.westportnow.com/index.php?/v2_5/comments/paul_emmett_62/.

2 Brad Ricca, *Super Boys: The Amazing Adventures of Jerry Siegel and Joe Shuster* (New York: St. Martin's, 2013), 104.

3 Neal Gabler, *Walt Disney: The Triumph of the American Imagination* (New York: Knopf, 2006), 196–198.

4 Lawrence Van Gelder, "Long Islanders: A Pioneer in Profiting on Famous Names," *New York Times*, April 7, 1985.

5 Ian Gordon, *Comic Strips and Consumer Culture, 1890–1945* (Washington, DC: Smithsonian Institution Press, 1998).

6 Michael J. Hayde, *Flights of Fantasy: The Unauthorized but True Story of Radio & TV's Adventures of Superman* (Albany, GA: BearManor Media, 2009), 28.

7 Ibid., 36.

8 Ibid., 39–40.

9 Ibid., 40.

10 The advertisement is reproduced ibid., 44.

11 Ibid., 49–56.

12 Robert Lesser, *A Celebration of Comic Art and Memorabilia* (New York: Hawthorn Books, 1975), 81, 129; David Longest, *Character Toys and Collectibles: Second Series* (Paducah, KY: Collector Books, 1987), 155.

13 Jack Liebowitz to Jerry Siegel, May 2, 1940. The letter can be found in *Siegel v. Warner Bros. Entm't, Inc.*, Case 2:04-cv-08400-SGL-RZ (C.D. Cal. 2009), Document 353-3, filed August 5, 2008. Unless otherwise stated, letters cited are from this source.

14 Gerard Jones, *Men of Tomorrow: Geeks, Gangsters, and the Birth of the Comic Book* (New York: Basic Books, 2005), 35. Jones does not cite a source. Hayde notes that Republic Pictures announced the Superman deal in its 1940–1941 press book and scripted a fifteen-part movie serial. Hayde, *Flights of Fantasy*, 43.

15 For the reprint, see *Superman Chronicles 10* (New York: DC Comics, 2012).

16 Steve Younis, "Superman and the Phone Booth," Superman Home Page,

accessed October 26, 2014, http://www.supermanhomepage.com/other/other.php?topic=phonebooth.

17 Available at DC Entertainment, accessed March 31, 2015, http://www.shopdcentertainment.com/product/superman+phonebooth+phone+case+for+iphone+and+galaxy+smezpip003.do?sortby=ourPicks&refType=&from=f.

18 Ian Gordon, "The Moral World of Superman and the American War in Vietnam," *Journal of Graphic Novels and Comics* 6, no. 2 (2015): 173.

19 John Dower, *War without Mercy: Race and Power in the Pacific War* (New York: Pantheon, 1986).

20 "The Black Narcissus," *The Adventures of Superman*, episode 4, broadcast October 15, 1942, accessed March 13, 2015, https://archive.org/details/Superman_page05.

21 "The Black Narcissus," *The Adventures of Superman*, episode 5, broadcast October 16, 1942, accessed March 13, 2015, https://archive.org/details/Superman_page05.

22 Hugh Rockoff, "Keep on Scrapping: The Salvage Drives of World War II," NBER Working Paper 13418, National Bureau of Economic Research, Cambridge, MA, September 2007, http://www.nber.org/papers/w13418; Susan Strasser, *Waste and Want: A Social History of Trash* (New York: Henry Holt, 1999).

23 "Fund for Neediest Tops $200,000 Mark," *New York Times*, December 27, 1940; "$3,097 Contributed for the Neediest," *New York Times*, January 6, 1943; "New Citizen Helps the Neediest Fund," *New York Times*, January 1, 1944.

24 Fredric Wertham, "The Comics . . . Very Funny!," *Saturday Review of Literature*, May 29, 1948, 6–7, 27–29; reprinted in *Reader's Digest*, August 1948, 15.

25 Gordon, *Comic Strips and Consumer Culture*, 136–137.

26 Eco, "Myth," 22.

27 Rayna Denison, "It's a Bird! It's a Plane! No, It's DVD! Superman, Smallville, and the Production (of) Melodrama," in *Film and Comics*, ed. Ian Gordon, Mark Jancovich, and Matthew P. McAllister (Jackson: University Press of Mississippi, 2007), 160–179; Matthew P. McAllister, Ian Gordon, and Mark Jancovich, "Blockbuster Meets Superhero Comic, or Art House Meets Graphic Novel? The Contradictory Relationship between Film and Comic Art," *Journal of Popular Film and Television* 34, no. 3 (2006): 108–114.

28 Gary Arnold, "Hollywood's Super Holiday: It's 'Superman'!; Will the Ageless Man of Steel Triumph at the Box Office?," *Washington Post*, December 10, 1978; Aljean Harmetz, "The Marketing of Superman and His Paraphernalia," *New York Times*, June 21, 1981.

29 Connie Bruck, *Master of the Game* (New York: Simon and Schuster, 1994); Van Gelder, "Long Islanders."

30 Jeremy Taylor, "Now Where Did I Park the Batmobile?," *Daily Mail*, August 6, 2011, http://www.dailymail.co.uk/home/moslive/article-2021924/Batmobile-

James-Bond-Now-did-I-park-car.html; James May, "Why the Corgi James Bond Aston Martin DB5 Is the Most Significant Car Ever," *Sunday Times*, January 18, 2015.

31 *DC Comics v. Jerry Powers*, 465 F. Supp. 843 (S.D.N.Y. 1978); 1978 U.S. Dist. LEXIS 13963.

32 Licensing Corporation of America marketing book, 1979, accessed January 25, 2014, http://www.plaidstallions.com/dc/lca.html: "1978 Superman Toshiba Coffee Maker Ad," Collecting Superman, accessed March 20, 2015, http://collectingsuperman.com/?p=2108; Gillette's then-subsidiary PaperMate brought out a series of Superman PrestoMagix instant transfers in 1978. PrestoMagix, accessed March 20, 2015, http://prestomag.tumblr.com/page/6.

33 Licensing Corporation of America marketing book, 1979.

34 Jason Sacks, Jim Beard, Dave Dykema, Keith Dallas, and John Wells, *American Comic Book Chronicles: The 1970s, 1970–1979* (Raleigh, NC: TwoMorrows, 2014), 247–248.

35 Ibid., 248. The comic book store owner, and also distributor, at the time Robert Beerbohm has expressed this view numerous times, including in an email to the Comix Scholars list, March 8, 2015.

36 Robert Beerbohm, "Secret Origins of the Direct Market, Part One," *Comic Book Artist* 6 (1999): 80–91; Robert Beerbohm, "Secret Origins of the Direct Market, Part Two," *Comic Book Artist* 7 (2000): 116–125.

37 Peter Bart, "Superman Faces New Hurdles: Publishers of Comic Books Showing Decline," *New York Times*, September 23, 1962.

38 All products listed on Amazon.com, accessed May 4, 2015.

39 *Superman* #159 (February 1963); *Superman* #383 (May 1983).

40 In 1982, to match the purchasing power of one million 1962 dollars required $3,197,577.

41 In a 2007 interview with the financial website The Motley Fool, Marvel editor in chief Joe Quesada described Marvel's comic books as "the R&D for the company." Tim Beyers, "Marvel's R&D Machine," The Motley Fool, March 1, 2007, http://www.fool.com/investing/general/2007/03/01/marvels-rd-machine.aspx.

42 George Gene Gustines, "Film Trailer Aids Sales of 'Watchmen' Novel," *New York Times*, August 14, 2008.

43 Heidi MacDonald, "Goodbye 1700: DC's New York Offices Close for Good Today," *Comics Beat*, April 10, 2015, http://www.comicsbeat.com/goodbye-1700-dcs-new-york-offices-close-for-good-today/.

44 "The People Beat," *San Antonio Express-News*, July 18, 2001; Phil Rosenthal, "A Lot of Nerve," *Chicago Sun-Times*, May 16, 2001; "Frankenvision," *Toronto Star*, October 26, 2002; Walt Belcher, "Here's Reality: 14 Days of Meeting

Stars," *Tampa Tribune*, July 16, 2001; Charlie McCollum, "ABC, WB Schedules Get Major Retooling," *San Jose Mercury News*, May 16, 2001.

45 *Smallville*, season 10, episode 18, aired April 22, 2011.

46 *Siegel v. Warner Bros. Entm't, Inc.*, No. 2:04-cv-08400-SGL-RZ (C.D. Cal. 2009), Expert Report of Steven D. Sills, Document 281-2, filed December 10, 2007.

47 Gord Lacey, "Lois & Clark: The New Adventures of Superman—It's a Bird, It's a Plane, It's an Announcement!," TV Shows on DVD, March 14, 2005, http://www.tvshowsondvd.com/news/Lois-Clark-New-Adventures-Superman/3116; "Adventures of Superman—The Complete 1st Season," TV Shows on DVD, accessed April 13, 2015, http://www.tvshowsondvd.com/releases/Adventures-Superman-Complete-1st-Season/4994.

48 Geoff Boucher, "'Smallville' Tom Welling on Saying Goodbye to Superman," *Los Angeles Times*, May 5, 2011, http://herocomplex.latimes.com/tv/smallville-tom-welling-on-saying-goodbye-to-superman/.

49 "Smallville Toys Around with the Justice League," *TV Guide News*, September 17, 2007, http://www.tvguide.com/news/smallville-toys-justice-16692/.

50 Whitney Pastorek, "The 'Aquaman' Pilot Is a Hit on iTunes," *Entertainment Weekly*, August 4, 2006, http://www.ew.com/article/2006/08/04/aquamanpilot-hit-itunes.

51 Matthew Freeman, "Advertising the Yellow Brick Road: Historicizing the Industrial Emergence of Transmedia Storytelling," *International Journal of Communication* 8 (2014): 2371–2372.

52 Stephen Herskovitz and Malcolm Crystal, "The Essential Brand Persona: Storytelling and Branding," *Journal of Business Strategy* 31, no. 3 (2010): 21–28; Stephen Denning, "Effective Storytelling: Strategic Business Narrative Techniques," *Strategy & Leadership* 34, no. 1 (2006): 42–48.

53 "July 2014 Comic Book Sales Figures," Comichron, accessed August 18, 2014, http://www.comichron.com/monthlycomicssales/2014/2014-07.html; "Man of Steel," Box Office Mojo, accessed August 18, 2014, http://www.boxofficemojo.com/movies/?id=superman2012.htm.

54 Tony Lisanti, "Top 150 Global Licensors," *Global License* 7, no. 2 (2014): T3.

55 Ted Johnson, "Judge: Superman Rights Transferred to DC Comics in 2001 Agreement," *Variety*, March 21, 2013, http://variety.com/2013/film/news/judge-superman-rights-transferred-to-dc-comics-in-2001-agreement-1200327258/; see numerous court documents in *Siegel*, No. 2:04-cv-08400-RZ.

EPILOGUE

1 Adam Gopnik, "What Did Jesus Do?," *New Yorker*, May 24, 2010, 73.

2 A list of "Easter eggs" in *Man of Steel* is offered at Andrew Dyce, "'Man of Steel' Easter Eggs, Trivia & References," Screen Rant, June 14, 2013, http://screenrant.com/man-of-steel-movie-easter-eggs-trivia-comic-book-references/.

BIBLIOGRAPHY

Agostino, Lauren, and A. L. Newberg. *Holding Kryptonite: Truth, Justice and America's First Superhero*. New York: Holmes and Watson, 2014.

Andrae, Thomas. *Creators of the Superheroes*. Neshannock, PA: Hermes, 2011.

———. "From Menace to Messiah: The History and Historicity of Superman." In *American Media and Mass Culture: Left Perspectives*, edited by Donald Lazure, 124–138. Berkeley: University of California Press, 1987.

Barker, Martin. *A Haunt of Fear*. London: Pluto, 1984.

Beaty, Bart. "Superhero Fan Service: Audience Strategies in the Contemporary Interlinked Hollywood Blockbuster." *Information Society* (forthcoming).

Beerbohm, Robert. "The Big Bang Theory of Comic Book History." *Comic Book Marketplace*, August 1977, 50–60.

———. "Secret Origins of the Direct Market, Part One." *Comic Book Artist* 6 (1999): 80–91.

———. "Secret Origins of the Direct Market, Part Two," *Comic Book Artist* 7 (2000): 116–125.

Benton, Mike. *The Comic Book in America: An Illustrated History*. Dallas: Taylor, 1989.

———. *Superhero Comics of the Golden Age: The Illustrated History*. Dallas: Taylor, 1992.

Blum, John Morton. *V Was for Victory: Politics and American Culture during World War II*. New York: Harcourt Brace Jovanovich, 1976.

Bonazzi, Robert. *Man in the Mirror: John Howard Griffin and the Story of "Black Like Me."* Maryknoll, NY: Orbis Books, 1997.

Boym, Svetlana. *The Future of Nostalgia*. New York: Basic Books, 2001.

Bruck, Connie. *Master of the Game*. New York: Simon and Schuster, 1994.

Byrne, John. "Superman: A Personal View." In *Superman: The Man of Steel*, vi–viii. New York: Ballantine Books, 1988.

Cabarga, Leslie. *The Fleischer Story*. Boston: Da Capo, 1988.

Cassidy, Paul. "An Approach to the Profession of the Comic Strip Cartooning Based upon an Analytical Survey of Current Trends and Personal Experiences." Master's thesis, University of Wisconsin, 1942.

Chartier, Roger. "Texts, Printing, Readings." In *The New Cultural History*, edited by Lynn Hunt, 154–175. Berkeley: University of California Press, 1989.

Cheng, John. *Astounding Wonder: Imagining Science and Science Fiction in Interwar America*. Philadelphia: University of Pennsylvania Press, 2012.

Corey. Herbert. "Your Son's a Better Soldier than You Were." *Nation's Business*, September 1942, 42–44.

Cowan, Ruth Schwartz. "Ambivalent Dreams: Women and the Home after World War II." *Journal of Women's History* 13, no. 3 (2001): 151–152.

———. *More Work for Mother: The Ironies of Household Technology from the Open Hearth to the Microwave*. New York: Basic Books, 1983.

Daniels, Les. *DC Comics: Sixty Years of the World's Favorite Comic Book Heroes*. Boston: Bulfinch, 1995.

———. *Superman: The Complete History: The Life and Times of the Man of Steel*. San Francisco: Chronicle Books, 1998.

DeGrazia, Edward. *Censorship Landmarks*. New York: R. R. Bowker, 1969.

De Haven, Tom. *Our Hero: Superman on Earth*. New Haven, CT: Yale University Press, 2010.

Denison, Rayna. "It's a Bird! It's a Plane! No, It's DVD! Superman, Smallville, and the Production (of) Melodrama." In *Film and Comics*, edited by Ian Gordon, Mark Jancovich, and Matthew P. McAllister, 160–179. Jackson: University Press of Mississippi, 2007.

Denning, Stephen. "Effective Storytelling: Strategic Business Narrative Techniques." *Strategy & Leadership* 34, no. 1 (2006): 42–48.

DeSanto, Tom. Introduction to *Superman: Red Son*, by Mark Millar. New York: DC Comics, 2004.

Dower, John. *War without Mercy: Race and Power in the Pacific War*. New York: Pantheon, 1986.

Eco, Umberto. "Apocalittici e integrati: La cultura italiana e le comunicazioni di massa" (Apocalyptic and integrated: Italian culture and mass communications). In *Apocalittici e integrati: Comunicazioni di massa e teorie della cultura di massa* (Apocalyptic and integrated: Mass communications and theories of mass culture). 1964. Reprint, Milan: RCS, 1996.

———. "The Myth of Superman." Translated by Natalie Chilton. *Diacritics* 2 (1972): 14–22. Originally published as "Il mito di Superman e la *dissoluzione* del tempo," in *Demitizzazione e imagine*, edited by E. Castelli (Padua: Cedam, 1962).

Engelhardt, Tom. "The Strawberry Shortcake Strategy." In *Watching Television: A Pantheon Guide to Popular Culture*, edited by Todd Gitlin, 68–110. New York: Pantheon, 1986.

Feiffer, Jules. *The Great Comic Book Heroes*. New York: Doubleday, 1965.

Franklin, Benjamin. "Pennsylvania Assembly: Reply to the Governor, November 11, 1755." In *The Papers of Benjamin Franklin*, edited by Leonard W. Labaroo, vol. 6., 242. New Haven, CT: Yale University Press, 1963.

Freeman, Matthew. "Advertising the Yellow Brick Road: Historicizing the Industrial Emergence of Transmedia Storytelling." *International Journal of Communication* 8 (2014): 2371–2372.

Friedrich, Otto. "Up, Up and Away!!!" *Time*, March 14, 1988, 69–74.

Gabilliet, Jean-Paul. *Of Comics and Men: A Cultural History of American Comic Books*. Jackson: University Press of Mississippi, 2010.

Gabler, Neal. *Walt Disney: The Triumph of the American Imagination*. New York: Knopf, 2006.

Geertz, Clifford. *Interpretation of Cultures: Selected Essays*. New York: Basic Books, 1973.

Gopnik, Adam. "What Did Jesus Do?," *New Yorker*, May 24, 2010, 72–77.

Gordon, Ian. *Comic Strips and Consumer Culture, 1890–1945*. Washington, DC: Smithsonian Institution Press, 1998.

——. "The Moral World of Superman and the American War in Vietnam." *Journal of Graphic Novels and Comics* 6, no. 2 (2015): 172–181.

——. "Nostalgia, Myth, and Ideology: Visions of Superman at the End of the American Century." In *Comics and Ideology*, edited by Matthew McAllister, Edward Sewell, and Ian Gordon, 177–193. New York: Peter Lang, 2001.

Griffin, John Howard. *Black Like Me*. Boston: Houghton Mifflin, 1961.

Gwenllian-Jones, Sara. "Web Wars: Online TV Fandom and Studio Censorship." In *Must See TV: Designing Schedules, Finding Audiences, Transforming Technologies*, edited by Mark Jancovich and James Lyons, 163–177. London: BFI, 2002.

Hajdu, David. *The Ten-Cent Plague: The Great Comic-Book Scare and How It Changed America*. New York: Farrar, Straus and Giroux, 2008.

Harris, Neil. "Who Owns Our Myths? Heroism and Copyright in an Age of Mass Culture." In *Cultural Excursions: Marketing Appetites and Cultural Tastes in Modern America*, 233–249. Chicago: University of Chicago Press, 1990.

Harvey, Robert. *The Art of the Comic Book: An Aesthetic History*. Jackson: University Press of Mississippi, 1996.

Hayde, Michael J. *Flights of Fantasy: The Unauthorized but True Story of Radio & TV's Adventures of Superman*. Albany, GA: BearManor Media, 2009.

Healey, Karen. "When Fangirls Perform: The Gendered Fan Identity in Superhero Comics Fandom." In *The Contemporary Comic Book Superhero*, edited by Angela Ndalianis, 144–163. New York: Routledge, 2009.

Herskovitz, Stephen, and Malcolm Crystal. "The Essential Brand Persona: Storytelling and Branding." *Journal of Business Strategy* 31, no. 3 (2010): 21–28.

Jack Kirby's Fourth World Omnibus: Volume 1. New York: DC Comics, 2007.

Jameson, Fredric. "Postmodernism and Consumer Society." In *The Anti-aesthetic: Essays on Postmodern Culture*, edited by Hal Foster, 111–125. Port Townsend, WA: Bay, 1983.

Jenkins, Henry. *Convergence Culture: Where Old and New Media Collide*. New York: NYU Press, 2006.

——. "'Just Men in Tights': Rewriting Silver Age Comics in an Era of Multiplicity." In *Men in Tights: Comic Book Superheroes*, edited by Angela Ndalianis, 16–43. New York: Routledge, 2009.

Jones, Gerard. *Men of Tomorrow: Geeks, Gangsters, and the Birth of the Comic Book*. New York: Basic Books, 2005.

Kemp, Martin. *Christ to Coke: How Image Becomes Icon*. New York: Oxford University Press, 2011.

Knight, Jack, and Jean Ensminger. "Conflict over Changing Social Norms: Bargaining, Ideology, and Enforcement." In *The New Institutionalism in Sociology*, edited by Mary C. Brinton and Victor Nee, 105–126. Stanford, CA: Stanford University Press, 1998.

Kobler, John. "Up, Up and Away! The Rise of Superman Inc." *Saturday Evening Post*, June 21, 1941.

Lasch, Christopher. "The Politics of Nostalgia." *Harper's*, November 1984, 65–70.

——. *The True and Only Heaven*. New York: Norton, 1991.

Lent, John. *Pulp Demons: International Dimensions of the Postwar Anti-Comics Campaign*. Madison, NJ: Fairleigh Dickinson University Press, 1999.

Lesser, Robert. *A Celebration of Comic Art and Memorabilia*. New York: Hawthorn Books, 1975.

Lévi-Strauss, Claude. *Structural Anthropology*. London: Allen Lane, 1968.

Levitt Steven D., and Stephen J. Dubner. *Freakonomics: A Rogue Economist Explores the Hidden Side of Everything*. New York: William Morrow, 2005.

Lisanti, Tony. "Top 150 Global Licensors." *Global License* 7, no. 2 (2014): T3.

Longest, David. *Character Toys and Collectibles: Second Series*. Paducah, KY: Collector Books, 1987.

Maggin, Elliot S. Introduction to *Kingdom Come*, by Mark Waid and Alex Ross, 5–7. New York: DC Comics, 2006.

May, Elaine Tyler. *Homeward Bound: American Families in the Cold War Era*. New York: Basic Books, 1988.

McAllister, Matthew P., Ian Gordon, and Mark Jancovich. "Blockbuster Meets Superhero Comic, or Art House Meets Graphic Novel? The Contradictory Relationship between Film and Comic Art." *Journal of Popular Film and Television* 34, no. 3 (2006): 108–114.

McCabe, Joseph. "Speeding Bullets and Changing Lanes." In *The Man from Krypton: A Closer Look at Superman*, edited by Glenn Yeffeth, 161–173. Dallas: BenBella Books, 2006.

Millar, Mark. *Superman: Red Son*. New York: DC Comics, 2004.

Mitchell, Steven E. "Evil Harvest: Investigating the Comic Book, 1948–1955." Master's thesis, Arkansas State University, 1982.

Montgomery, David. *The Fall of the House of Labor: The Workplace, the State, and American Labor Activism, 1865–1925*. New York: Cambridge University Press, 1987.

Murray, Janet Horowitz. *Hamlet on the Holodeck: The Future of Narrative in Cyberspace*. New York: Free Press, 1997.

Ndalianis, Angela. "Enter the Aleph—Superhero Worlds and Hypertime Realities." In *Men in Tights: Comic Book Superheroes*, edited by Angela Ndalianis, 270–290. New York: Routledge, 2009.

New York State Joint Legislative Committee to Study the Publication of Comics. *Report of the New York State Joint Legislative Committee to Study the Publication of Comics*. Legislative document no. 37. 1954.

Parker, Felan. "Official Apocrypha: *Elseworlds, What If . . . ?* and the Transmedia Franchise." Paper presented at New Narrative Conference, Toronto, May 2010.

Penley, Constance. "Feminism, Psychoanalysis, and the Study of Popular Culture." In *Cultural Studies*, edited by Lawrence Grossberg, Cary Nelson, and Paula A. Treichler, 479–500. New York: Routledge, 1992.

Regalado, Aldo J. *Bending Steel: Modernity and the American Superhero*. Jackson: University Press of Mississippi, 2015.

Ricca, Brad. *Super Boys: The Amazing Adventures of Jerry Siegel and Joe Shuster*. New York: St. Martin's, 2013.

Rockoff, Hugh. "Keep on Scrapping: The Salvage Drives of World War II." NBER Working Paper 13418. National Bureau of Economic Research, Cambridge, MA, September 2007. http://www.nber.org/papers/w13418.

Sacks, Jason, Jim Beard, Dave Dykema, Keith Dallas, and John Wells. *American Comic Book Chronicles: The 1970s, 1970–1979*. Raleigh, NC: TwoMorrows, 2014.

Saunders, Benjamin. *Do the Gods Wear Capes? Spirituality, Fantasy, and Superheroes*. New York: Continuum, 2011.

Schelly, Billy. *The Golden Age of Comic Fandom*. Seattle: Hamster, 2003.

Siegel, Jerry, Jack Schiff, Wayne Boring, Jack Burnley, and Whitney Ellsworth. *Superman: The Golden Age Sundays, 1943–1946*. San Diego: Idea and Design Works, 2013.

Smith, Adam. *The Wealth of Nations: An Inquiry into the Nature and Causes of the Wealth of Nations*. 1776. Reprint, Petersfield, UK: Harriman House, 2007.

Staiger, Janet. *Media Reception Studies*. New York: NYU Press, 2005.

Stewart, Susan. *On Longing: Narratives of the Miniature, the Gigantic, the Souvenir, the Collection*. Baltimore: Johns Hopkins University Press, 1984.

Strasser, Susan. *Satisfaction Guaranteed: The Making of the American Mass Market*. New York: Pantheon, 1989.

———. *Waste and Want: A Social History of Trash*. New York: Henry Holt, 2000.

Summers, Harrison B., ed. *A Thirty-Year History of Programs Carried on National Radio Networks in the United States, 1926–1956.* Salem, NH: Ayer, 1986.

Superman Chronicles 10. New York: DC Comics, 2012.

Superman in the Fifties. New York: DC Comics, 2002.

Superman in the Seventies. New York: DC Comics, 2000.

Superman in the Sixties. New York: DC Comics, 1999.

"Superman's Dilemma." *Time,* April 13, 1942.

Tollin, Anthony. *Superman on Radio.* Schiller Park, IL: Radio Spirits, 1997.

Tye, Larry. *Superman: The High-Flying History of America's Most Enduring Hero.* New York: Random House, 2012.

Vico, Giambattista. *Selected Writings.* New York: Cambridge University Press, 1982.

Waid, Mark, and Alex Ross. *Kingdom Come.* New York: DC Comics, 2006.

Wall, Wendy. *Inventing the "American Way": The Politics of Consensus from the New Deal to the Civil Rights Movement.* New York: Oxford University Press, 2008.

Wertham, Fredric. "The Comics . . . Very Funny!" *Saturday Review of Literature,* May 29, 1948, 6–7, 27–29.

———. *The Seduction of the Innocent.* New York: Holt, Rinehart and Winston, 1954.

———. *The World of Fanzines.* Carbondale: Southern Illinois University Press, 1973.

Westbrook, Robert B. "'I Want a Girl, Just Like the Girl That Married Harry James': American Women and the Problem of Political Obligation in World War II." *American Quarterly* 42, no. 4 (1990): 587–614

Wheldon, Glen. *Superman: The Unauthorized Biography.* Hoboken, NJ: Wiley, 2013.

Williams, William Appleman. *The Tragedy of American Diplomacy.* 2nd ed. New York: Dell, 1972.

Wolfe, Tom. "The 'Me' Decade and the Third Great Awakening." *New York,* August 23, 1976. http://nymag.com/news/features/45938/.

Wright, Bradford W. *Comic Book Nation: The Transformation of Youth Culture in America.* Baltimore: Johns Hopkins University Press, 2001.

Yockey, Matt. "Somewhere in Time: Utopia and the Return of Superman." *Velvet Light Trap* 61 (2008): 26–37.

Zieger, Robert. *American Workers, American Unions, 1920–1985.* Baltimore: Johns Hopkins University, 1986.

INDEX

Ian Gordon is a professor of American history at the National University of Singapore. His book *Comic Strips and Consumer Culture* (1998) is widely cited and used by historians and scholars of the media. He has coedited two collections of scholarly writings on comics: *Comics & Ideology* (2001) and *Film and Comic Books* (2007). His work on comics includes articles on Superman, *Maus*, and Australian comic strips. He is an international contributing editor to the *Journal of American History* and on the editorial board of several journals including the *Journal of Graphic Novels and Comics, Popular Communication, Studies in Comics*, and *ImageText*.